Contemporary Cultures

EDITED BY

Brice Obermeyer

EMPORIA STATE UNIVERSITY

Linus
Publications, Inc.

Published by Linus Publications, Inc.

Ronkonkoma, NY 11779

ISBN 10: 1-60797-343-X

ISBN 13: 978-1-60797-343-0

Printed in the United States of America.

This book is printed on acid-free paper.

Print Number   5   4   3   2   1

TABLE OF CONTENTS

ACKNOWLEDGMENTS

Anthropological theory by SAGE PUBLICATIONS LTD.. Reproduced with permission of SAGE PUBLICATIONS LTD. in the format Photocopy for a coursepack via Copyright Clearance Center.

Talking from 9 to 5 : women and men at work by TANNEN, DEBORAH Reproduced with permission of WILLIAM MORROW & COMPANY INC. in the format Photocopy for a coursepack via Copyright Clearance Center.

Man the hunter by Lee, Richard B.; et al Reproduced with permission of TRANSACTION-ALDINE in the format Photocopy for a coursepack via Copyright Clearance Center.

The Sciences by NEW YORK ACADEMY OF SCIENCES Reproduced with permission of NEW YORK ACADEMY OF SCIENCES in the format Photocopy for a coursepack via Copyright Clearance Center.

Our kind : who we are, where we came from, where we are going by HARRIS, MARVIN Reproduced with permission of HARPERCOLLINS PUBLISHERS, INC. in the format Photocopy for a coursepack via Copyright Clearance Center.

Indian givers : how the Indians of the Americas transformed the world by WEATHERFORD, JACK M. Reproduced with permission of RANDOM HOUSE, INC. in the format Photocopy for a coursepack via Copyright Clearance Center.

Women and the family in rural Taiwan by WOLF, MARGERY Reproduced with permission of STANFORD UNIVERSITY PRESS in the format Photocopy for a coursepack via Copyright Clearance Center.

Natural history by AMERICAN MUSEUM OF NATURAL HISTORY Reproduced with permission of NATURAL HISTORY MAGAZINE, INC.

Psychology today by SUSSEX PUBLISHERS, LLC. Reproduced with permission of SUSSEX PUBLISHERS, LLC

Reprinted with kind permission from Springer Science and Buiness Media: Society, "The Kindness of Strangers" September /October 2007, Robin Fox

Conformity & Conflict: Readings in Cultural Anthropology, 13th Ed. by Spradley, James & McCurdy, David W. (2009) Reproduced with permission of PEARSON EDUCATION, INC.

1

ANTHROPOLOGY AND THE STUDY OF CULTURE

CHAPTER ONE

Culture and Ethnography

Culture, as its name suggests, lies at the heart of cultural anthropology. And the concept of **culture,** along with ethnography, sets anthropology apart from other social and behavioral sciences. Let us look more closely at these concepts.

To understand what anthropologists mean by *culture,* imagine yourself in a foreign setting, such as a market town in India, forgetting what you might already know about that country. You step off a bus onto a dusty street where you are immediately confronted by strange sights, sounds, and smells. Men dress in Western clothes, but of a different style. Some women drape themselves in long shawls that entirely cover their bodies. They peer at you through a small gap in this garment as they walk by. Buildings are one- or two-story affairs, open at the front so you can see inside. Near you some people sit on wicker chairs eating strange foods. Most unusual is how people talk. They utter vocalizations unlike any you have ever heard, and you wonder how they can possibly understand each other. But obviously they do, since their behavior seems organized and purposeful.

Scenes such as this confronted early explorers, missionaries, and anthropologists, and from their observations an obvious point emerged. People living in various parts of the world looked and behaved in dramatically different ways. And these differences correlated with groups. The people of India had customs different from those of the Papuans; the British did not act and dress like the Iroquois.

Two possible explanations for group differences came to mind. Some argued that group behavior was inherited. Dahomeans of the African Gold Coast, for example, were characterized as particularly "clever and adaptive" by one British colonial official, while, according to the same authority, another African group was "happy-go-lucky and improvident." Usually implied in such statements was the idea that group members were born that way. Such thinking persists to the present and in its most malignant extreme takes the form of racism.

But a second explanation also emerged. Perhaps, rather than a product of inheritance, the behavior characteristic of a group was learned. The way people dressed, what they ate, how they talked—all these could more easily be explained as acquisitions. Thus a baby born on the African Gold Coast would, if immediately transported to China and raised like other children there, grow up to dress, eat, and talk like a Chinese. Cultural anthropologists focus on the explanation of learned behavior.

The idea of learning, and a need to label the lifestyles associated with particular groups, led to the definition of culture. In 1871, British anthropologist Sir Edward Burnet Tylor argued that "Culture ... is that complex whole which includes knowledge, belief, art, law, morals, custom, and any other capabilities and habits acquired by man as a member of society."[1] The definition we present here places more emphasis on the importance of knowledge than does Tylor's. We will say that *culture is the learned and shared knowledge that people use to generate behavior and interpret experience.*

Important to this definition is the idea that culture is a kind of knowledge, not behavior. It is in people's heads. It reflects the mental categories they learn from others as they grow up. It helps them *generate* behavior and *interpret* what they experience. At the moment of birth, we lack a culture. We don't yet have a system of beliefs, knowledge, and patterns of customary behavior. But from that moment until we die, each of us participates in a kind of universal schooling that teaches us our native culture. Laughing and smiling are genetic responses, but as infants we soon learn when to smile, when to laugh, and even how to laugh. We also inherit the potential to cry, but we must learn our cultural rules for when crying is appropriate.

As we learn our culture, we acquire a way to interpret experience. For example, Americans learn that dogs are like little people in furry suits. Dogs live in our houses, eat our food, share our beds. They hold a place in our hearts; their loss causes us to grieve. Villagers in India, on the other hand, often view dogs as pests that are useful only for hunting (in those few parts of the country where one still can hunt) and as watchdogs. Quiet days in Indian villages are often punctuated by the yelp of a dog that has been threatened or actually hurt by its master or a bystander.

---

[1]Edward Burnet Tylor, *Primitive Culture* (New York: Harper Torchbooks, Harper & Row, 1958; originally published by John Murray, London, 1871), p. 1.

Clearly, it is not the dogs that are different in these two societies. Rather, it is the meaning that dogs have for people that varies. And such meaning is cultural; it is learned as part of growing up in each group.

There are two basic kinds of culture, explicit and tacit. **Explicit culture** is cultural knowledge that people can talk about. As you grow up, for example, you learn that there are words for many things you encounter. There are items such as *clothes,* actions such as *playing,* emotional states such as *sadness,* ways to talk such as *yelling,* and people such as *mother.* Recognizing that culture may be explicit is important to the ethnographic process discussed below. If people have words for cultural categories, anthropologists can use interviews or observations of people talking to uncover them. Because so much culture is explicit, words—both spoken and written—become essential to the discovery and understanding of a culture.

Tacit culture is cultural knowledge that people lack words for. For example, as we grow up we learn to recognize and use a limited number of sound categories such as /d/, /e/, and /f/. Although anthropological linguists have given sound categories a name *(phonemes),* nonlinguists lack such a term. Instead, we learn our sound categories by hearing and replicating them and we use them unconsciously. No parent said, "Now let's work on our phonemes tonight, dear," to us when we were little.

Anthropologist Edward Hall pioneered the study of tacit culture. He noted, for example, that middle-class North Americans observe four speaking distances—intimate, personal, social, and public—without naming them. (Hall, not his informants, invented the terms above.) Hall also noticed that people from other societies observed different tacit speaking distances, so that a Latin American's closer (than North American) personal speaking distance made North Americans uncomfortable because it seemed intimate. Because it is unspoken, tacit culture can be discovered only through behavioral observation.

Ethnography is the process of discovering and describing a particular culture. It involves anthropologists in an intimate and personal activity as they attempt to learn how the members of a particular group see their worlds.

But which groups qualify as culture-bearing units? How does the anthropologist identify the existence of a culture to study? This was not a difficult question when anthropology was a new science. As Tylor's definition notes, culture was the whole way of life of a people. To find it, one sought out distinctive ethnic units, such as Bhil tribals in India or Apaches in the American Southwest. Anything one learned from such people would be part of their culture.

But discrete cultures of this sort are becoming more difficult to find. The world is increasingly divided into large national societies, each subdivided into a myriad of subgroups. Anthropologists are finding it increasingly attractive to study such subgroups, because they form the arena for most of life in complex society. And this is where the concept of the microculture enters the scene.

Microcultures are systems of cultural knowledge characteristic of subgroups within larger societies. Members of a microculture will usually share much of what they know with everyone in the greater society but will possess a special cultural knowledge that is unique to the subgroup. For example, a college fraternity has a microculture within the context of a university and a nation. Its members have special daily routines, jokes, and meanings for events. It is this shared knowledge that makes up their microculture and that can serve as the basis for ethnographic study. More and more, anthropologists are turning to the study of microcultures, using the same ethnographic techniques they employ when they investigate the broader culture of an ethnic or national group.

More than anything else, it is ethnography that is anthropology's unique contribution to social science. Most scientists, including many who view people in social context, approach their research as **detached observers.** As social scientists, they observe the human subjects of their study, categorize what they see, and generate theory to account for their findings. They work from the outside, creating a system of knowledge to account for other people's behavior. Although this is a legitimate and often useful way to conduct research, it is not the main task of ethnography.

Ethnographers seek out the insider's viewpoint. Because culture is the knowledge people use to generate behavior and interpret experience, the ethnographer seeks to understand group members' behavior from the inside, or cultural, perspective. Instead of looking for a **subject** to observe, ethnographers look for an **informant** to teach them the culture. Just as a child learns its native culture from parents and other people in its social environment, the ethnographer learns another culture by inferring folk categories from the observation of behavior and by asking informants what things mean.

Anthropologists employ many strategies during field research to understand another culture better. But all strategies and all research ultimately rest on the cooperation of informants. An informant is neither a subject in a scientific experiment nor a **respondent** who answers the investigator's questions. An informant is a teacher who has a special kind of pupil: a professional anthropologist. In this unique relationship a transformation occurs in the anthropologist's understanding of an alien culture. It is the informant who transforms the anthropologist from a tourist into an ethnographer. The informant may be a child who explains how to play hopscotch, a cocktail waitress who teaches the anthropologist to serve drinks and to encourage customers to leave tips, an elderly man who teaches the anthropologist to build an igloo, or a grandmother who explains the intricacies of Zapotec kinship. Almost any individual who has acquired a repertoire of cultural behavior can become an informant.

Ethnography is not as easy to do as we might think. For one thing, North Americans are not taught to be good listeners. We prefer to observe and draw our own conclusions. We like a sense of control in social contexts; passive listening is a sign of weakness in our culture. But listening and learning from others is at the heart of ethnography, and we must put aside our discomfort with the student role.

It is also not easy for informants to teach us about their cultures. Culture often lies below a conscious level. A major ethnographic task is to help informants remember their culture.

Naive realism may also impede ethnography. **Naive realism** is the belief that people everywhere see the world in the same way. It may, for example, lead the unwary ethnographer to assume that beauty is the same for all people everywhere or, to use our previous example, that dogs should mean the same thing in India as they do in the United States. If an ethnographer fails to control his or her own naive realism, inside cultural meanings will surely be overlooked.

Culture shock and ethnocentrism may also stand in the way of ethnographers. **Culture shock** is a state of anxiety that results from cross-cultural misunderstanding. Immersed alone in another society, the ethnographer understands few of the culturally defined rules for behavior and interpretation used by his or her hosts. The result is anxiety about proper action and an inability to interact appropriately in the new context.

Ethnocentrism can be just as much of a liability. **Ethnocentrism** is the belief and feeling that one's own culture is best. It reflects our tendency to judge other people's beliefs and behavior using values of our own native culture. Thus if we come from a society that abhors painful treatment of animals, we are likely to react with anger when an Indian villager hits a dog with a rock. Our feeling is ethnocentric.

It is impossible to rid ourselves entirely of the cultural values that make us ethnocentric when we do ethnography. But it is important to control our ethnocentric feeling in the field if we are to learn from informants. Informants resent negative judgment.

Finally, the role assigned to ethnographers by informants affects the quality of what can be learned. Ethnography is a personal enterprise, as all the articles in this section illustrate. Unlike survey research using questionnaires or short interviews, ethnography requires prolonged social contact. Informants will assign the ethnographer some kind of role and what that turns out to be will affect research.

The selections in Part One illustrate several points about culture and ethnography. The first piece, by the late James Spradley, takes a close look at the concept of culture and its role in ethnographic research. The second, by Richard Lee, illustrates how a simple act of giving can have a dramatically different cultural meaning in two societies, leading to cross-cultural misunderstanding. Laura Bohannan's article deals with the concept of naive realism and its role in cross-cultural misunderstanding. When she tells the classic story of *Hamlet* to African Tiv elders, the plot takes on an entirely different meaning as they use their own cultural knowledge in its interpretation. In the fourth selection, Claire Sterk describes how she conducted ethnographic field research under difficult circumstances. She sought to learn the culture of prostitutes working in New York City and Atlanta as part of a broader research interest in the spread and control of AIDS. The fifth article, by George Gmelch, explores how naive realism nearly ended a student's field research in Barbados.

Key Terms

culture	informant
culture shock	microcultures
detached observer	naive realism
ethnocentrism	respondent
ethnography	subject
explicit culture	tacit culture

CHAPTER TWO

Using Anthropology

David W. McCurdy

Some disciplines, such as economics, have an obvious relationship to the nonacademic world. Economic theory, although generated as part of basic research, may often prove useful for understanding the "real" economy. Anthropology, on the other hand, does not seem so applicable. In this article, David McCurdy discusses some of the professional applications of anthropology and argues that there is a basic anthropological perspective that can help anyone cope with the everyday world. He uses the case of a company manager to illustrate this point, asserting that ethnographic "qualitative" research is an important tool for use in the nonacademic world.

In 1990 a student whom I had not seen for fifteen years stopped by my office. He had returned for his college reunion and thought it would be interesting to catch up on news about his (and my) major department, anthropology. The conversation, however, soon shifted from college events to his own life. Following graduation and a stint in the Peace Corps, he noted, he had begun to study for his license as a ship's engineer. He had attended the Maritime Academy and worked for years on freighters. He was finally granted his license, he continued, and currently held the engineer's position on a container ship that made regular trips between Seattle and Alaska. He soon would be promoted to chief engineer and be at the top of his profession.

As he talked, he made an observation about anthropology that may seem surprising. His background in the discipline, he said, had helped him significantly in his work. He found it useful as he went about his daily tasks, maintaining his ship's complex engines and machinery, his relationships with the crew, and his contacts with land-based management.

And his is not an unusual case. Over the years, several anthropology graduates have made the same observation. One, for example, is a community organizer who feels that the cross-cultural perspective he learned in anthropology helps him mediate disputes and facilitate decision making in a multiethnic neighborhood. Another, who works as an advertising account executive, claims that anthropology helps her discover what products mean to customers. This, in turn, permits her to design more effective ad campaigns. A third says she finds anthropology an invaluable tool as she arranges interviews and writes copy. She is a producer for a metropolitan television news program. I have heard the same opinion expressed by many others, including the executive editor of a magazine for home weavers, the founder of a fencing school, a housewife, a physician, several lawyers, the kitchen manager for a catering firm, and a high school teacher.

The idea that anthropology can be useful is also supported by the experience of many new Ph.D.s. A recent survey has shown, for the first time, that more new doctorates in anthropology find employment in professional settings than in college teaching or scholarly research, and the list of nonacademic work settings revealed by the survey is remarkably broad. There is a biological anthropologist, for example, who conducts research on nutrition for a company that manufactures infant formula. A cultural anthropologist works for a major car manufacturer, researching such questions as how employees adapt to working overseas, and how they relate to conditions on domestic production lines. Others formulate government policy; plan patient care in hospitals; design overseas development projects; run famine relief programs; consult on tropical forest management; and advise on product development, advertising campaigns, and marketing strategy for corporations.

This new-found application of cultural anthropology comes as a surprise to many Americans. Unlike political science, for example, which has a name that logically connects it with practical political and legal professions, there is nothing in the term *anthropology* that tells most Americans how it might be useful.

The research subject of anthropology also makes it more difficult to comprehend. Political scientists investigate political processes, structures, and motivations. Economists look at the production and exchange of goods and services. Psychologists study differences and similarities among individuals. The research of cultural anthropologists, on the other hand, is more difficult to characterize. Instead of a focus on particular human institutions, such as politics, law, and economics, anthropologists are interested in cross-cultural differences and similarities among the world's many groups.

This interest produces a broad view of human behavior that gives anthropology its special cross-cultural flavor. It also produces a unique research strategy, called *ethnography*, that tends to be qualitative rather than quantitative. Whereas other social sciences moved toward *quantitative methods* of research designed to test theory by using survey questionnaires and structured, repetitive observations, most anthropologists conduct *qualitative research* designed to elicit the cultural knowledge of the people they seek to understand. To do this, anthropologists often live and work with their subjects, called *informants* within the discipline. The result is a highly detailed ethnographic description of the categories and rules people consult when they behave, and the meanings that things and actions have for them.

It is this ethnographic approach, or cultural perspective, that I think makes anthropology useful in such a broad range of everyday settings. I particularly find important the special anthropological understanding of the culture concept, ethnographic field methods, and social analysis. To illustrate these assertions, let us take a single case in detail, that of a manager working for a large corporation who consciously used the ethnographic approach to solve a persistent company problem.

The Problem

The manager, whom we will name Susan Stanton, works for a large multinational corporation called UTC (not the company's real name). UTC is divided into a number of parts, including divisions, subdivisions, departments, and other units designed to facilitate its highly varied business enterprises. The company is well-diversified, engaging in research, manufacturing, and customer services. In addition to serving a wide cross-section of public and private customers, it also works on a variety of government contracts for both military and nonmilitary agencies.

One of its divisions is educational. UTC has established a large number of customer outlets in cities throughout the United States, forming what it calls its "customer outlet network." They are staffed by educational personnel who are trained to offer a variety of special courses and enrichment programs. These courses and programs are marketed mainly to other businesses or to individuals who desire special training or practical information. For example, a small company might have UTC provide its employees with computer training, including instruction on hardware, programming, computer languages, and computer program applications. Another company might ask for instruction on effective management or accounting procedures. The outlets' courses for individuals include such topics as how to get a job, writing a resume, or enlarging your own business.

To organize and manage its customer outlet network, UTC has created a special division. The division office is located at the corporate headquarters and is responsible for developing new courses, improving old ones, training customer outlet personnel, and marketing customer outlet courses, or "products" as they are called inside the company. The division also has departments that develop, produce, and distribute the special learning materials used in customer outlet courses. These include books, pamphlets, video and audio tapes and cassettes, slides, overlays, and films. These materials are stored in a warehouse and are shipped, as they are ordered, to customer outlets around the country.

It is with this division that Susan Stanton first worked as a manager. She had started her career with the company in a small section of the division that designed various program materials. She had worked her way into management, holding a series of increasingly important positions. She was then asked to take over the management of a part of the division that had the manufacture, storage, and shipment of learning materials as one of its responsibilities.

But there was a catch. She was given this new management position with instructions to solve a persistent, although vaguely defined, problem. "Improve the service," they had told her, and "get control of the warehouse inventory." In this case, "service" meant the process of filling orders sent in by customer outlets for various materials stored in the warehouse. The admonition to improve the service seemed to indicate that service was poor, but all she was told about the situation was that customer outlet personnel complained about the service; she did not know exactly why or what "poor" meant.

In addition, inventory was "out of control." Later she was to discover the extent of the difficulty.

> We had a problem with inventory. The computer would say we had two hundred of some kind of book in stock, yet it was back ordered because there was nothing on the shelf. We were supposed to have the book but physically there was nothing there. I'm going, "Uh, we have a small problem. The computer never lies, like your bank statement, so why don't we have the books?"

If inventory was difficult to manage, so were the warehouse employees. They were described by another manager as "a bunch of knuckle draggers. All they care about is getting their money. They are lazy and don't last long at the job." Strangely, the company did not view the actions of the warehouse workers as a major problem. Only later did Susan Stanton tie in poor morale in the warehouse with the other problems she had been given to solve.

Management by Defense

Although Stanton would take the ethnographic approach to management problems, that was not what many other managers did. They took a defensive stance, a position opposite to the discovery procedures of ethnography. Their major concern—like that of many people in positions of leadership and responsibility—was to protect their authority and their ability to manage and to get things done. Indeed, Stanton also shared this need. But their solution to maintaining their position was different from hers. For them, claiming ignorance and asking questions—the hallmark of the ethnographic approach—is a sign of weakness. Instead of discovering what is going on when they take on a new management assignment, they often impose new work rules and procedures. Employees learn to fear the arrival of new managers because their appearance usually means a host of new, unrealistic demands. They respond by hiding what they actually do, withholding information that would be useful to the manager. Usually, everyone's performance suffers.

Poor performance leads to elaborate excuses as managers attempt to blame the troubles on others. Stanton described this tendency.

> When I came into the new job, this other manager said, "Guess what? You have got a warehouse. You are now the proud owner of a forklift and a bunch of knuckle draggers." And I thought, management's perception of those people is very low. They are treating them as dispensable, that you can't do anything with them. They say the workers don't have any career motives. They don't care if they do a good job. You have to force them to do anything. You can't motivate them. It's only a warehouse, other managers were saying. You can't really do that much about the problems there so why don't you just sort of try to keep it under control.

Other managers diminished the importance of the problem itself. It was not "poor service" that was the trouble. The warehouse was doing the best it could with what it had. It was just that the customers—the staff at the customer outlets—were complainers. As Susan Stanton noted:

The people providing the service thought that outlet staff were complainers. They said, "Staff complain about everything. But it can't be that way. We have checked it all out and it isn't that bad."

Making excuses and blaming others lead to low morale and a depressed self-image. Problems essentially are pushed aside in favor of a "let's just get by" philosophy.

Ethnographic Management

By contrast, managers take the offensive when they use ethnographic techniques. That is what Stanton did when she assumed her new managerial assignment over the learning materials manufacturing and distribution system. To understand what the ethnographic approach means, however, we must first look briefly at what anthropologists do when they conduct ethnographic field research. Our discussion necessarily involves a look at the concepts of culture and microculture as well as ethnography. For as we will shortly point out, companies have cultures of their own, a point that has recently received national attention; but more important for the problem we are describing here, companies are normally divided into subgroups, each with its own microculture. It is these cultures and microcultures that anthropologically trained managers can study ethnographically, just as fieldworkers might investigate the culture of a Kung band living in the Kalahari Desert of West Africa or the Gypsies living in San Francisco.

Ethnography refers to the process of discovering and describing culture, so it is important to discuss this general and often elusive concept. There are numerous definitions of culture, each stressing particular sets of attributes. The definition we employ here is especially appropriate for ethnographic field work. We may define culture as the acquired knowledge that people use to generate behavior and interpret experience. In growing up, one learns a system of cultural knowledge appropriate to the group. For example, an American child learns to chew with a closed mouth because that is the cultural rule. The child's parents interpret open-mouthed chewing as an infraction and tell the child to chew "properly." A person uses such cultural knowledge throughout life to guide actions and to give meaning to surroundings.

Because culture is learned, and because people can easily generate new cultural knowledge as they adapt to other people and things, human behavior and perceptions can vary dramatically from one group to another. In parts of India, for example, children learn to chew "properly" with their mouths open. Their cultural worlds are quite different from the ones found in the United States.

Cultures are associated with groups of people. Traditionally, anthropologists associated culture with relatively distinctive ethnic groups. *Culture* referred to the whole life-way of a society, and particular cultures could be named. Anthropologists talked of German culture, Ibo culture, and Bhil culture. Culture was everything that was distinctive about the group.

Culture is still applied in this manner today, but with the advent of complex societies and a growing interest among anthropologists in understanding them, the culture concept has also been used in a more limited way. Complex societies such as our own are composed of thousands of groups. Members of these groups usually share the national culture, including a language and a huge inventory of knowledge for doing things, but the groups themselves have specific cultures of their own. For example, if you were to walk into the regional office of a stock brokerage firm, you would hear the people there talking an apparently foreign language. You might stand in the "bull pen," listen to brokers make "cold calls," "sell short," "negotiate a waffle," or get ready to go to a "dog and pony show." The fact that an event such as this feels strange when you first encounter them is strong evidence to support the notion that you don't yet know the culture that organizes them. We call such specialized groups *microcultures*.

We are surrounded by microcultures, participating in a few, encountering many others. Our family has a microculture. So may our neighborhood, our college, and even our dormitory floor. The waitress who serves us lunch at the corner restaurant shares a culture with her co-workers. So do bank tellers at our local savings and loan. Kin, occupational groups, and recreational associations each tend to display special microcultures. Such cultures can be, and now often are, studied by anthropologists interested in understanding life in complex American society.

The concept of microculture is essential to Susan Stanton as she begins to attack management problems at UTC because she assumes that conflict between different microcultural groups is most likely at the bottom of the difficulty. One microculture she could focus on is UTC company culture. She knows, for example, that there are a variety of rules and expectations—written and unwritten—for how things should be done at the company. She must dress in her "corporates," for example, consisting of a neutral-colored suit, stockings, and conservative shoes. UTC also espouses values about the way employees should be treated, how people are supposed to feel about company products, and a variety of other things that set that particular organization apart from other businesses.

But the specific problems that afflicted the departments under Stanton's jurisdiction had little to do with UTC's corporate culture. They seemed rather to be the result of misunderstanding and misconnection between two units, the warehouse and the customer outlets. Each had its own microculture. Each could be investigated to discover any information that might lead to a solution of the problems she had been given.

Such investigation would depend on the extent of Stanton's ethnographic training. As an undergraduate in college, she had learned how to conduct ethnographic interviews, observe behavior, and analyze and interpret data. She was not a professional anthropologist, but she felt she was a good enough ethnographer to discover some relevant aspects of microcultures at UTC.

Ethnography is the process of discovering and describing a culture. For example, an anthropologist who travels to India to conduct a study of village culture will use ethnographic techniques. The anthropologist will move into a community, occupy a house, watch people's daily routines, attend rituals, and spend hours interviewing informants. The goal is to discover a detailed picture of what is going on by seeing village culture through the eyes of informants. The anthropologist wants the insider's perspective. Villagers become teachers, patiently explaining different aspects of their culture, praising the anthropologist for acting correctly and appearing to understand, laughing when the anthropologist makes mistakes or seems confused. When the anthropologist knows what to do and can explain in local terms what is going on or what is likely to happen, real progress has been made. The clearest evidence of such progress is when informants say, "You are almost human now," or "You are beginning to talk just like us."

The greatest enemy of good ethnography is the preconceived notion. Anthropologists do not conduct ethnographic research by telling informants what they are like based on earlier views of them. They teach the anthropologist how to see their world: the anthropologist does not tell them what their world should really be like. All too often in business, a new manager will take over a department and begin to impose changes on its personnel to fit a preconceived perception of them. The fact that the manager's efforts are likely to fail makes sense in light of this ignorance. The manager doesn't know the micro culture. Nor has he or she asked employees about it.

But can a corporate manager really do ethnography? After all, managers have positions of authority to maintain, as we noted earlier. It is all right for professional anthropologists to enter the field and act ignorant; they don't have a position to maintain and they don't have to continue to live with their informants. The key to the problem appears to be the "grace period." Most managers are given one by their employees when they are new on the job. A new manager cannot be expected to know everything. It is permissible to ask basic questions. The grace period may last only a month or two, but it is usually long enough to find out valuable information.

This is the opportunity that Susan Stanton saw as she assumed direction of the warehouse distribution system. As she described it:

> I could use the first month, actually the first six weeks, to find out what was going on, to act dumb and find out what people actually did and why. I talked to end customers. I talked to salespeople, people who were trying to sell things to help customer outlets with their needs. I talked to coordinators at headquarters staff who were trying to help all these customer outlets do their jobs and listened to what kinds of complaints they had heard. I talked to the customer outlet people and the guys in the warehouse. I had this six-week grace period where I could go in and say, "I don't know anything about this. If you were in my position, what would you do, or what would make the biggest difference, and why would it make a difference?" You want to find out what the world they are operating in is like. What do they value? And people were excited because I was asking and listening and, by God, intending to do something about it instead of just disappearing again.

As we shall see shortly, Stanton's approach to the problem worked. But it also resulted in an unexpected bonus. Her ethnographic approach symbolized unexpected interest and concern to her employees. That, combined with realistic management, gave her a position of respect and authority. Their feelings for her were expressed by one warehouse worker when he said:

> When she [Susan] was going to be transferred to another job, we gave her a party. We took her to this country-and-western place and we all got to dance with the boss. We told her that she was the first manager who ever tried to understand what it was like to work in the warehouse. We thought she would come in like the other managers and make a lot of changes that didn't make sense. But she didn't. She made it work better for us.

Problems and Causes

An immediate benefit of her ethnographic inquiry was a much clearer view of what poor service meant to customer outlet personnel. Stanton discovered that learning materials, such as books and cassettes, took too long to arrive after they were ordered. Worse, material did not arrive in the correct quantities. Sometimes there would be too many items, but more often there were too few, a particularly galling discrepancy since customer outlets were charged for what they ordered, not what they received. Books also arrived in poor condition, their covers ripped or scratched, edges frayed, and ends gouged and dented. This, too, bothered customer outlet staff because they were often visited by potential customers who were not impressed by the poor condition of their supplies. Shortages and scruffy books did nothing to retain regular customers either.

The causes of these problems and the difficulties with warehouse inventory also emerged from ethnographic inquiry. Stanton discovered, for example, that most customer outlets operated in large cities, where often they were housed in tall buildings. Materials shipped to their office address often ended up sitting in ground-level lobbies, because few of the buildings had receiving docks or facilities. Books and other items also arrived in large boxes, weighing up to a hundred pounds. Outlet staff, most of whom were women, had to go down to the lobby, open those boxes that were too heavy for them to carry, and haul armloads of supplies up the elevator to the office. Not only was this time-consuming, but customer outlet staff felt it was beneath their dignity to do such work. They were educated specialists, after all.

The poor condition of the books was also readily explained. By packing items loosely in such large boxes, warehouse workers ensured trouble in transit. Books rattled around with ease, smashing into each other and the side of the box. The result was torn covers and frayed edges. Clearly no one had designed the packing and shipping process with customer outlet staff in mind.

The process, of course, originated in the central warehouse, and here as well, ethnographic data yielded interesting information about the causes of the problem. Stanton learned, for example, how materials were stored in loose stacks on the warehouse shelves. When orders arrived at the warehouse, usually through the mail, they were placed in a pile and filled in turn (although there were times when special preference was given to some customer outlets). A warehouse employee filled an order by first checking it against the stock recorded by the computer, then going to the appropriate shelves and picking the items by hand. Items were packed in the large boxes and addressed to customer outlets. With the order complete, the employee was supposed to enter the number of items picked and shipped in the computer so that inventory would be up to date.

But, Stanton discovered, workers in the warehouse were under pressure to work quickly. They often fell behind because materials the computer said were in stock were not there, and because picking by hand took so long. Their solution to the problem of speed resulted in a procedure that even further confused company records.

> Most of the people in the warehouse didn't try to count well. People were looking at the books on the shelves and were going, "Eh, that looks like the right number. You want ten? Gee, that looks like about ten." Most of the time the numbers they shipped were wrong.

The causes of inaccurate amounts in shipping were thus revealed. Later, Stanton discovered that books also disappeared in customer outlet building lobbies. While staff members carried some of the materials upstairs, people passing by the open boxes helped themselves.

Other problems with inventory also became clear. UTC employees, who sometimes walked through the warehouse, would often pick up interesting materials from the loosely stacked shelves. More important, rushed workers often neglected to update records in the computer.

The Shrink-Wrap Solution

The detailed discovery of the nature and causes of service and inventory problems suggested a relatively painless solution to Stanton. If she had taken a defensive management position and failed to learn the insider's point of view, she might have resorted to more usual remedies that were impractical and unworkable. Worker retraining is a common answer to corporate difficulties, but it is difficult to accomplish and often fails. Pay incentives, punishments, and motivation enhancements such as prizes and quotas are also frequently tried. But they tend not to work because they don't address fundamental causes.

Shrink-wrapping books and other materials did. Shrink-wrapping is a packaging method in which clear plastic sheeting is placed around items to be packaged, then through a rapid heating and cooling process, shrunk into a tight covering. The plastic molds itself like a tight skin around the things it contains, preventing any internal movement or external contamination. Stanton described her decision.

> I decided to have the books shrink-wrapped. For a few cents more, before the books ever arrived in the warehouse, I had them shrink-wrapped in quantities of five and ten. I made it part of the contract with the people who produced the books for us.

On the first day that shrink-wrapped books arrived at the warehouse, Stanton discovered that they were immediately unwrapped by workers who thought a new impediment had been placed in their way. But the positive effect of shrink-wrapping soon became apparent. For example, most customer outlets ordered books in units of fives and tens. Warehouse personnel could now easily count out orders in fives and tens, instead of having to count each book or estimate numbers in piles. Suddenly, orders filled at the warehouse contained the correct number of items.

Employees were also able to work more quickly, since they no longer had to count each book. Orders were filled faster, the customer outlet staff was pleased, and warehouse employees no longer felt the pressure of time so intensely. Shrink-wrapped materials also traveled more securely. Books, protected by their plastic covering, arrived in good condition, again delighting the personnel at customer outlets.

Stanton also changed the way materials were shipped, based on what she had learned from talking to employees. She limited the maximum size of shipments to twenty-five pounds by using smaller boxes. She also had packages marked "inside delivery" so that deliverymen would carry the materials directly to the customer outlet offices. If they failed to do so, boxes were light enough to carry upstairs. No longer would items be lost in skyscraper lobbies.

Inventory control became more effective. Because they could package and ship materials more quickly, the worker in the warehouse had enough time to enter the size and nature of shipments in the computer. Other UTC employees no longer walked off with books from the warehouse, because the shrink-wrapped bundles were larger and more conspicuous, and because taking five or ten books is more like stealing than "borrowing" one.

Finally, the improved service dramatically changed morale in the division. Customer outlet staff members, with their new and improved service, felt that finally someone had cared about them. They were more positive and they let people at corporate headquarters know about their feelings. "What's happening down there?" they asked. "The guys in the warehouse must be taking vitamins."

Morale soared in the warehouse. For the first time, other people liked the service workers there provided. Turnover decreased as pride in their work rose. They began to care more about the job, working faster with greater care. Managers who had previously given up on the "knuckle draggers" now asked openly about what had got into them.

Stanton believes the ethnographic approach is the key. She has managers who work for her read anthropology, especially books on ethnography, and she insists that they "find out what is going on."

Conclusion

Anthropology is, before all, an academic discipline with a strong emphasis on scholarship and basic research. But, as we have also seen, anthropology is a discipline that contains several intellectual tools—the concept of culture, the ethnographic approach to fieldwork, a cross-cultural perspective, a holistic view of human behavior—that make it useful in a broad range of nonacademic settings. In particular, it is the ability to do qualitative research that makes anthropologists successful in the professional world.

A few years ago an anthropologist consultant was asked by a utility company to answer a puzzling question: Why were its suburban customers, whose questionnaire responses indicated an attempt at conservation, failing to reduce their consumption of natural gas? To answer the question, the anthropologist conducted ethnographic interviews with members of several families, listening as they told him about how warm they liked their houses and how they set the heat throughout the day. He also received permission to install several video cameras aimed at thermostats in private houses. When the results were in, the answer to the question was deceptively simple: Fathers fill out questionnaires and turn down thermostats; wives, children, and cleaning workers, all of whom, in this case, spent time in the houses when fathers were absent, turn them up. Conservation, the anthropologist concluded, would have to involve family decisions, not just admonitions to save gas.

Over the past two or three years, anthropology's usefulness in the world of work has been discovered by the United States press. For example, *U.S. News and World Report* carried a story in 1998 entitled "Into the Wild Unknown of Workplace Culture: Anthropologists Revitalize Their Discipline," which traced changing trends in academic anthropology and highlighted the growth of the discipline's penetration of the business world.[1] Included in the article were examples of useful ethnography, such as the discovery by one anthropologist consultant that rank-and-file union members were upset with shop stewards because the latter spent more time recruiting new members than responding to grievances. In another instance, the article reported on the work of anthropologist Ken Erickson. Hired to find out why immigrant meatpackers had launched a wildcat strike, he was able to show that the workers struck because they felt their supervisors treated

---

1   Brendan I. Koerner, "Into the Wild Unknown of Workplace Culture: Anthropologists Revitalize Their Discipline," *U.S. News & World Report*, **August 10**, 1998, p. 56.

them as unskilled laborers, not because there was a language problem, as proposed by management. The workers had developed elaborate strategies to work quickly, effectively, and safely that were ignored or unknown to their supervisors.

In 1999, *USA Today* carried a story that further emphasized anthropology's usefulness. Entitled "Hot Asset in Corporate: Anthropology Degrees," the article began with, "Don't throw away the MBA degree yet. But as companies go global and crave leaders for a diverse workforce, a new hot degree is emerging for aspiring executives: anthropology."[2] The piece carried numerous examples—the hiring of anthropologist Steve Barnett as a vice president at Citicorp following his discovery of the early warning signs that identify people who do not pay credit card bills; the case of Hallmark, which sent anthropologists into immigrant homes to discover how holidays and birthdays are celebrated so that the company could design appropriate cards for such occasions; the example of a marketing consultant firm that sent anthropologists into bathrooms to watch how women shave their legs, and in the process, to discover what women want in a razor.

The article also listed executives who stressed how important their anthropology degree has been for their business successes. Motorola corporate lawyer Robert Faulkner says that the anthropology degree he received before going to law school has become increasingly valuable in his management job. Warned by his father that most problems are people problems, Michael Koss, CEO of the Koss headphone company, is another example. He received his anthropology degree from Beloit College. Katherine Burr, CEO of The Hanseatic Group, has an MA in anthropology and was quoted as saying, "My competitive edge came completely out of anthropology. The world is so unknown, changes so rapidly. Preconceptions can kill you." The article concluded with the observations of Ken Erickson of the Center for Ethnographic Research. "It takes trained observation. Observation is what anthropologists are trained to do."

In short, cultural anthropology has entered the world of business over the past twenty years. I argue that the key to its special utility and value in the commercial world is the ethnographic approach. Anthropologists have this ethnographic field experience and a sense of how social systems work and how people use their cultural knowledge. They have the special background, originally developed to discover and describe the cultural knowledge and behavior of unknown societies, needed to, in the words of Susan Stanton, "find out what is going on."

---

2   Del Jones, "Hot Asset in Corporate: Anthropology Degrees," *USA Today*, February 18, 1999, section B, p. 1.

Review Questions

1. What kinds of jobs do professional anthropologists do?

2. What is special about anthropology that makes fundamental knowledge of it valuable to some jobs?

3. What is meant by *qualitative research?* Why is such research valuable to business and government?

4. What difficulties did the company manager described in this article face? What solutions did she invent to deal with them? How did her knowledge of anthropology help her with this problem?

5. Why is ethnography useful in everyday life? Can you think of situations in which you could use ethnographic research?

2

CULTURE

CHAPTER THREE

Culture Change and Applied Anthropology

Nowhere in the world do human affairs remain precisely constant from year to year. New ways of doing things mark the history of even the most stable groups. Change occurs when an Australian aboriginal dreams about a new myth and teaches it to the members of his band; when a loader in a restaurant kitchen invents a way to stack plates more quickly in the dishwasher; or when a New Guinea Big Man cites the traditional beliefs about ghosts to justify the existence of a new political office devised by a colonial government. Wherever people interpret their natural and social worlds in a new way, cultural change has occurred. Broad or narrow, leisurely or rapid, such change is part of life in every society.

Culture change can originate from two sources: innovation and borrowing. **Innovation** is the invention of qualitatively new forms. It involves the recombination of what people already know into something different. For example, Canadian Joseph-Armand Bombardier became an innovator when he mated tracks, designed to propel earth-moving equipment, to a small bus that originally ran on tires, producing the first snowmobile in the 1950s. Later, the Skolt Lapps of Finland joined him as innovators when they adapted his now smaller, more refined snowmobile for herding reindeer in 1961. The Lapp innovation was not the vehicle itself. That was borrowed. What was new was the use of the vehicle in herding, something usually done by men on skis.

Innovations are more likely to occur and to be adopted during stressful times when traditional culture no longer works well. Bombardier, for example, began work on his snowmobile after he was unable to reach medical help in time to save the life of his critically ill son during a Canadian winter storm. Frustrated by the slowness of his horse and sleigh, he set out to create a faster vehicle.

The other basis of culture change is **borrowing.** Borrowing—or **diffusion,** as it is sometimes called—refers to the adoption of something new from another group. Tobacco, for example, was first domesticated and grown in the New World but quickly diffused to Europe and Asia after 1492. Such items as the umbrella, pajamas, Arabic numerals, and perhaps even the technology to make steel came to Europe from India. Ideologies and religions may diffuse from one society to another.

An extreme diffusionist view has been used to explain most human achievements. For example, author Erich von Daniken argues that features of ancient New World civilizations were brought by space invaders. Englishman G. Elliot Smith claimed that Mayan and Aztec culture diffused from Egypt. Thor Hey-erdahl sailed a reed boat, the *Ra II,* from Africa to South America to prove that an Egyptian cultural origin was possible for New World civilization.

Whether something is an innovation or borrowed, it must pass through a process of **social acceptance** before it can become part of a culture. Indeed many, if not most, novel ideas and things remain unattractive and relegated to obscurity. To achieve social acceptance, an innovation must become known to the members of a society, must be accepted as valid, and must fit into a system of cultural knowledge revised to accept it.

Several principles facilitate social acceptance. If a change wins the support of a person in authority, it may gain the approval of others. Timing is also important. It would have made little sense for a Lapp to attempt the introduction of snowmobiles when there was no snow or when the men who do the reindeer herding were scattered over their vast grazing territory. Other factors also affect social acceptance. Changes have a greater chance of acceptance if they meet a felt need, if they appeal to peoples prestige (in societies where prestige is important), and if they provide some continuity with traditional customs.

Change may take place under a variety of conditions, from the apparently dull day-to-day routine of a stable society to the frantic climate of a revolution. One situation that has occupied many anthropologists interested in change is **cultural contact,** particularly situations of contact where one society politically dominates another. World history is replete with examples of such domination, which vary in outcome from annihilation—in the case of the Tasmanians and hundreds of tribes in North and South America, Africa, Asia, and even ancient Europe—to the political rule that indentured countless millions of people to colonial powers.

The process of change caused by these conditions is called **acculturation.** Acculturation results from cultural contact. Acculturative change may affect dominant societies as well as subordinate ones. After their ascendance in India, for example, the British came to wear *khaki* clothes, live in *bungalows,* and trek through *jungles*—all Indian concepts.

But those who are subordinated experience the most far-reaching changes in their way of life. From politically independent, self-sufficient people, they usually become subordinate and dependent. Sweeping changes in social structure and values may occur, along with a resulting social disorganization.

Although the age of colonial empires is largely over, the destruction of tribal culture continues at a rapid pace today. As we saw in Reed's article in Part Three of this book, hundreds of thousands of Amazonian Indians have already perished in the last few years because of intrusive frontier and development programs. Following almost exactly the pattern of past colonial exploitation, modern governments bent on "progress" displace and often kill off indigenous tribal populations. The frequent failure of development, coupled with its damaging impact on native peoples, has caused many anthropologists to reassess their role. As a result, more and more anthropologists have become part of native resistance to outside intrusion.

A less dramatic, but in many ways no less important, agent of change is the world economy. No longer can most people live in self-sufficient isolation. Their future is inevitably tied in with an overall system of market exchange. Take the Marshall Islanders described by anthropologist Michael Rynkiewich, for example. Although they cultivate to meet their own subsistence needs, they also raise coconuts for sale on the world market. Receipts from the coconut crop go to pay for outboard motors and gasoline, cooking utensils, and a variety of other goods they don't manufacture themselves but have come to depend on. Several major American food companies have now eliminated coconut oil from their products because of its high level of saturated fat. This loss has created lower demand for copra (dried coconut meat), from which the oil is pressed. Reduced demand, in turn, may cause substantial losses to the Marshall Islanders. A people who once could subsist independently have now become prisoners of the world economic system.

Anthropologists may themselves become agents of change, applying their work to practical problems. **Applied anthropology,** as opposed to academic anthropology, includes any use of anthropological knowledge to influence social interaction, to maintain or change social institutions, or to direct the course of cultural change. There are four basic uses of anthropology contained within the applied field: adjustment anthropology, administrative anthropology, action anthropology, and advocate anthropology.

Adjustment anthropology uses anthropological knowledge to make social interaction more predictable among people who operate with different cultural codes. For example, take the anthropologists who consult with companies and government agencies about intercultural communication. It is often their job to train Americans to interpret the cultural rules that govern interaction in another society. For a businessperson who will work in Latin America, the anthropologist may point out the appropriate culturally defined speaking distances, ways to sit, definitions of time, topics of conversation, times for business talk, and so on. All of these activities would be classified as adjustment anthropology.

Administrative anthropology uses anthropological knowledge for planned change by those who are external to the local cultural group. It is the use of anthropological knowledge by a person with the power to make decisions. If an anthropologist provides knowledge to a mayor about the culture of constituents, he or she is engaged in administrative anthropology. So would advisers to chief administrators of U.S. trust territories such as once existed in places like the Marshall Islands.

Action anthropology uses anthropological knowledge for planned change by the local cultural group. The anthropologist acts as a catalyst, providing information but avoiding decision making, which remains in the hands of the people affected by the decisions.

Advocate anthropology uses anthropological knowledge by the anthropologist to increase the power of self-determination of a particular cultural group. Instead of focusing on the process of innovation, the anthropologist centers attention on discovering the sources of power and how a group can gain access to them. James Spradley took such action when he studied tramps in 1968. He discovered that police and courts systematically deprived tramps of their power to control their lives and of the rights accorded normal citizens. By releasing his findings to the Seattle newspapers, he helped tramps gain additional power and weakened the control of Seattle authorities.

Whether they are doing administrative, advocate, adjustment, or action anthropology, anthropologists take, at least in part, a qualitative approach. They do ethnography, discover the cultural knowledge of their informants, and apply this information in the ways discussed previously. In contrast to the quantitative data so often prized by other social scientists, they use the insider's viewpoint to discover problems, to advise, and to generate policy.

The articles in this part illustrate several aspects of cultural change and applied anthropology. The first, by Terence Turner, relates the case of how one people, the Kayapo of the Brazilian Amazon, have successfully resisted external threats to their existence as a people. By uniting Indians, environmental groups, and legislators, and using the international media, they have managed to protect and expand their forest area and advance the international environmental cause. The second updated selection, by medical anthropologist Sonia Patten, describes her experience as an applied anthropologist. Working with USAID funding, she and a team of specialists designed a program using milk goats to improve children's nutrition in Malawi. The third article, by David McCurdy, discusses the modern uses of anthropology. From studies of General Motors workers, to program assessment for people with AIDS, to participation in government health projects, to international counseling, professional anthropologists put their discipline to work. In this article, McCurdy looks at one way in which the ethnographic perspective can be put to work in a business setting. Finally, in the last article, John Omohundro tackles a question often asked by students: "What do you do with an anthropology major?" Basing his answer on years of work with his institution's career development office, he argues that anthropology teaches a number of skills that are useful in the world of work. The trick, he notes, is for students to translate these skills into resume language that employers can understand.

Key Terms

acculturation
action anthropology
adjustment anthropology
administrative anthropology
advocate anthropology
applied anthropology

borrowing
cultural contact
diffusion
innovation
social acceptance

CHAPTER FOUR

Eating Christmas in the Kalahari

Richard Borshay Lee

What happens when an anthropologist living among the !Kung of Africa decides to be generous and to share a large animal with everyone at Christmastime? This compelling account of the misunderstanding and confusion that resulted takes the reader deeper into the nature of culture. Richard Lee carefully traces how the !Kung perceived his generosity and taught the anthropologist something about his own culture.

The !Kung Bushmen's knowledge of Christmas is thirdhand. The London Missionary Society brought the holiday to the southern Tswana tribes in the early nineteenth century. Later, native catechists spread the idea far and wide among the Bantu-speaking pastoralists, even in the remotest corners of the Kalahari Desert. The Bushmen's idea of the Christmas story, stripped to its essentials, is "praise the birth of white man's god-chief"; what keeps their interest in the holiday high is the Tswana-Herero custom of slaughtering an ox for his Bushmen neighbors as an annual goodwill gesture. Since the 1930s, part of the Bushmen's annual round of activities has included a December congregation at the cattle posts for trading, marriage brokering, and several days of trance dance feasting at which the local Tswana headman is host.

As a social anthropologist working with !Kung Bushmen, I found that the Christmas ox custom suited my purposes. I had come to the Kalahari to study the hunting and gathering subsistence economy of the !Kung, and to accomplish this it was essential not to provide them with food, share my own food, or interfere in any way with their food-gathering activities. While liberal handouts of tobacco and medical supplies were appreciated, they were scarcely adequate to erase the glaring disparity in wealth between the anthropologist, who maintained a two-month inventory of canned goods, and the Bushmen, who rarely had a day's supply of food on hand. My approach, while paying off in terms of data, left me open to frequent accusations of stinginess and hardheartedness. By their lights, I was a miser.

The Christmas ox was to be my way of saying thank you for the cooperation of the past year; and since it was to be our last Christmas in the field, I was determined to slaughter the largest, meatiest ox that money could buy, insuring that the feast and trance dance would be a success.

Through December I kept my eyes open at the wells as the cattle were brought down for watering. Several animals were offered, but none had quite the grossness that I had in mind. Then, ten days before the holiday, a Herero friend led an ox of astonishing size and mass up to our camp. It was solid black, stood five feet high at the shoulder, had a five-foot span of horns, and must have weighed 1,200 pounds on the hoof. Food consumption calculations are my specialty, and I quickly figured that bones and viscera aside, there was enough meat—at least four pounds—for every man, woman, and child of the 150 Bushmen in the vicinity of /ai/ai who were expected at the feast.

Having found the right animal at last, I paid the Herero £20 ($56) and asked him to keep the beast with his herd until Christmas day. The next morning word spread among the people that the big solid black one was the ox chosen by /ontah (my Bushman name; it means, roughly, "whitey") for the Christmas feast. That afternoon I received the first delegation. Ben!a, an outspoken sixty-year-old mother of five, came to the point slowly.

"Where were you planning to eat Christmas?"

"Right here at /ai/ai," I replied.

"Alone or with others?"

"I expect to invite all the people to eat Christmas with me."

"Eat what?"

"I have purchased Yehave's black ox, and I am going to slaughter and cook it."

"That's what we were told at the well but refused to believe it until we heard it from yourself."

"Well, it's the black one," I replied expansively, although wondering what she was driving at.

"Oh, no!" Ben!a groaned, turning to her group. "They were right." Turning back to me she asked, "Do you expect us to eat that bag of bones?"

"Bag of bones! It's the biggest ox at /ai/ai."

"Big, yes, but old. And thin. Everybody knows there's no meat on that old ox. What did you expect us to eat off it, the horns?"

Everybody chuckled at Benla's one-liner as they walked away, but all I could manage was a weak grin.

That evening it was the turn of the young men. They came to sit at our evening fire. /gaugo, about my age, spoke to me man-to-man.

"/ontah, you have always been square with us," he lied. "What has happened to change your heart? That sack of guts and bones of Yehave's will hardly feed one camp, let alone all the Bushmen around /ai/ai." And he proceeded to enumerate the seven camps in the /ai/ai vicinity, family by family. "Perhaps you have forgotten that we are not few, but many. Or are you too blind to tell the difference between a proper cow and an old wreck? That ox is thin to the point of death."

"Look, you guys," I retorted, "that is a beautiful animal, and I'm sure you will eat it with pleasure at Christmas."

"Of course we will eat it; it's food. But it won't fill us up to the point where we will have enough strength to dance. We will eat and go home to bed with stomachs rumbling."

That night as we turned in, I asked my wife, Nancy, "What did you think of the black ox?"

"It looked enormous to me. Why?"

"Well, about eight different people have told me I got gypped; that the ox is nothing but bones."

"What's the angle?" Nancy asked. "Did they have a better one to sell?"

"No, they just said that it was going to be a grim Christmas because there won't be enough meat to go around. Maybe I'll get an independent judge to look at the beast in the morning."

Bright and early, Halingisi, a Tswana cattle owner, appeared at our camp. But before I could ask him to give me his opinion on Yehave's black ox, he gave me the eye signal that indicated a confidential chat. We left the camp and sat down.

"/ontah, I'm surprised at you; you've lived here for three years and still haven't learned anything about cattle."

"But what else can a person do but choose the biggest, strongest animal one can find?" I retorted.

"Look, just because an animal is big doesn't mean that it has plenty of meat on it. The black one was a beauty when it was younger, but now it is thin to the point of death."

"Well, I've already bought it. What can I do at this stage?"

"Bought it already? I thought you were just considering it. Well, you'll have to kill it and serve it, I suppose. But don't expect much of a dance to follow."

My spirits dropped rapidly. I could believe that Ben!a and /gaugo just might be putting me on about the black ox, but Halingisi seemed to be an impartial critic. I went around that day feeling as though I had bought a lemon of a used car.

In the afternoon it was Tomazo's turn. Tomazo is a fine hunter, a top trance performer . ... and one of my most reliable informants. He approached the subject of the Christmas cow as part of my continuing Bushman education.

"My friend, the way it is with us Bushmen," he began, "is that we love meat. And even more than that, we love fat. When we hunt we always search for the fat ones, the ones dripping with layers of white fat: fat that turns into a clear, thick oil in the cooking pot, fat that slides down your gullet, fills your stomach and gives you a roaring diarrhea," he rhapsodized.

"So, feeling as we do," he continued, "it gives us pain to be served such a scrawny thing as Yehave's black ox. It is big, yes, and no doubt its giant bones are good for soup, but fat is what we really crave, and so we will eat Christmas this year with a heavy heart."

The prospect of a gloomy Christmas now had me worried, so I asked Tomazo what I could do about it.

"Look for a fat one, a young one . . . smaller, but fat. Fat enough to make us //gom (evacuate the bowels), then we will be happy."

My suspicions were aroused when Tomazo said that he happened to know a young, fat, barren cow that the owner was willing to part with. Was Tomazo working on commission, I wondered? But I dispelled this unworthy thought when we approached the Herero owner of the cow in question and found that he had decided not to sell.

The scrawny wreck of a Christmas ox now became the talk of the /ai/ai water hole and was the first news told to the outlying groups as they began to come in from the bush for the feast. What finally convinced me that real trouble might be brewing was the visit from u!au, an old conservative with a reputation for fierceness. His nickname meant spear and referred to an incident thirty years ago in which he had speared a man to death. He had an intense manner; fixing me with his eyes, he said in clipped tones:

"I have only just heard about the black ox today, or else I would have come here earlier. /ontah, do you honestly think you can serve meat like that to people and avoid a fight?" He paused, letting the implications sink in. "I don't mean fight you, /ontah; you are a white man. I mean a fight between Bushmen. There are many fierce ones here, and with such a small quantity of meat to distribute, how can you give everybody a fair share? Someone is sure to accuse another of taking too much or hogging all the choice pieces. Then you will see what happens when some go hungry while others eat."

The possibility of at least a serious argument struck me as all too real. I had witnessed the tension that surrounds the distribution of meat from a kudu or gemsbok kill, and had documented many arguments that sprang up from a real or imagined slight in meat distribution. The owners of a kill may spend up to two hours arranging and rearranging the piles of meat under the gaze of a circle of recipients before handing them out. And I knew that the Christmas feast at /ai/ai would be bringing together groups that had feuded in the past.

Convinced now of the gravity of the situation, I went in earnest to search for a second cow; but all my inquiries failed to turn one up.

The Christmas feast was evidently going to be a disaster, and the incessant complaints about the meagerness of the ox had already taken the fun out of it for me. Moreover, I was getting bored with the wisecracks, and after losing my temper a few times, I resolved to serve the beast anyway. If the meat fell short, the hell with it. In the Bushmen idiom, I announced to all who would listen:

"I am a poor man and blind. If I have chosen one that is too old and too thin, we will eat it anyway and see if there is enough meat there to quiet the rumbling of our stomachs."

On hearing this speech, Ben!a offered me a rare word of comfort. "It's thin," she said philosophically, "but the bones will make a good soup."

At dawn Christmas morning, instinct told me to turn over the butchering and cooking to a friend and take off with Nancy to spend Christmas alone in the bush. But curiosity kept me from retreating. I wanted to see what such a scrawny ox looked like on butchering, and if there *was* going to be a fight, I wanted to catch every word of it. Anthropologists are incurable that way.

The great beast was driven up to our dancing ground, and a shot in the forehead dropped it in its tracks. Then, freshly cut branches were heaped around the fallen carcass to receive the meat. Ten men volunteered to help with the cutting. I asked /gaugo to make the breast bone cut. This cut, which begins the butchering process for most large game, offers easy access for removal of the viscera. But it also allows the hunter to spot-check the amount of fat on an animal. A fat game animal carries a white layer up to an inch thick on the chest, while in a thin

one, the knife will quickly cut to bone. All eyes fixed on his hand as /
gaugo, dwarfed by the great carcass, knelt to the breast. The first cut
opened a pool of solid white in the black skin. The second and third
cut widened and deepened the creamy white. Still no bone. It was pure
fat; it must have been two inches thick.

"Hey /gau," I burst out, "that ox is loaded with fat. What's this
about the ox being too thin to bother eating? Are you out of your mind?"

"Fat?" /gau shot back. "You call that fat? This wreck is thin, sick,
dead!" And he broke out laughing. So did everyone else. They rolled
on the ground, paralyzed with laughter. Everybody laughed except me;
I was thinking.

I ran back to the tent and burst in just as Nancy was getting up.
"Hey, the black ox. It's fat as hell! They were kidding about it being
too thin to eat. It was a joke or something. A put-on. Everyone is really
delighted with it."

"Some joke," my wife replied. "It was so funny that you were ready
to pack up and leave /ai/ai."

If it had indeed been a joke, it had been an extraordinarily
convincing one, and tinged, I thought, with more than a touch of
malice, as many jokes are. Nevertheless, that it was a joke lifted my
spirits considerably, and I returned to the butchering site where the
shape of the ox was rapidly disappearing under the axes and knives of
the butchers. The atmosphere had become festive. Grinning broadly,
their arms covered with blood well past the elbow, men packed chunks
of meat into the big cast-iron cooking pots, fifty pounds to the load,
and muttered and chuckled all the while about the thinness and
worthlessness of the animal and /ontah's poor judgment.

We danced and ate that ox two days and two nights; we cooked
and distributed fourteen potfuls of meat and no one went home hungry
and no fights broke out.

But the "joke" stayed in my mind. I had a growing feeling that
something important had happened in my relationship with the
Bushmen and that the clue lay in the meaning of the joke. Several days
later, when most of the people had dispersed back to the bush camps,
I raised the question with Hakekgose, a Tswana man who had grown
up among the !Kung, married a !Kung girl, and who probably knew
their culture better than any other non-Bushman.

"With us whites," I began, "Christmas is supposed to be the day
of friendship and brotherly love. What I can't figure out is why the
Bushmen went to such lengths to criticize and belittle the ox I had
bought for the feast. The animal was perfectly good and their jokes and
wisecracks practically ruined the holiday for me."

"So it really did bother you," said Hakekgose. "Well, that's the way they always talk. When I take my rifle and go hunting with them, if I miss, they laugh at me for the rest of the day. But even if I hit and bring one down, it's no better. To them, the kill is always too small or too old or too thin; and as we sit down on the kill site to cook and eat the liver, they keep grumbling, even with their mouths full of meat. They say things like, 'Oh, this is awful! What a worthless animal! Whatever made me think that this Tswana rascal could hunt!' "

"Is this the way outsiders are treated?" I asked.

"No, it is their custom; they talk that way to each other, too. Go and ask them."

/gaugo had been one of the most enthusiastic in making me feel bad about the merit of the Christmas ox. I sought him out first.

"Why did you tell me the black ox was worthless, when you could see that it was loaded with fat and meat?"

"It is our way," he said, smiling. "We always like to fool people about that. Say there is a Bushman who has been hunting. He must not come home and announce like a braggart, 'I have killed a big one in the bush!' He must first sit down in silence until I or someone else comes up to his fire and asks, 'What did you see today?' He replies quietly, 'Ah, I'm no good for hunting. I saw nothing at all [pause] just a little tiny one.' Then I smile to myself," /gaugo continued, "because I know he has killed something big.

"In the morning we make up a party of four or five people to cut up and carry the meat back to the camp. When we arrive at the kill we examine it and cry out, 'You mean to say you have dragged us all the way out here in order to make us cart home your pile of bones? Oh, if I had known it was this thin I wouldn't have come.' Another one pipes up, 'People, to think I gave up a nice day in the shade for this. At home we may be hungry, but at least we have nice cool water to drink.' If the horns are big, someone says, 'Did you think that somehow you were going to boil down the horns for soup?'

"To all this you must respond in kind. 'I agree,' you say, 'this one is not worth the effort; let's just cook the liver for strength and leave the rest for the hyenas. It is not too late to hunt today and even a duiker or a steenbok would be better than this mess.'

"Then you set to work nevertheless; butcher the animal, carry the meat back to the camp and everyone eats," /gaugo concluded.

Things were beginning to make sense. Next, I went to Tomazo. He corroborated /gaugo's story of the obligatory insults over a kill and added a few details of his own.

"But," I asked, "why insult a man after he has gone to all that trouble to track and kill an animal and when he is going to share the meat with you so that your children will have something to eat?"

"Arrogance," was his cryptic answer.

"Arrogance?"

"Yes, when a young man kills much meat he comes to think of himself as a chief or a big man, and he thinks of the rest of us as his servants or inferiors. We can't accept this. We refuse one who boasts, for someday his pride will make him kill somebody. So we always speak of his meat as worthless. This way we cool his heart and make him gentle."

"But why didn't you tell me this before?" I asked Tomazo with some heat.

"Because you never asked me," said Tomazo, echoing the refrain that has come to haunt every field ethnographer.

The pieces now fell into place. I had known for a long time that in situations of social conflict with Bushmen I held all the cards. I was the only source of tobacco in a thousand square miles, and I was not incapable of cutting an individual off for noncooperation. Though my boycott never lasted longer than a few days, it was an indication of my strength. People resented my presence at the water hole, yet simultaneously dreaded my leaving. In short I was a perfect target for the charge of arrogance and for the Bushman tactic of enforcing humility.

I had been taught an object lesson by the Bushmen; it had come from an unexpected corner and had hurt me in a vulnerable area. For the big black ox was to be the one totally generous, unstinting act of my year at /ai/ai and I was quite unprepared for the reaction I received.

As I read it, their message was this: There are no totally generous acts. All "acts" have an element of calculation. One black ox slaughtered at Christmas does not wipe out a year of careful manipulation of gifts given to serve your own ends. After all, to kill an animal and share the meat with people is really no more than the Bushmen do for each other every day and with far less fanfare.

In the end, I had to admire how the Bushmen had played out the farce— collectively straight-faced to the end. Curiously, the episode reminded me of the *Good Soldier Schweik* and his marvelous encounters with authority. Like Schweik, the Bushmen had retained a thoroughgoing skepticism of good intentions. Was it this independence of spirit, I wondered, that had kept them culturally viable in the face of generations of contact with more powerful societies, both black and white? The thought that the Bushmen were alive and well in the Kalahari was strangely comforting. Perhaps, armed with that independence and with their superb knowledge of their environment, they might yet survive the future.

Review Questions

1. What was the basis of the misunderstanding experienced by Lee when he gave an ox for the Christmas feast held by the !Kung?

2. Construct a model of cross-cultural misunderstanding, using the information presented by Lee in this article.

3. Why do you think the !Kung ridicule and denigrate people who have been successful hunters or who have provided them with a Christmas ox? Why do Americans expect people to be grateful to receive gifts?

3

LANGUAGE

CHAPTER FIVE

Language and Communication

Culture is a system of symbols that allows us to represent and communicate our experience. We are surrounded by symbols: the flag, a new automobile, a diamond ring, billboard pictures, and, of course, spoken words.

A **symbol** is anything that we can perceive with our senses that stands for something else. Almost anything we experience can come to have symbolic meaning. Every symbol has a referent that it calls to our attention. The term *lawn*, for example, refers to a field of grass plants. When we communicate with symbols, we call attention not only to the referent but also to numerous connotations of the symbol. In U.S. culture we associate lawns with places such as homes and golf courses; actions such as mowing, fertilizing, and raking; and activities such as backyard games and barbeques. Human beings have the capacity to assign meaning to anything they experience in an arbitrary fashion, which allows limitless possibilities for communication.

Symbols greatly simplify the task of communication. Once we learn that a word such as *barn*, for example, stands for a certain type of building, we can communicate about a whole range of specific buildings that fit into the category. And we can communicate about barns in their absence; we can even invent flying barns and dream about barns. Symbols make it possible to communicate the immense variety of human experience, whether past or present, tangible or intangible, good or bad.

Many channels are available to human beings for symbolic communication: sound, sight, touch, and smell. Language, our most highly developed communication system, uses the channel of sound (or, for some deaf people, sight). **Language** is a system of cultural knowledge used to generate and interpret speech. It is a feature of every culture and a distinctive characteristic of the human animal. **Speech** refers to the behavior that produces vocal sounds. Our distinction between language and speech is like the one made between culture and behavior. Language is part of culture, the system of knowledge that generates behavior. Speech is the behavior generated and interpreted by language.

Every language is composed of three subsystems for dealing with vocal symbols: phonology, grammar, and semantics. Let's look briefly at each of these.

Phonology consists of the categories and rules for forming vocal symbols. It is concerned not directly with meaning but with the formation and recognition of the vocal sounds to which we assign meaning. For example, if you utter the word *bat*, you have followed a special set of rules for producing and ordering sound categories characteristic of the English language.

A basic element defined by phonological rules for every language is the phoneme. **Phonemes** are the minimal categories of speech sounds that serve to keep utterances apart. For example, speakers of English know that the words *bat, cat, mat, hat, rat,* and *fat* are different utterances because they hear the sounds /b/, /c/, /m/, /h/, /r/, and /f/ as different categories of sounds. In English, each of these is a phoneme. Our language contains a limited number of phonemes from which we construct all our vocal symbols.

Phonemes are arbitrarily constructed, however. Each phoneme actually classifies slightly different sounds as though they were the same. Different languages may divide up the same range of speech sounds into different sound categories. For example, speakers of English treat the sound /t/ as a single phoneme. Hindi speakers take the same general range and divide it into four phonemes: /t/, /tʰ/, /T/, and /Tʰ/. (The lowercase *t*'s are made with the tongue against the front teeth, while the uppercase *T*'s are made by touching the tongue to the roof of the mouth further back than would be normal for an English speaker. The *h* indicates a puff of air, called *aspiration*, associated with the *t* sound.) Americans are likely to miss important distinctions among Hindi words because they hear these four different phonemes as a single one. Hindi speakers, on the other hand, tend to hear more than one sound category as they listen to English speakers pronounce *t*'s. The situation is reversed for /w/ and /v/. We treat these as two phonemes, whereas Hindi speakers hear them as one. For them, the English words *wine* and *vine* sound the same.

Phonology also includes rules for ordering different sounds. Even when we try to talk nonsense, we usually create words that follow English phonological rules. It would be unlikely, for example, for us ever to begin a word with the phoneme /ng/—usually written in English as "ing." It must come at the end or in the middle of words.

Grammar is the second subsystem of language. **Grammar** refers to the categories and rules for combining vocal symbols. No grammar contains rules for combining every word or element of meaning in the language. If this were the case, grammar would be so unwieldy that no one could learn all the rules in a lifetime. Every grammar deals with *categories* of symbols, such as the ones we call *nouns* and *verbs*. Once you know the rules covering a particular category, you can use it in appropriate combinations.

Morphemes are the categories in any language that carry meaning. They are minimal units of meaning that cannot be subdivided. Morphemes occur in more complex patterns than you may think. The term *bats*, for example, is actually two morphemes, /bat/ meaning a flying mammal and /s/ meaning plural. Even more confusing, two different morphemes may have the same sound shape. /Bat/ can refer to a wooden club used in baseball as well as a flying mammal.

The third subsystem of every language is semantics. **Semantics** refers to the categories and rules for relating vocal symbols to their referents. Like the rules of grammar, semantic rules are simple instructions for combining things; they instruct us to combine words with what they refer to. A symbol can be said to *refer* because it focuses our attention and makes us take account of something. For example, /bat/ refers to a family of flying mammals, as we have already noted.

Language regularly occurs in a social context, and to understand its use fully it is important to recognize its relation to sociolinguistic rules. **Sociolinguistic rules** combine meaningful utterances with social situations into appropriate messages.

Although language is the most important human vehicle for communication, almost anything we can sense may represent a **nonlinguistic symbol** that conveys meaning. The way we sit, how we use our eyes, how we dress, the car we own, the number of bathrooms in our house—all these things carry symbolic meaning. We learn what they mean as we acquire culture. Indeed, a major reason we feel so uncomfortable when we enter a group from a strange culture is our inability to decode our host's symbolic world.

The articles in Part Two illustrate several important aspects of language and communication. The first, by Sarah Boxer, describes the way the U.S. armed forces (and by extension people in general) use words to influence how listeners will define events. To do so, she traces the history of how military operations receive their names and points out that today, names such as "Just Cause" may actually create negative as well as positive images in an audience. Article 7, by Deborah Tannen, looks at another aspect of language—conversation styles. Focusing on the different speaking styles of men and women in the workplace, she describes and analyzes how conversational styles themselves carry meaning and unwittingly lead to misunderstanding. In the third selection, Jennifer Boehlke illustrates the concept of speech acts, which are ways to talk. Based on her ethnography of tattooists at a tattoo and piercing parlor, she describes the speech act called *juicing*, which is used by tattooists to persuade clients to get tattoos, reduce their fear, reinforce their decisions, and spend more money. The final article, by Belle Mellor, describes how anthropologists have been hired to discover the ways people use technical communication devices, such as cell phones, computers, and landlines.

Key Terms

grammar
language
morphemes
nonlinguistic symbol
phonemes

phonology
semantics
sociolinguistic rules
speech
symbol

CHAPTER SIX

Conversation Style: Talking on the Job

Deborah Tannen

In this piece excerpted from her book about conversation in the workplace, Deborah Tannen discusses a tacit dimension of communication, conversation style. Looking at the different ways men and women approach or avoid asking for help on the job, she argues that gender differences in conversation style are responsible not only for miscommunication but also for misguided evaluations and moral judgments about the performance and character of co-workers.

People have different conversational styles, influenced by the part of the country they grew up in, their ethnic backgrounds and those of their parents, their age, class, and gender. But conversational style is invisible. Unaware that these and other aspects of our backgrounds influence our ways of talking, we think we are simply saying what we mean. Because we don't realize that others' styles are different, we are often frustrated in conversations. Rather than seeing the culprit as differing styles, we attribute troubles to others' intentions (she doesn't like me), abilities (he's stupid), or character (she's rude, he's inconsiderate), our own failure (what's wrong with me?), or the failure of a relationship (we just can't communicate)....

Although I am aware of the many influences on conversational style and have spent most of my career studying and writing about them . . . style differences influenced by gender receive particular attention [here]. This is not only because these are the differences people most want to hear about (although this is so and is a factor), but also because there is something fundamental about our categorization by gender. When you spot a person walking down the street toward you, you immediately and automatically identify that person as male or female. You will not necessarily try to determine which state they are from, what their class background is, or what country their grandparents came from. A secondary identification, in some places and times, may be about race. But, while we may envision a day when a director will be able to cast actors for a play without reference to race, can we imagine a time when actors can be cast without reference to their sex?

Few elements of our identities come as close to our sense of who we are as gender. If you mistake people's cultural background—you thought they were Greek, but they turn out to be Italian; you assumed they'd grown up in Texas, but it turns out they're from Kentucky; you say "Merry Christmas" and they say, "we don't celebrate Christmas; we're Muslim"—it catches you off guard and you rearrange the mental frame through which you view them. But if someone you thought was male turns out to be female—like the jazz musician Billy Tipton, whose own adopted sons never suspected that their father was a woman until the coroner broke the news to them after his (her) death—the required adjustment is staggering. Even infants discriminate between males and females and react differently depending on which they confront.

Perhaps it is because our sense of gender is so deeply rooted that people are inclined to hear descriptions of gender patterns as statements about gender *identity*—in other words, as absolute differences rather than a matter of degree and percentages, and as universal rather than culturally mediated. The patterns I describe are based on observations of particular speakers in a particular place and time: mostly (but not exclusively) middle-class Americans of European background working in offices at the present time. Other cultures evince very different patterns of talk associated with gender—and correspondingly different assumptions about the "natures" of women and men. I don't put a lot of store in talk about "natures" or what is "natural." People in every culture will tell you that the behaviors common in their own culture are "natural." I also don't put a lot of store in people's explanations that their way of talking is a natural response to their environment, as there is always an equally natural and opposite way of responding to the same environment. We all tend to regard the way things are as the way things have to be—as only natural.

The reason ways of talking, like other ways of conducting our daily lives, come to seem natural is that the behaviors that make up our lives are ritualized. Indeed, the "ritual" character of interaction is at the heart of this book. Having grown up in a particular culture, we learn to do things as the people we encounter do them, so the vast majority of our decisions about how to speak become automatic. You see someone you know, you ask "How are you?," chat, then take your leave, never pausing to ponder the many ways you could handle this interaction differently—and would, if you lived in a different culture. Just as an American automatically extends a hand for a handshake while a Japanese automatically bows, what the American and Japanese find it natural to say is a matter of convention learned over a lifetime.

No one understood the ritual nature of everyday life better than sociologist Erving Goffman, who also understood the fundamental role played by gender in organizing our daily rituals. In his article "The Arrangement Between the Sexes," Goffman pointed out that we tend to say "sex-linked" when what we mean is "sex-class-linked." When hearing that a behavior is "sex-linked," people often conclude that the behavior is to be found in every individual of that group, and that it is somehow inherent in their sex, as if it came hooked to a chromosome. Goffman suggests the term "genderism" (on the model, I assume, of "mannerism," not of "sexism") for "a sex-class linked individual behavioral practice." This is the spirit in which I intend references to gendered patterns of behavior: not to imply that there is anything inherently male or female about particular ways of talking, nor to claim that every individual man or woman adheres to the pattern, but rather to observe that a larger percentage of women or men *as a group* talk in a particular way, or individual women and men *are more likely* to talk one way or the other.

That individuals do not always fit the pattern associated with their gender does not mean that the pattern is not typical. Because more women or men speak in a particular way, that way of speaking becomes associated with women or men—or, rather, it is the other way around: More women or men learn to speak particular ways *because* those ways are associated with their own gender. And individual men or women who speak in ways associated with the other gender will pay a price for departing from cultural expectations.

If my concept of how gender displays itself in everyday life has been influenced by Goffman, the focus of my research—talk—and my method for studying it grow directly out of my own discipline, linguistics. My understanding of what goes on when people talk to each other is based on observing and listening as well as tape-recording, transcribing, and analyzing conversation. In response to my book *You Just Don't Understand*, I was contacted by people at many companies who asked whether I could help them apply the insights in that book to the problem of "the glass ceiling": Why weren't women advancing as quickly as the men who were hired at the same time? And more generally, they wanted to understand how to integrate women as well as others who were historically not "typical" employees into the increasingly diverse workforce. I realized that in order to offer insight, I needed to observe what was really going on in the workplace. . . .

Women and Men Talking on the Job

Amy was a manager with a problem: She had just read a final report written by Donald, and she felt it was woefully inadequate. She faced the unsavory task of telling him to do it over. When she met with Donald, she made sure to soften the blow by beginning with praise, telling him everything about his report that was good. Then she went on to explain what was lacking and what needed to be done to make it acceptable. She was pleased with the diplomatic way she had managed to deliver the bad news. Thanks to her thoughtfulness in starting with praise, Donald was able to listen to the criticism and seemed to understand what was needed. But when the revised report appeared on her desk, Amy was shocked. Donald had made only minor, superficial changes, and none of the necessary ones. The next meeting with him did not go well. He was incensed that she was now telling him his report was not acceptable and accused her of having misled him. "You told me before it was fine," he protested.

Amy thought she had been diplomatic; Donald thought she had been dishonest. The praise she intended to soften the message "This is unacceptable" sounded to him like the message itself: "This is fine." So what she regarded as the main point—the needed changes—came across to him as optional suggestions, because he had already registered her praise as the main point. She felt he hadn't listened to her. He thought she had changed her mind and was making him pay the price.

Work days are filled with conversations about getting the job done. Most of these conversations succeed, but too many end in impasses like this. It could be that Amy is a capricious boss whose wishes are whims, and it could be that Donald is a temperamental employee who can't hear criticism no matter how it is phrased. But I don't think either was the case in this instance. I believe this was one of innumerable misunderstandings caused by differences in conversational style. Amy delivered the criticism in a way that seemed to her self-evidently considerate, a way she would have preferred to receive criticism herself:

taking into account the other person's feelings, making sure he knew that her ultimate negative assessment of his report didn't mean she had no appreciation of his abilities. She offered the praise as a sweetener to help the nasty-tasting news go down. But Donald didn't expect criticism to be delivered in that way, so he mistook the praise as her overall assessment rather than a preamble to it.

This conversation could have taken place between two women or two men. But I do not think it is a coincidence that it occurred between a man and a woman. . . . Conversational rituals common among men often involve using opposition such as banter, joking, teasing, and playful put-downs, and expending effort to avoid the one-down position in the interaction. Conversational rituals common among women are often ways of maintaining an appearance of equality, taking into account the effect of the exchange on the other person, and expending effort to downplay the speakers' authority so they can get the job done without flexing their muscles in an obvious way.

When everyone present is familiar with these conventions, they work well. But when ways of speaking are not recognized as conventions, they are taken literally, with negative results on both sides. Men whose oppositional strategies are interpreted literally may be seen as hostile when they are not, and their efforts to ensure that they avoid appearing one-down may be taken as arrogance. When women use conversational strategies designed to avoid appearing boastful and to take the other person's feelings into account, they may be seen as less confident and competent than they really are. As a result, both women and men often feel they are not getting sufficient credit for what they have done, are not being listened to, are not getting ahead as fast as they should.

When I talk about women's and men's characteristic ways of speaking, I always emphasize that both styles make sense and are equally valid in themselves, though the difference in styles may cause trouble in interaction. In a sense, when two people form a private relationship of love or friendship, the bubble of their interaction is a world unto itself, even though they both come with the prior experience of their families, their community, and a lifetime of conversations. But someone who takes a job is entering a world that is already functioning, with its own characteristic style already in place. Although there are many influences such as regional background, the type of industry involved, whether it is a family business or a large corporation, in general, workplaces that have previously had men in positions of power have already established male-style interaction as the norm. In that sense, women, and others whose styles are different, are not starting out equal, but are at a disadvantage. Though talking at work is quite similar to talking in private, it is a very different enterprise in many ways.

When not Asking Directions is Dangerous to Your Health

If conversational-style differences lead to troublesome outcomes in work as well as private settings, there are some work settings where the outcomes of style are a matter of life and death. Healthcare professionals are often in such situations. So are airline pilots.

Of all the examples of women's and men's characteristic styles that I discussed in *You Just Don't Understand,* the one that (to my surprise) attracted the most attention was the question "Why don't men like to stop and ask for directions?" Again and again, in the responses of audiences, talk-show hosts, letter writers, journalists, and conversationalists, this question seemed to crystallize the frustration many people had experienced in their own lives. And my explanation seems to have rung true: that men are more likely to be aware that asking for directions, or for any kind of help, puts them in a one-down position.

With regard to asking directions, women and men are keenly aware of the advantages of their own style. Women frequently observe how much time they would save if their husbands simply stopped and asked someone instead of driving around trying in vain to find a destination themselves. But I have also been told by men that it makes sense not to ask directions because you learn a lot about a neighborhood, as well as about navigation, by driving around and finding your own way.

But some situations are more risky than others. A Hollywood talk-show producer told me that she had been flying with her father in his private airplane when he was running out of gas and uncertain about the precise location of the local landing strip he was heading for. Beginning to panic, the woman said, "Daddy! Why don't you radio the control tower and ask them where to land?" He answered, "I don't want them to think I'm lost." This story had a happy ending, else the woman would not have been alive to tell it to me.

Some time later, I repeated this anecdote to a man at a cocktail party—a man who had just told me that the bit about directions was his favorite part of my book, and who, it turned out, was also an amateur pilot. He then went on to tell me that he had had a similar experience. When learning to fly, he got lost on his first solo flight. He did not want to humiliate himself by tuning his radio to the FAA emergency frequency and asking for help, so he flew around looking for a place to land. He spotted an open area that looked like a landing field, headed for it—and found himself deplaning in what seemed like a deliberately hidden landing strip that was mercifully deserted at the time. Fearing he had stumbled upon an enterprise he was not supposed to be aware of, let alone poking around in, he climbed back into the plane, relieved that he had not gotten into trouble. He managed to find his way back to his home airport as well, before he ran out of gas. He maintained, however, that he was certain that more than a few small-plane crashes have occurred because other amateur pilots who did not want to admit they were lost were less lucky. In light of this, the amusing question of why men prefer not to stop and ask for directions stops being funny.

The moral of the story is not that men should immediately change and train themselves to ask directions when they're in doubt, any more than women should immediately stop asking directions and start honing their navigational skills by finding their way on their own. The moral is flexibility: Sticking to habit in the face of all challenges is not so smart if it ends up getting you killed. If we all understood our own styles and knew their limits and their alternatives, we'd be better off—especially at work, where the results of what we do have repercussions for co-workers and the company, as well as for our own futures.

To Ask or Not to Ask

An intern on duty at a hospital had a decision to make. A patient had been admitted with a condition he recognized, and he recalled the appropriate medication. But that medication was recommended for a number of conditions, in different dosages. He wasn't quite sure what dose was right for this condition. He had to make a quick decision: Would he interrupt the supervising resident during a meeting to check the dose, or would he make his best guess and go for it?

What was at stake? First and foremost, the welfare, and maybe even the life, of the patient. But something else was at stake too—the reputation, and eventually the career, of the intern. If he interrupted the resident to ask about the dosage, he was making a public statement about what he didn't know, as well as making himself something of a nuisance. In this case, he went with his guess, and there were no negative effects. But, as with small-plane crashes, one wonders how many medical errors have resulted from decisions to guess rather than ask.

It is clear that not asking questions can have disastrous consequences in medical settings, but asking questions can also have negative consequences. A physician wrote to me about a related experience that occurred during her medical training. She received a low grade from her supervising physician. It took her by surprise because she knew that she was one of the best interns in her group. She asked her supervisor for an explanation, and he replied that she didn't know as much as the others. She knew from her day-to-day dealings with her peers that she was one of the most knowledgeable, not the least. So she asked what evidence had led him to his conclusion. And he told her, "You ask more questions."

There is evidence that men are less likely to ask questions in a public situation, where asking will reveal their lack of knowledge. One such piece of evidence is a study done in a university classroom, where sociolinguist Kate Remlinger noticed that women students asked the professor more questions than men students did. As part of her study, Remlinger interviewed six students at length, three men and three women. All three men told her that they would not ask questions in class if there was something they did not understand, Instead, they said they would try to find the answer later by reading the textbook, asking a friend, or, as a last resort, asking the professor in private during office hours. As one young man put it, "If it's vague to me, I usually don't ask. I'd rather go home and look it up."

Of course, this does not mean that no men will ask questions when they are in doubt, nor that all women will; the differences, as always, are a matter of likelihood and degree. As always, cultural differences play a role too. It is not unusual for American professors to admit their own ignorance when they do not know the answer to a student's question, but there are many cultures in which professors would not, and students from those cultures may judge American professors by those standards. A student from the Middle East told a professor at a California university that she had just lost all respect for one of his colleagues. The reason: She had asked a question in class, and the offending professor had replied, "I don't know offhand, but I'll find out for you."

The physician who asked her supervisor why he gave her a negative evaluation may be unusual in having been told directly what behavior led to the misjudgment of her skill. But in talking to doctors and doctors-in-training around the country, I have learned that there is nothing exceptional about her experience, that it is common for interns and residents to conceal their ignorance by not asking questions, since those who do ask are judged less capable. Yet it seems that many women who are more likely than men to ask questions (just as women are more likely to stop and ask for directions when they're lost) are unaware that they may make a negative impression at the same time that they get information. Their antennae have not been attuned to making sure they don't appear one-down.

This pattern runs counter to two stereotypes about male and female styles: that men are more focused on information and that women are more sensitive. In regard to classroom behavior, it seems that the women who ask questions are more focused on information, whereas the men who refrain from doing so are more focused on interaction—the impression their asking will make on others. In this situation, it is the men who are more sensitive to the impression made on others by their behavior, although their concern is, ultimately, the effect on themselves rather than on others. And this sensitivity is likely to make them look better in the world of work. Realizing this puts the intern's decision in a troubling perspective. He had to choose between putting his career at risk and putting the patient's health at risk.

It is easy to see benefits of both styles: Someone willing to ask questions has ready access to a great deal of information—all that is known by the people she can ask. But just as men have told me that asking directions is useless since the person you ask may not know and may give you the wrong answer, some people feel they are more certain to get the right information if they read it in a book, and they are learning more by finding it themselves. On the other hand, energy may be wasted looking up information someone else has at hand, and I have heard complaints from people who feel they were sent on wild-goose chases by colleagues who didn't want to admit they really were not sure of what they pretended to know.

The reluctance to say "I don't know" can have serious consequences for an entire company—and did: On Friday, June 17, 1994, a computer problem prevented Fidelity Investments from calculating the value of 166 mutual funds. Rather than report that the values for these funds were not available, a manager decided to report to the National Association of Securities Dealers that the values of these funds had not changed from the day before. Unfortunately, June 17 turned out to be a bad day in the financial markets, so the values of Fidelity's funds that were published in newspapers around the country stood out as noticeably higher than those of other funds. Besides the cost and inconvenience to brokerage firms who had to re-compute their customers' accounts, and the injustice to investors who made decisions to buy or sell based on inaccurate information, the company was mightily embarrassed and forced to apologize publicly. Clearly this was an instance in which it would have been preferable to say, "We don't know."

Flexibility, again, is key. There are many situations in which it serves one well to be self-reliant and discreet about revealing doubt or ignorance, and others in which it is wise to admit what you don't know.

Review Questions

1. What does Tannen mean by *conversational style?*

2. What is the important style difference in the way men and women ask for directions or help, according to Tannen?

3. What is Tannen's hypothesis about why males avoid asking other people for directions?

4. In Tannen's perspective, what conclusions do men and women draw about each other when they display typically different approaches to asking directions?

4

SUBSISTENCE
STRATEGIES AND
ECONOMIC SYSTEMS

CHAPTER SEVEN

Ecology and Subsistence

Ecology is the relationship of an organism to other elements within its environmental sphere. Every species, no matter how simple or complex, fits into a larger complex ecological system; each adapts to its ecological niche unless rapid environmental alterations outstrip the organism's ability and potential to adapt successfully. An important aim of ecological studies is to show how organisms fit within particular environments. Such studies also look at the effect environments have on the shape and behavior of life forms.

Every species has adapted biologically through genetically produced variation and natural selection. For example, the bipedal (two-footed) locomotion characteristic of humans is one possible adaptation to walking on the ground. It also permitted our ancestors to carry food, tools, weapons, and almost anything else they desired, enabling them to range out from a home base and bring things back for others to share.

Biological processes have led to another important human characteristic, the development of a large and complex brain. The human brain is capable of holding an enormous inventory of information. With it, we can classify the parts of our environment and retain instructions for complex ways to deal with the things in our world. Because we can communicate our knowledge symbolically through language, we are able to teach one another. Instead of a genetic code that directs behavior automatically, we operate with a learned cultural code. Culture gives us the ability to behave in a much wider variety of ways and to change rapidly in new situations. With culture, people have been able to live successfully in almost every part of the world.

Cultural ecology is the way people use their culture to adapt to particular environments. All people live in a **physical environment,** the world they can experience through their senses, but they will conceive of it in terms that seem most important to their adaptive needs and cultural perspective. We call this perspective the **cultural environment.**

All human societies must provide for the material needs of their members. People everywhere have to eat, clothe themselves, provide shelter against the elements, and take care of social requirements such as hospitality, gift giving, and proper dress.

Societies employ several different strategies to meet their material needs, strategies that affect their complexity and internal organization as well as relationships to the natural environment and to other human groups. Anthropologists often use these **subsistence strategies** to classify different groups into five types: hunter-gatherers, horticulturalists, pastoralists, agriculturalists, and industrialists. Let us look briefly at each of these.

People who rely on **hunting and gathering** depend on wild plants and animals for subsistence. Hunter-gatherers forage for food, moving to different parts of their territories as supplies of plants, animals, and water grow scarce. They live in small bands of from 10 to 50 people and are typically egalitarian, leading a life marked by sharing and cooperation. Because hunter-gatherer bands are so small, they tend to lack formal political, legal, and religious structure, although members have regular ways to make group decisions, settle disputes, and deal ritually with the questions of death, adversity, social value, and world identification.

Hunter-gatherers tend to see themselves as part of the environment, not masters of it. This view shapes a religious ritual aimed at the maintenance and restoration of environmental harmony. All people lived as hunter-gatherers until about 10,000 years ago, when the first human groups began to farm and dwell in more permanent settlements. Today few hunter-gatherers survive. Most have lost their habitats to more powerful groups bent on economic and political exploitation.

Horticulture represents the earliest farming strategy, one that continues on a diminishing basis among many groups today. Horticulturalists garden. They often use a technique called **slash-and-burn agriculture,** which requires them to clear and burn over wild land and, with the aid of a digging stick, sow seeds in the ashes. When fields lose their fertility after a few years, they are abandoned and new land is cleared. Although horticulturalists farm, they often continue to forage for wild foods and still feel closely related to the natural environment.

Horticulture requires a substantial amount of undeveloped land, so overall population densities must remain fairly low. But the strategy permits higher population densities than hunting and gathering, so horticulturalists tend to live in larger permanent settlements numbering from 50 to 250 individuals. (Some horticultural societies have produced chiefdomships with much larger administrative and religious town centers.) Although they are still small by our standards, horticultural communities are large enough to require more complex organizational strategies. They often display more elaborate kinship systems based on descent, political structures that include headmen or chiefs, political alliances, religions characterized by belief in a variety of supernatural beings, and the beginnings of social inequality. Many of today's so-called tribal peoples are horticulturalists.

Pastoralism is a subsistence strategy based on the herding of domesticated animals such as cattle, goats, sheep, and camels. Although herding strategies vary from one environment to another, pastoralists share some general attributes. They move on a regular basis during the year to take advantage of fresh sources of water and fodder for their animals. They usually congregate in large encampments for part of the year when food and water are plentiful, then divide into smaller groups when these resources become scarce. Pastoralists often display a strong sense of group identity and pride, a fierce independence, and skill at war and raiding. Despite attempts by modern governments to place them in permanent settlements, many pastoral groups in Africa and Asia continue their nomadic lifestyle.

Agriculture is still a common subsistence strategy in many parts of the world. *Agriculture* refers to a kind of farming based on the intensive cultivation of permanent land holdings. Agriculturalists usually use plows and organic fertilizers and may irrigate their fields in dry conditions.

Agrarian societies are marked by a high degree of social complexity. They are often organized as nation-states with armies and bureaucracies, social stratification, markets, extended families and kin groups, and some occupational specialization. Religion takes on a formal structure and is organized as a separate institution.

The term **industrialism** labels the final kind of subsistence strategy. Ours is an industrial society, as is much of the Western, and more recently, the Asian world. Industrial nations are highly complex; they display an extensive variety of subgroups and social statuses. Industrial societies tend to be dominated by market economies in which goods and services are exchanged on the basis of price, supply, and demand. There is a high degree of economic specialization, and mass marketing may lead to a depersonalization of human relations. Religious, legal, political, and economic systems find expression as separate institutions in a way that might look disjointed to hunter-gatherers or others from smaller, more integrated societies.

The study of cultural ecology involves more than an understanding of people's basic subsistence strategies. Each society exists in a distinctive environment. Although a group may share many subsistence methods with other societies, there are always special environmental needs that shape productive techniques. Andean farmers, for example, have developed approximately 3,000 varieties of potatoes to meet the demands of growing conditions at different elevations in their mountain habitat. Bhil farmers in India have learned to create fields by damming up small streams in their rugged Aravalli hill villages. Otherwise, they would find it difficult to cultivate there at all. American farmers learned to "contour-plow" parallel to slopes in response to water erosion and now increasingly use plowless (no-till) farming to prevent the wind from carrying away precious topsoil.

No matter how successful their microenvironmental adjustments are, most groups in the world now face more serious adaptive challenges. One difficulty is the exploitation of their lands by outsiders, who are often unconstrained by adaptive necessity. A second is the need to overexploit the environment to meet market demand. (See Part Four for articles on market pressures.) In either case, many local peoples find that their traditional subsistence techniques no longer work. They have lost control of their own environmental adjustment and must struggle to adapt to outsiders and what is left of their habitat.

Finally, just as humans adapt culturally to their environments, altering them in the process, environments may biologically adapt to humans. For example, intensive agriculture in the United States provides greater food sources for deer. In response, the number of deer has risen by as much as 400 percent. Animals domesticated by humans, such as cows, pigs, chickens, sheep, goats, dogs, and cats, have also experienced both genetic modification and increased numbers from their association with people. Less obviously, microbes have evolved to take advantage of the growing human presence. Some subsist on human wastes; others, including many that cause epidemic diseases, have evolved to subsist on people themselves.

The !Kung, described by Richard Lee in the first selection, provide an excellent example of a traditional foraging lifestyle. The update to this article by Richard Lee and Megan Biesele show that the same bands of people who once lived on wild foods in the Kalahari now find themselves confined to small government-mandated settlements. Cattle herders tend their animals on the desert lands once occupied by the !Kung. The second article, by Jared Diamond, describes the fate of Easter Islanders who overexploited their small island ecosystem. The example serves as a warning to people everywhere as populations grow and resources diminish. The third article, by Bernard Nietschmann, details the impact of the international market system on a local subsistence economy. Motivated by money, Miskito Indians came to be dependent on outsiders for food and found themselves unable to meet their traditional reciprocal obligations. Readers should note that most Miskito Indians were displaced from their traditional communities and occupations by the Sandinista government of Nicaragua after this article was written. Many have not returned to their former homes. The fourth selection, by Richard Reed, is a sobering reminder of what can happen to a horticultural people who once subsisted in harmony with their tropical forest habitat, but who now find themselves being displaced by colonists. These outsiders have stripped the forest bare. Nevertheless, the horticultural model is emerging as the most economical solution for sustained use of the forest in today's world.

Key Terms

agriculture   industrialism
cultural ecology   pastoralism
cultural environment   physical environment
ecology   slash-and-burn agriculture
horticulture   subsistence strategies
hunting and gathering

CHAPTER EIGHT

The Hunters: Scarce Resources in the Kalahari

Richard Borshay Lee

Until about 10,000 years ago, everyone in the world survived by hunting and gathering wild foods. They lived in intimate association with their natural environments and employed a complex variety of strategies to forage for food and other necessities of life. Agriculture displaced foraging as the main subsistence technique over the next few thousand years, but some hunter-gatherers lived on in the more remote parts of the world. This study by Richard Lee was done in the early 1960s and describes the important features of one of the last foraging groups, the Ju/'hoansi-!Kung living in the Kalahari Desert. It argues against the idea, held by many anthropologists at that time, that hunter-gatherers live a precarious, hand-to-mouth existence. Instead, Lee found that the !Kung, depending more on vegetable foods than meat, actually spent little time collecting food and managed to live long and fruitful lives in their difficult desert home. The update by Lee and Megan Biesele that appears at the end of the article details the events that have led the !Kung to settle down permanently to life as small-scale farmers and cattle raisers.

The current anthropological view of hunter-gatherer subsistence rests on two questionable assumptions. First is the notion that these people are primarily dependent on the hunting of game animals, and second is the assumption that their way of life is generally a precarious and arduous struggle for existence.

Recent data on living hunter-gatherers show a radically different picture. We have learned that in many societies, plant and marine resources are far more important than are game animals in the diet. More important, it is becoming clear that, with few conspicuous exceptions, the hunter-gatherer subsistence base is at least routine and reliable and at best surprisingly abundant. Anthropologists have consistently tended to underestimate the viability of even those "marginal isolates" of hunting peoples that have been available to ethnographers.

The purpose of this paper is to analyze the food-getting activities of one such "marginal" people, the !Kung Bushmen of the Kalahari Desert. Three related questions are posed: How do the Bushmen make a living? How easy or difficult is it for them to do this? What kinds of evidence are necessary to measure and evaluate the precariousness or security of a way of life? And after the relevant data are presented, two further questions are asked: What makes this security of life possible? To what extent are the Bushmen typical of hunter-gatherers in general?

Bushman Subsistence

The !Kung Bushmen of Botswana are an apt case for analysis. They inhabit the semi-arid northwest region of the Kalahari Desert. With only six to nine inches of rainfall per year, this is, by any account, a marginal environment for human habitation. In fact, it is precisely the unattractiveness of their homeland that has kept the !Kung isolated from extensive contact with their agricultural and pastoral neighbors.

Fieldwork was carried out in the Dobe area, a line of eight permanent water-holes near the South-West Africa border and 125 miles south of the Okavango River. The population of the Dobe area consists of 466 Bushmen, including 379 permanent residents living in independent camps or associated with Bantu cattle posts, as well as 87 seasonal visitors. The Bushmen share the area with some 340 Bantu pastoralists largely of the Herero and Tswana tribes. The ethnographic present refers to the period of fieldwork: October 1963 to January 1965.

The Bushmen living in independent camps lack firearms, livestock, and agriculture. Apart from occasional visits to the Herero for milk, these !Kung are entirely dependent upon hunting and gathering for their subsistence. Politically they are under the nominal authority of the Tswana headman, although they pay no taxes and receive very few government services. European presence amounts to one overnight government patrol every six to eight weeks. Although Dobe-area !Kung have had some contact with outsiders since the 1880s, the majority of them continue to hunt and gather because there is no viable alternative locally available to them.

Each of the fourteen independent camps is associated with one of the permanent waterholes. During the dry season (May-October) the entire population is clustered around these wells. Table 1 shows the numbers at each well at the end of the 1964 dry season. Two wells had no camp residents and one large well supported five camps. The number of camps at each well and the size of each camp changed frequently during the course of the year. The "camp" is an open aggregate of cooperating persons which changes in size and composition from day to day. Therefore, I have avoided the term "band" in describing the !Kung Bushman living groups.

Each waterhole has a hinterland lying within a six-mile radius that is regularly exploited for vegetable and animal foods. These areas are not territories in the zoological sense, since they are not defended against outsiders. Rather, they constitute the resources that lie within a convenient walking distance of a waterhole. The camp is a self-sufficient subsistence unit. The members move out each day to hunt and gather, and return in the evening to pool the collected foods in such a way that every person present receives an equitable share. Trade in foodstuffs

TABLE 1: NUMBERS AND DISTRIBUTION OF RESIDENT BUSHMEN AND BANTU BY WATERHOLE*

Name of Waterhole	No. of Camps	Population of Camps	Other Bushmen	Total Bushmen	Bantu
Dobe	2	37	—	37	—
!angwa	1	16	23	39	84
Bate	2	30	12	42	21
!ubi	1	19	—	19	65
!gose	3	52	9	61	18
/ai/ai	5	94	13	107	67
!xabe	—	—	8	8	12
Mahopa	—	—	23	23	73
Total	14	248	88	336	340

* Figures do not include 130 Bushmen outside area on the date of census.

between camps is minimal; personnel do move freely from camp to camp, however. The net effect is of a population constantly in motion. On the average, an individual spends a third of his time living only with close relatives, a third visiting other camps, and a third entertaining visitors from other camps.

Because of the strong emphasis on sharing, and the frequency of movement, surplus accumulation of storable plant foods and dried meat is kept to a minimum. There is rarely more than two or three days' supply of food on hand in a camp at any time. The result of this lack of surplus is that a constant subsistence effort must be maintained throughout the year. Unlike agriculturalists, who work hard during the planting and harvesting seasons and undergo "seasonal unemployment" for several months, the Bushmen hunter-gatherers collect food every third or fourth day throughout the year.

Vegetable foods comprise from 60 to 80 percent of the total diet by weight, and collecting involves two or three days of work per woman per week. The men also collect plants and small animals, but their major contribution to the diet is the hunting of medium and large game. The men are conscientious but not particularly successful hunters; although men's and women's work input is roughly equivalent in terms of man-day of effort, the women provide two to three times as much food by weight as the men.

Table 2 summarizes the seasonal activity cycle observed among the Dobe-area !Kung in 1964. For the greater part of the year, food is locally abundant and easily collected. It is only during the end of the dry season in September and October, when desirable foods have been eaten out in the immediate vicinity of the waterholes, that the people have to plan longer hikes of 10 to 15 miles and carry their own water to those areas where the mongongo nut is still available. The important point is that food is a constant, but distance required to reach food is a variable; it is short in the summer, fall, and early winter, and reaches its maximum in the spring.

This analysis attempts to provide quantitative measures of subsistence status, including data on the following topics: abundance and variety of resources, diet selectivity, range size and population density, the composition of the work force, the ratio of work to leisure time, and the caloric and protein levels in the diet. The value of quantitative data is that they can be used comparatively and also may be useful in archeological reconstruction. In addition, one can avoid the pitfalls of subjective and qualitative impressions; for example, statements about food "anxiety" have proven to be difficult to generalize across cultures.

TABLE 2: THE BUSHMAN ANNUAL ROUND

	Jan.	Feb.	Mar.	April	May	June	July	Aug.	Sept.	Oct.	Nov.	Dec.
Season	Summer Rains			Autumn Dry			Winter Dry			Spring Dry		First Rains
Availability of water	Temporary summer pools everywhere			Large summer pools			Permanent waterholes only					Summer pools developing
Group moves	Widely dispersed at summer pools			At large summer pools			All population restricted to permanent waterholes					Moving out to summer pools
Men's subsistence activities	1. Hunting with bow, arrows, and dogs (year-round) 2. Running down immatures 3. Some gathering (year-round)					Trapping small game in snares				Running down newborn animals		
Women's subsistence activities	1. Gathering of mongongo nuts (year-round) 2. Fruits, berries, melons					Roots, bulbs, resins				Roots, leafy greens		
Ritual activities	Dancing, trance performances, and ritual curing (year-round)											
				Boys' initiation*								†
Relative subsistence hardship			Water-food distance minimal			Increasing distance from water to food				Water-food distance minimal		

*Held once every five years; none in 1963-64.

† New Year's: Bushmen join the celebrations of their missionized Bantu neighbors.

Abundance and Variety of Resources

It is impossible to define "abundance" of resources absolutely. However, one index of *relative* abundance is whether or not a population exhausts all the food available from a given area. By this criterion, the habitat of the Dobe-area Bushmen is abundant in naturally occurring foods. By far the most important food is the mongongo (mangetti) nut (*Ricinodendron rautanenii* Schinz). Although tens of thousands of pounds of these nuts are harvested and eaten each year, thousands more rot on the ground each year for want of picking.

The mongongo nut, because of its abundance and reliability, alone accounts for 50 percent of the vegetable diet by weight. In this respect it resembles a cultivated staple crop such as maize or rice. Nutritionally it is even more remarkable, for it contains five times the calories and ten times the protein per cooked unit of the cereal crops. The average daily per capita consumption of 300 nuts yields about 1,260 calories and 56 grams of protein. This modest portion, weighing only about 7.5 ounces, contains the caloric equivalent of 2.5 pounds of cooked rice and the protein equivalent of 14 ounces of lean beef.

Furthermore, the mongongo nut is drought resistant, and it will still be abundant in the dry years when cultivated crops may fail. The extremely hard outer shell protects the inner kernel from rot and allows the nuts to be harvested for up to twelve months after they have fallen to the ground. A diet based on mongongo nuts is in fact more reliable than one based on cultivated foods, and it is not surprising, therefore, that when a Bushman was asked why he hadn't taken to agriculture, he replied: "Why should we plant, when there are so many mongongo nuts in the world?"

Apart from the mongongo, the Bushmen have available eighty-four other species of edible food plants, including twenty-nine species of fruits, berries, and melons and thirty species of roots and bulbs. The existence of this variety allows for a wide range of alternatives in subsistence strategy. During the summer months the Bushmen have no problem other than to choose among the tastiest and most easily collected foods. Many species, which are quite edible but less attractive, are bypassed, so that gathering never exhausts *all* the available plant foods of an area. During the dry season the diet becomes much more eclectic and the many species of roots, bulbs, and edible resins make an important contribution. It is this broad base that provides an essential margin of safety during the end of the dry season, when the mongongo nut forests are difficult to reach. In addition, it is likely that these rarely utilized species provide important nutritional and mineral trace elements that may be lacking in the more popular foods.

Diet Selectivity

If the Bushmen were living close to the "starvation" level, then one would expect them to exploit every available source of nutrition. That their life is well above this level is indicated by the data in Table 3. Here all the edible plant species are arranged in classes according to the frequency with which they were observed to be eaten. It should be noted that although there are some eighty-five species available, about 90 percent of the vegetable diet by weight is drawn from only twenty-three species. In other words, 75 percent of the listed species provide only 10 percent of the food value.

In their meat-eating habits, the Bushmen show a similar selectivity. Of the 223 local species of animals known and named by the Bushmen, 54 species are classified as edible, and of these only 17 species were hunted on a regular basis. Only a handful of the dozens of edible species of small mammals, birds, reptiles, and insects that occur locally are regarded as food. Such animals as rodents, snakes, lizards, termites, and grasshoppers, which in the literature are included in the Bushman diet, are despised by the Bushmen of the Dobe area.

Range Size and Population Density

The necessity to travel long distances, the high frequency of moves, and the maintenance of populations at low densities are also features commonly associated with the hunting and gathering way of life. Density estimates for hunters in western North America and Australia have ranged from 3 persons/square mile to as low as 1 person/100 square miles. In 1963-65, the resident and visiting Bushmen were observed to utilize an area of about 1,000 square miles during the course of the annual round for an effective population density of 41 persons/100 square miles. Within this area, however, the amount of ground covered by members of an individual camp was surprisingly small. A day's round-trip of twelve miles serves to define a "core" area six miles in radius surrounding each water point. By fanning out in all directions from their well, the members of a camp can gain access to the food resources of well over 100 square miles of territory within a two-hour hike. Except for a few weeks each year, areas lying beyond this six-mile radius are rarely utilized, even though they are no less rich in plants and game than are the core areas.

Although the Bushmen move their camps frequently (five or six times a year), they do not move them very far. A rainy season camp in the nut forests is rarely more than ten or twelve miles from the home

TABLE 3: !KUNG BUSHMAN PLANT FOODS

Food Class	Part Eaten								Total Number of Species in Class	Totals (Percentages)	
	Fruit and Nut	Bean and Root	Fruit and Stalk	Root, Bulb	Fruit, Berry, Melon	Resin	Leaves	Seed, Bean		Estimated Contribution by Weight to Vegetable Diet	Estimated Contribution of Each Species
i. Primary Eaten daily throughout year (mongongo) nut	1	—	—	—	—	—	—	—	1	c.50	c.50*
ii. Major Eaten daily in season	1	1	1	1	4	—	—	—	8	c.25	c.3†
iii. Minor Eaten several times per week in season	—	—	—	7	3	2	2	—	14	c.15	c.1
iv. Supplementary Eaten when classes I-III locally unavailable	—	—	—	9	12	10	1	—	32	c.7	c.0.2
v. Rare Eaten several times per year	—	—	—	9	4	—	—	—	13	c.3	c.0.1‡
vi. Problematic Edible but not observed to be eaten	—	—	—	4	6	4	1	2	17	nil	nil
Total Species	2	1	1	30	29	16	4	2	85	100	—

* 1 species constitutes 50 percent of the vegetable diet by weight.
† 23 species constitute 90 percent of the vegetable diet by weigh.
‡ 62 species constitute the remaining 10 percent of the diet.

waterhole, and often new campsites are occupied only a few hundred yards away from the previous one. By these criteria, the Bushmen do not lead a free-ranging nomadic way of life. For example, they do not undertake long marches of 30 to 100 miles to get food, since this task can be readily fulfilled within a day's walk of home base. When such long marches do occur they are invariably for visiting, trading, and marriage arrangements, and should not be confused with the normal routine of subsistence.

Demographic Factors

Another indicator of the harshness of a way of life is the age at which people die. Ever since Hobbes characterized life in the state of nature as "nasty, brutish and short," the assumption has been that hunting and gathering is so rigorous that members of such societies are rapidly worn out and meet an early death. Silberbauer, for example, says of the Gwi Bushmen of the central Kalahari that "life expectancy ... is difficult to calculate, but I do not believe that many live beyond 45." And Coon has said of hunters in general:

> The practice of abandoning the hopelessly ill and aged has been observed in many parts of the world. It is always done by people living in poor environments where it is necessary to move about frequently to obtain food, where food is scarce, and transportation difficult. ... Among peoples who are forced to live in this way the oldest generation, the generation of individuals who have passed their physical peak, is reduced in numbers and influence. There is no body of elders to hand on tradition and control the affairs of younger men and women, and no formal system of age grading.

The !Kung Bushmen of the Dobe area flatly contradict this view. In a total population of 466, no fewer than 46 individuals (17 men and 29 women) were determined to be over sixty years of age, a proportion that compares favorably to the percentage of elderly in industrialized populations.

The aged hold a respected position in Bushmen society and are the effective leaders of the camps. Senilicide is extremely rare. Long after their productive years have passed, the old people are fed and cared for by their children and grandchildren. The blind, the senile, and the crippled are respected for the special ritual and technical skills they possess. For instance, the four elders at !gose waterhole were totally or partially blind, but this handicap did not prevent their active participation in decision making and ritual curing.

Another significant feature of the composition of the work force is the late assumption of adult responsibility by the adolescents. Young people are not expected to provide food regularly until they are married. Girls typically marry between the ages of fifteen and twenty, and boys about five years later, so that it is not unusual to find healthy, active teenagers visiting from camp to camp while their older relatives provide food for them.

As a result, the people in the twenty to sixty age group support a surprisingly large percentage of nonproductive young and old people. About 40 percent of the population in camps contributes little to the food supplies. This allocation of work to young and middle-aged adults allows for a relatively carefree childhood and adolescence and a relatively unstrenuous old age.

Leisure and Work

Another important index of ease or difficulty of subsistence is the amount of time devoted to the food quest. Hunting has usually been regarded by social scientists as a way of life in which merely keeping alive is so formidable a task that members of such societies lack the leisure time necessary to "build culture." The !Kung Bushmen would appear to conform to the rule, for as Lorna Marshall says:

> It is vividly apparent that among the !Kung Bushmen, ethos, or "the spirit which actuates manners and customs," is survival. Their time and energies are almost wholly given to this task, for life in their environment requires that they spend their days mainly in procuring food.

It is certainly true that getting food is the most important single activity in Bushman life. However, this statement would apply equally well to small-scale agricultural and pastoral societies too. How much time is *actually* devoted to the food quest is fortunately an empirical question. And an analysis of the work effort of the Dobe Bushmen shows some unexpected results. From July 6 to August 2, 1964, I recorded all the daily activities of the Bushmen living at the Dobe waterhole. Because of the coming and going of visitors, the camp population fluctuated in size day by day, from a low of 23 to a high of 40, with a mean of 31.8 persons. Each day some of the adult members of the camp went out to hunt and/or gather while others stayed home or went visiting. The daily recording of all personnel on hand made it possible to calculate the number of man-days of work as a percentage of total number of man-days of consumption.

Although the Bushmen do not organize their activities on the basis of a seven-day week, I have divided the data this way to make them more intelligible. The workweek was calculated to show how many days out of seven each adult spent in subsistence activities (Table 4, Column 7). Week II has been eliminated from the totals since the investigator contributed food. In week I, the people spent an average of 2.3 days in subsistence activities, in week II, 1.9 days, and in week IV, 3.2 days. In all, the adults of the Dobe camp worked about two and a half days a week. Since the average working day was about six hours long, the fact emerges that !Kung Bushmen of Dobe, despite their harsh environment, devote from twelve to nineteen hours a week to getting food. Even the hardest-working individual in the camp, a man named ≠oma who went out hunting on sixteen of the twenty-eight days, spent a maximum of thirty-two hours a week in the food quest.

TABLE 4 SUMMARY OF DOBE WORK DIARY

week	(1) Mean Group Size	(2) Adult-Days	(3) Child-Days	(4) Total Man-Days of Consumption	(5) Man-Days of Work	(6) Meat (lbs.)	(7) Average Workweek/ Adult	(8) Index of Subsistence Effort
I	25.6	114	65	179	37	104	2.3	.21
(July 6-12)	(23-29)							
II	28.3	125	73	198	22	80	1.2	.11
(July 13-19)	(23-27)							
III	34.3	156	84	240	42	177	1.9	.18
(July 20-26)	(29-40)							
IV	35.6	167	82	249	77	129	3.2	.31
(July 27-Aug. 2)	(32-40)							
4-wk. total	30.9	562	304	866	178	490	2.2	.21
Adjusted total*	31.8	437	231	668	156	410	2.5	.23

*See text

Key: Column 1: Mean group size $= \dfrac{\text{total man-days of consumption}}{7}$.

Column 7: Workweek = the number of workdays per adult per week.

Column 8: Index of subsistence effort $= \dfrac{\text{man-days of work}}{\text{man-days of consumption}}$

(e.g., in Week I, the value of "S" = 21, i.e., 21 days of work/100 days of consumption or 1 workday produces food for 5 consumption days).

Because the Bushmen do not amass a surplus of foods, there are no seasons of exceptionally intensive activities such as planting and harvesting, and no seasons of unemployment. The level of work observed is an accurate reflection of the effort required to meet the immediate caloric needs of the group. This work diary covers the midwinter dry season, a period when food is neither at its most plentiful nor at its scarcest levels, and the diary documents the transition from better to worse conditions (see Table 5). During the fourth week the gatherers were making overnight trips to camps in the mongongo nut forests seven to ten miles distant from the waterhole. These longer trips account for the rise in the level of work, from twelve or thirteen to nineteen hours per week.

If food getting occupies such a small proportion of a Bushman's waking hours, then how *do* people allocate their time? A woman gathers on one day enough food to feed her family for three days, and spends the rest of her time resting in camp, doing embroidery, visiting other camps, or entertaining visitors from other camps. For each day at home, kitchen routines, such as cooking, nut cracking, collecting firewood, and fetching water, occupy one to three hours of her time. This rhythm of steady work and steady leisure is maintained throughout the year.

The hunters tend to work more frequently than the women, but their schedule is uneven. It is not unusual for a man to hunt avidly for a week and then do nothing at all for two or three weeks. Since hunting is an unpredictable business and subject to magical control, hunters sometimes experience a run of bad luck and stop hunting for a month or longer. During these periods, visiting, entertaining, and especially dancing are the primary activities of men. (Unlike the Hadza, gambling is only a minor leisure activity.)

The trance dance is the focus of Bushman ritual life; over 50 percent of the men have trained as trance-performers and regularly enter trance during the course of the all-night dances. At some camps, trance dances occur as frequently as two or three times a week, and those who have entered trances the night before rarely go out hunting the following day. ... In a camp with five or more hunters, there are usually two or three who are actively hunting and several others who are inactive. The net effect is to phase the hunting and non-hunting so that a fairly steady supply of meat is brought into camp.

Caloric Returns

Is the modest work effort of the Bushmen sufficient to provide the calories necessary to maintain the health of the population? Or have the !Kung, in common with some agricultural peoples, adjusted to a permanently substandard nutritional level?

TABLE 5 CALORIC AND PROTEIN LEVELS IN THE !KUNG BUSHMAN DIET, JULY-AUGUST, 1964

Per-Capita Consumption					
Class of Food	Percentage Contribution to Diet by Weight	Weight in Grams	Protein in Grams	Calories per Person per Day	Percentage Caloric Contribution of Meat and Vegetables
Meat	37	230	34.5	690	33
Mongongo nuts	33	210	56.7	1,260	67
Other vegetable foods	30	190	1.9	190	
Total all sources	100	630	93.1	2,140	100

During my fieldwork I did not encounter any cases of kwashiorkor, the most common nutritional disease in the children of African agricultural societies. However, without medical examinations, it is impossible to exclude the possibility that subclinical signs of malnutrition existed.

Another measure of nutritional adequacy is the average consumption of calories and proteins per person per day. The estimate for the Bushmen is based on observations of the weights of foods of known composition that were brought into Dobe camp on each day of the study period. The per-capita figure is obtained by dividing the total weight of foodstuffs by the total number of persons in the camp. These results are set out in detail elsewhere and can only be summarized here. During the study period 410 pounds of meat were brought in by the hunters of the Dobe camp, for a daily share of nine ounces of meat per person. About 700 pounds of vegetables were gathered and consumed during the same period. Table 5 sets out the calories and proteins available per capita in the !Kung Bushman diet from meat, mongongo nuts, and other vegetable sources.

This output of 2,140 calories and 93.1 grams of protein per person per day may be compared with the Recommended Daily Allowances (RDA) for persons of the small size and stature but vigorous activity regime of the !Kung Bushmen. The RDA for Bushmen can be estimated at 1,975 calories and 60 grams of protein per person per day. Thus it is apparent that food output exceeds energy requirements by 165 calories and 33 grams of protein. One can tentatively conclude that even a modest subsistence effort of two or three days' work per week is enough to provide an adequate diet for the !Kung Bushmen.

The Security of Bushman Life

I have attempted to evaluate the subsistence base of one contemporary hunter-gatherer society living in a marginal environment. The !Kung Bushmen have available to them some relatively abundant high-quality foods, and they do not have to walk very far or work very hard to get them. Furthermore, this modest work effort provides sufficient calories to support not only active adults, but also a large number of middle-aged and elderly people. The Bushmen do not have to press their youngsters into the service of the food quest, nor do they have to dispose of the oldsters after they have ceased to be productive.

The evidence presented assumes an added significance because this security of life was observed during the third year of one of the most severe droughts in South Africa's history. Most of the 576,000 people of Botswana are pastoralists and agriculturalists. After the crops had failed three years in succession and over 100,000 head of cattle had died on the range for lack of water, the World Food Program of the United Nations instituted a famine relief program which has grown to include 180,000 people, over 30 percent of the population. This program did not touch the Dobe area in the isolated northwest corner of the country, and the Herero and Tswana women there were able to feed their families only by joining the Bushman women to forage for wild foods. Thus the natural plant resources of the Dobe area were carrying a higher proportion of population than would be the case in years when the Bantu harvested crops. Yet this added pressure on the land did not seem to adversely affect the Bushmen.

In one sense it was unfortunate that the period of my fieldwork happened to coincide with the drought, since I was unable to witness a "typical" annual subsistence cycle. However, in another sense, the coincidence was a lucky one, for the drought put the Bushmen and their subsistence system to the acid test and, in terms of adaptation to scarce resources, they passed with flying colors. One can postulate that their subsistence base would be even more substantial during years of higher rainfall.

What are the crucial factors that make this way of life possible? I suggest that the primary factor is the Bushmen's strong emphasis on vegetable food sources. Although hunting involves a great deal of effort and prestige, plant foods provide from 60 to 80 percent of the annual diet by weight. Meat has come to be regarded as a special treat; when available, it is welcomed as a break from the routine of vegetable foods, but it is never depended upon as a staple. No one ever goes hungry when hunting fails.

The reason for this emphasis is not hard to find. Vegetable foods are abundant, sedentary, and predictable. They grow in the same place year after year, and the gatherer is guaranteed a day's return of food for a day's expenditure of energy. Game animals, by contrast, are scarce, mobile, unpredictable, and difficult to catch. A hunter has no guarantee of success and may in fact go for days or weeks without killing a large mammal. During the study period, there were eleven men in the Dobe camp, of whom four did no hunting at all. The seven active men spent a total of 78 man-days hunting, and this work input yielded eighteen animals killed, or one kill for every four man-days of hunting. The probability of any one hunter making a kill on a given day was 0.23. By contrast, the probability of a woman finding plant food on a given day was 1.00. In other words, hunting and gathering are not equally felicitous subsistence alternatives.

Consider the productivity per man-hour of the two kinds of subsistence activities. One man-hour of hunting produces about 100 edible calories, and of gathering, 240 calories. Gathering is thus seen to be 2.4 times more productive than hunting. In short, hunting is a *high-risk, low-return* subsistence activity, while gathering is a *low-risk, high-return* subsistence activity.

It is not at all contradictory that the hunting complex holds a central place in the Bushmen ethos and that meat is valued more highly than vegetable foods. Analogously, steak is valued more highly than potatoes in the food preferences of our own society. In both situations the meat is more "costly" than the vegetable food. In the Bushman case, the cost of food can be measured in terms of time and energy expended. By this standard, 1,000 calories of meat "costs" ten man-hours, while the "cost" of 1,000 calories of vegetable foods is only four man-hours. Further, it is to be expected that the less predictable, more expensive food source would have a greater accretion of myth and ritual built up around it than would the routine staples of life, which rarely if ever fail.

Conclusions

Three points ought to be stressed. First, life in the state of nature is not necessarily nasty, brutish, and short. The Dobe-area Bushmen live well today on wild plants and meat, in spite of the fact that they are confined to the least productive portion of the range in which

Bushman peoples were formerly found. It is likely that an even more substantial subsistence would have been characteristic of these hunters and gatherers in the past, when they had the pick of African habitats to choose from.

Second, the basis of Bushman diet is derived from sources other than meat. This emphasis makes good ecological sense to the !Kung Bushmen and appears to be a common feature among hunters and gatherers in general. Since a 30 to 40 percent input of meat is such a consistent target for modern hunters in a variety of habitats, is it not reasonable to postulate a similar percentage for prehistoric hunters? Certainly the absence of plant remains on archeological sites is by itself not sufficient evidence for the absence of gathering. Recently abandoned Bushman campsites show a similar absence of vegetable remains, although this paper has clearly shown that plant foods comprise over 60 percent of the actual diet.

Finally, one gets the impression that hunting societies have been chosen by ethnologists to illustrate a dominant theme, such as the extreme importance of environment in the molding of certain cultures. Such a theme can best be exemplified by cases in which the technology is simple and/or the environment is harsh. This emphasis on the dramatic may have been pedagogically useful, but unfortunately it has led to the assumption that a precarious hunting subsistence base was characteristic of all cultures in the Pleistocene. This view of both modern and ancient hunters ought to be reconsidered. Specifically I am suggesting a shift in focus away from the dramatic and unusual cases, and toward a consideration of hunting and gathering as a persistent and well-adapted way of life.

Epilogue: The Ju/'hoansi in 1994[1]

In 1963 perhaps three-quarters of the Dobe Ju/'hoansi were living in camps based primarily on hunting and gathering while the rest were attached to Black cattle posts. Back then there had been no trading stores, schools, or clinics, no government feeding programs, boreholes, or airstrips, and no resident civil servants (apart from the tribally-appointed headman, his clerk, and constable). By 1994 all these institutions and facilities were in place and the Dobe people were well into their third decade of rapid social change; they had been transformed in a generation from a society of foragers, some of whom herded and worked for others, to a society of small-holders who eked out a living by herding, farming, and craft production, along with some hunting and gathering.

Ju villages today look like others in Botswana. The beehive-shaped grass huts are gone, replaced by semi-permanent mud-walled houses behind makeshift stockades to keep out cattle. Villages ceased to be circular and tight-knit. Twenty-five people who lived in a space twenty by twenty meters now spread themselves out in a line village several hundred meters long. Instead of looking across the central open space at each other, the houses face the kraal where cattle and goats are kept, inscribing spatially a symbolic shift from reliance on each other to reliance on property in the form of herds.

Hunting and gathering, which provided Dobe Ju with over 85 percent of their subsistence as recently as 1964, now supplies perhaps 30 percent of their food. The rest is made up of milk and meat from domestic stock, store-bought mealie (corn) meal, and vast quantities of heavily-sugared tea whitened with powdered milk. Game meat and foraged foods and occasional produce from gardens makes up the rest of the diet. However, for most of the 1980s government and foreign drought relief provided the bulk of the diet. . . .

In the long run, Dobe-area Ju/'hoansi face serious difficulties. Since 1975, wealthy Tswana have formed borehole syndicates to stake out ranches in remote areas. With 99-year leases, which can be bought and sold, ownership is tantamount to private tenure. By the late 1980s borehole drilling was approaching the Dobe area. If the Dobe Ju do not form borehole syndicates soon, with overseas help, their traditional foraging areas may be permanently cut off from them by commercial ranching.

Review Questions

1. How does Lee assess the day-to-day quality of !Kung life when they lived as foragers? How does this view compare with that held by many anthropologists in the early 1960s?

2. What evidence does Lee give to support his view about the !Kung?

3. According to Lee, !Kung children are not expected to work until after they are married; old people are supported and respected. How does this arrangement differ from behavior in our own society, and what might explain the difference?

1.   Excerpted from Richard B. Lee and Megan Biesele, "A Local Culture in the Global System: The Ju/'hoansi-!Kung Today," *General Anthropology* 1(1) (Fall 1994): pp. 1, 3-5.

4. What was a key to successful subsistence for the !Kung and other hunter-gatherers, according to Lee?

5. In what ways has life changed for the !Kung since 1964? What has caused these changes?

5

POLITICAL SYSTEMS

CHAPTER NINE

Reciprocity and the Power of Giving

Lee Cronk

As we saw in the introduction to Part Four, reciprocity constitutes an important exchange system in every society. At the heart of reciprocal exchange is the idea of giving. In this article, Lee Cronk explores the functions of giving using a variety of examples from societies around the world. Giving may be benevolent. It may be used to strengthen existing relationships or to form new ones. Gifts may also be used aggressively to "fight" people, to "flatten" them with generosity. Givers often gain position and prestige in this way. Gifts may also be used to place others in debt so that one can control them and require their loyalty. Cronk shows that, in every society, from !Kung hxaro exchange to American foreign aid, there are "strings attached" to giving that affect how people and groups relate to each other.

During a trek through the Rockies in the 1830s, Captain Benjamin Louis E. de Bonneville received a gift of a fine young horse from a Nez Percé chief. According to Washington Irving's account of the incident, the American explorer was aware that "a parting pledge was necessary on his own part, to prove that this friendship was reciprocated." Accordingly, he "placed a handsome rifle in the hands of the venerable chief; whose benevolent heart was evidently touched and gratified by this outward and visible sign of amity."

Even the earliest white settlers in New England understood that presents from natives required reciprocity, and by 1764, "Indian gift" was so common a phrase that the Massachusetts colonial historian Thomas Hutchinson identified it as "a proverbial expression, signifying a present for which an equivalent return is expected." Then, over time, the custom's meaning was lost. Indeed, the phrase now is used derisively, to refer to one who demands the return of a gift. How this cross-cultural misunderstanding occurred is unclear, but the poet Lewis Hyde, in his book *The Gift,* has imagined a scenario that probably approaches the truth.

Say that an Englishman newly arrived in America is welcomed to an Indian lodge with the present of a pipe. Thinking the pipe a wonderful artifact, he takes it home and sets it on his mantelpiece. When he later learns that the Indians expect to have the pipe back, as a gesture of goodwill, he is shocked by what he views as their short-lived generosity. The newcomer did not realize that, to the natives, the point of the gift was not to provide an interesting trinket but to inaugurate a friendly relationship that would be maintained through a series of mutual exchanges. Thus, his failure to reciprocate appeared not only rude and thoughtless but downright hostile. "White man keeping" was as offensive to native Americans as "Indian giving" was to settlers.

In fact, the Indians' tradition of gift giving is much more common than our own. Like our European ancestors, we think that presents ought to be offered freely, without strings attached. But through most of the world, the strings themselves are the main consideration. In some societies, gift giving is a tie between friends, a way of maintaining good relationships, whereas in others it has developed into an elaborate, expensive, and antagonistic ritual designed to humiliate rivals by showering them with wealth and obligating them to give more in return.

In truth, the dichotomy between the two traditions of gift giving is less behavioral than rhetorical: our generosity is not as unconditional as we would like to believe. Like European colonists, most modern Westerners are blind to the purpose of reciprocal gift giving, not only in non-Western societies but also, to some extent, in our own. Public declarations to the contrary, we, too, use gifts to nurture long-term relationships of mutual obligation, as well as to embarrass our rivals and to foster feelings of indebtedness. And this ethic touches all aspects of contemporary life, from the behavior of scientists in research networks to superpower diplomacy. Failing to acknowledge this fact, especially as we give money, machines, and technical advice to peoples around the world, we run the risk of being misinterpreted and, worse, of causing harm.

Much of what we know about the ethics of gift giving comes from the attempts of anthropologists to give things to the people they are studying. Richard Lee, of the University of Toronto, learned a difficult lesson from the !Kung hunter-gatherers, of the Kalahari desert, when, as a token of goodwill, he gave them an ox to slaughter at Christmas. Expecting gratitude, he was shocked when the !Kung complained about having to make do with such a scrawny "bag of bones." Only later did Lee learn, with relief, that the !Kung belittle all gifts. In their eyes, no act is completely generous, or free of calculation; ridiculing gifts is their way of diminishing the expected return and of enforcing humility on those who would use gifts to raise their own status within the group.

Rada Dyson-Hudson, of Cornell University, had a similar experience among the Turkana, a pastoral people of northwestern Kenya. To compensate her informants for their help, Dyson-Hudson gave away pots, maize meal, tobacco, and other items. The Turkana reaction was less than heartwarming. A typical response to a gift of a pot, for example, might be, "Where is the maize meal to go in this pot?" or, "Don't you have a bigger one to give me?" To the Turkana, these are legitimate and expected questions.

The Mukogodo, another group of Kenyan natives, responded in a similar way to gifts Beth Leech and I presented to them during our fieldwork in 1986. Clothing was never nice enough, containers never big enough, tobacco and candies never plentiful enough. Every gift horse was examined carefully, in the mouth and elsewhere. Like the !Kung, the Mukogodo believe that all gifts have an element of calculation, and they were right to think that ours were no exception. We needed their help, and their efforts to diminish our expectations and lessen their obligations to repay were as fair as our attempts to get on their good side.

The idea that gifts carry obligations is instilled early in life. When we gave Mukogodo children candies after visiting their villages, their mothers reminded them of the tie: "Remember these white people? They are the ones who gave you candy." They also reinforced the notion that gifts are meant to circulate, by asking their children to part with their precious candies, already in their mouths. Most of the youngsters reluctantly surrendered their sweets, only to have them immediately returned. A mother might take, at most, a symbolic nibble from her child's candy, just to drive home the lesson.

The way food, utensils, and other goods are received in many societies is only the first stage of the behavior surrounding gift giving. Although repayment is expected, it is crucial that it be deferred. To reciprocate at once indicates a desire to end the relationship, to cut the strings; delayed repayment makes the strings longer and stronger. This is especially clear on the Truk Islands, of Micronesia, where a special word—*niffag*—is used to designate objects moving through the island's exchange network. From the Trukese viewpoint, to return niffag on the same day it is received alters its nature from that of a gift to that of a sale, in which all that matters is material gain.

After deciding the proper time for response, a recipient must consider how to make repayment, and that is dictated largely by the motive behind the gift. Some exchange customs are designed solely to preserve a relationship. The !Kung have a system, called *hxaro*, in which little attention is paid to whether the items exchanged are equivalent. Richard Lee's informant !Xoma explained to him that "Hxaro is when I take a thing of value and give it to you. Later, much later, when you find some good thing, you give it back to me. When I find something good I will give it to you, and so we will pass the years together." When Lee tried to determine the exact exchange values of various items (Is a spear worth three strings of beads, two strings, or one?), !Xoma explained that any return would be all right: "You see, we don't trade with things, we trade with people!"

One of the most elaborate systems of reciprocal gift giving, known as *kula*, exists in a ring of islands off New Guinea. Kula gifts are limited largely to shell necklaces, called *soulava*, and armbands, called *mwali*. A necklace given at one time is answered months or years later with an armband, the necklaces usually circulating clockwise, and the armbands counterclockwise, through the archipelago. Kula shells vary in quality and value, and men gain fame and prestige by having their names associated with noteworthy necklaces or armbands. The shells also gain value from their association with famous and successful kula partners.

Although the act of giving gifts seems intrinsically benevolent, a gift's power to embarrass the recipient and to force repayment has, in some societies, made it attractive as a weapon. Such antagonistic generosity reached its most elaborate expression, during the late nineteenth century, among the Kwakiutl, of British Columbia.

The Kwakiutl were acutely conscious of status, and every tribal division, clan, and individual had a specific rank. Disputes about status were resolved by means of enormous ceremonies (which outsiders usually refer to by the Chinook Indian term *potlatch*), at which rivals competed for the honor and prestige of giving away the greatest amount of property. Although nearly everything of value was fair game—blankets, canoes, food, pots, and, until the mid-nineteenth century, even slaves—the most highly prized items were decorated sheets of beaten copper, shaped like shields and etched with designs in the distinctive style of the Northwest Coast Indians.

As with the kula necklaces and armbands, the value of a copper sheet was determined by its history—by where it had been and who had owned it—and a single sheet could be worth thousands of blankets, a fact often reflected in its name. One was called "Drawing All Property from the House," and another, "About Whose Possession All Are Quarreling." After the Kwakiutl began to acquire trade goods from the Hudson's Bay Company's Fort Rupert post, in 1849, the potlatches underwent a period of extreme inflation, and by the 1920s, when items of exchange included sewing machines and pool tables, tens of thousands of Hudson's Bay blankets might be given away during a single ceremony.

In the 1880s, after the Canadian government began to suppress warfare between tribes, potlatching also became a substitute for battle. As a Kwakiutl man once said to the anthropologist Franz Boas, "The time of fighting is past. . . . We do not fight now with weapons: we fight with property." The usual Kwakiutl word for potlatch was *p!Esa*, meaning to flatten (as when one flattens a rival under a pile of blankets), and the prospect of being given a large gift engendered real fear. Still, the Kwakiutl seemed to prefer the new "war of wealth" to the old "war of blood."

Gift giving has served as a substitute for war in other societies, as well. Among the Siuai, of the Solomon Islands, guests at feasts are referred to as attackers, while hosts are defenders, and invitations to feasts are given on short notice in the manner of "surprise attacks." And like the Kwakiutl of British Columbia, the Mount Hagen tribes of New Guinea use a system of gift giving called *moka* as a way of gaining prestige and shaming rivals. The goal is to become a tribal leader, a "big-man." One moka gift in the 1970s consisted of several hundred pigs, thousands of dollars in cash, some cows and wild birds, a truck, and a motorbike. The donor, quite pleased with himself, said to the recipient, "I have won. I have knocked you down by giving so much."

Although we tend not to recognize it as such, the ethic of reciprocal gift giving manifests itself throughout our own society, as well. We, too, often expect something, even if only gratitude and a sense of indebtedness, in exchange for gifts, and we use gifts to establish friendships and to manipulate our positions in society. As in non-Western societies, gift giving in America sometimes takes a benevolent and helpful form; at other times, the power of gifts to create obligations is used in a hostile way.

The Duke University anthropologist Carol Stack found a robust tradition of benevolent exchange in an Illinois ghetto known as the Flats, where poor blacks engage in a practice called swapping. Among residents of the Flats, wealth comes in spurts; hard times are frequent and unpredictable. Swapping, of clothes, food, furniture, and the like, is a way of guaranteeing security, of making sure that someone will be there to help out when one is in need and that one will get a share of any windfalls that come along.

Such networks of exchange are not limited to the poor, nor do they always involve objects. Just as the exchange of clothes creates a gift community in the Flats, so the swapping of knowledge may create one among scientists. Warren Hagstrom, a sociologist at the University of Wisconsin, in Madison, has pointed out that papers submitted to scientific journals often are called contributions, and, because no payment is received for them, they truly are gifts. In contrast, articles written for profit—such as this one—often are held in low esteem: scientific status can be achieved only through *giving* gifts of knowledge.

Recognition also can be traded upon, with scientists building up their gift-giving networks by paying careful attention to citations and acknowledgments. Like participants in kula exchange, they try to associate themselves with renowned and prestigious articles, books, and institutions. A desire for recognition, however, cannot be openly acknowledged as a motivation for research, and it is a rare scientist who is able to discuss such desires candidly. Hagstrom was able to find just one mathematician (whom he described as "something of a social isolate") to confirm that "junior mathematicians want recognition from big shots and, consequently, work in areas prized by them."

Hagstrom also points out that the inability of scientists to acknowledge a desire for recognition does not mean that such recognition is not expected by those who offer gifts of knowledge, any more than a kula trader believes it is all right if his trading partner does not answer his gift of a necklace with an armband. While failure to reciprocate in New Guinean society might once have meant warfare, among scientists it may cause factionalism and the creation of rivalries.

Whether in the Flats of Illinois or in the halls of academia, swapping is, for the most part, benign. But manipulative gift giving exists in modern societies, too—particularly in paternalistic government practices. The technique is to offer a present that cannot be repaid, coupled with a claim of beneficence and omniscience. The Johns Hopkins University anthropologist Grace Goodell documented one example in Iran's Khuzestan Province, which, because it contains most of the country's oil fields and is next door to Iraq, is a strategically sensitive area. Goodell focused on the World Bank-funded Dez irrigation project, a showpiece of the shah's ambitious "white revolution" development plan. The scheme involved the irrigation of tens of thousands of acres and the forced relocation of people from their villages to new, model towns. According to Goodell, the purpose behind dismantling local institutions was to enhance central government control of the region. Before development, each Khūzestāni village had been a miniature city-state, managing its own internal affairs and determining its own relations with outsiders. In the new settlements, decisions were made by government bureaucrats, not townsmen, whose autonomy was crushed under the weight of a large and strategically placed gift.

On a global scale, both the benevolent and aggressive dimensions of gift giving are at work in superpower diplomacy. Just as the Kwakiutl were left only with blankets with which to fight after warfare was banned, the United States and the Soviet Union now find, with war out of the question, that they are left only with gifts—called concessions— with which to do battle. Offers of military cutbacks are easy ways to score points in the public arena of international opinion and to shame rivals, and failure either to accept such offers or to respond with even more extreme proposals may be seen as cowardice or as bellicosity. Mikhail Gorbachev is a virtuoso, a master potlatcher, in this new kind of competition, and, predictably, Americans often see his offers of disarmament and openness as gifts with long strings attached. One reason U.S. officials were buoyed last December [1988], when, for the first time since the Second World War, the Soviet Union accepted American assistance, in the aftermath of the Armenian earthquake, is that it seemed to signal a wish for reciprocity rather than dominance— an unspoken understanding of the power of gifts to bind people together.

Japan, faced with a similar desire to expand its influence, also has begun to exploit gift giving in its international relations. In 1989, it will spend more than ten billion dollars on foreign aid, putting it ahead of the United States for the second consecutive year as the world's greatest donor nation. Although this move was publicly welcomed in the United States as the sharing of a burden, fears, too, were expressed that the resultant blow to American prestige might cause a further slip in our international status. Third World leaders also have complained that too much Japanese aid is targeted at countries in which Japan has an economic stake and that too much is restricted to the purchase of Japanese goods—that Japan's generosity has less to do with addressing the problems of underdeveloped countries than with exploiting those problems to its own advantage.

The danger in all of this is that wealthy nations may be competing for the prestige that comes from giving gifts at the expense of Third World nations. With assistance sometimes being given with more regard to the donors' status than to the recipients' welfare, it is no surprise that, in recent years, development aid often has been more effective in creating relationships of dependency, as in the case of Iran's Khū zestān irrigation scheme, than in producing real development. Nor that, given the fine line between donation and domination, offers of help are sometimes met with resistance, apprehension and, in extreme cases, such as the Iranian revolution, even violence.

The Indians understood a gift's ambivalent power to unify, antagonize, or subjugate. We, too, would do well to remember that a present can be a surprisingly potent thing, as dangerous in the hands of the ignorant as it is useful in the hands of the wise.

Review Questions

1. What does Cronk mean by *reciprocity?* What is the social outcome of reciprocal gift giving?

2. According to Cronk, what are some examples of benevolent gift giving?

3. How can giving be used to intimidate other people or groups? Give some examples cited by Cronk and think of some from your own experience.

4. How does Cronk classify gift-giving strategies such as government foreign aid? Can you think of other examples of the use of exchange as a political device?

CHAPTER TEN

Life without Chiefs

Marvin Harris

It may come as a surprise to most Americans, but there were, and in a few cases still are, societies in the world that lack formal political structure. Instead of presidents, mayors, senators, and directors of homeland security, there are headmen, big men, and chiefs who lead by their ability to persuade and impress without the authority to make people act. In this article, Marvin Harris traces the evolution of political leadership, associating headmen with small hunting and gathering societies marked by reciprocal exchange, and big men with slightly larger horticultural societies that employ redistributive exchange. Chiefs also occupied the center of redistribution systems but their societies were larger and chiefs could inherit their positions. He concludes that human biological inheritance was shaped by a hunter-gatherer existence; there is nothing inherited about the political formalism and social inequality that characterize large state societies.

Can humans exist without some people ruling and others being ruled? To look at the modern world, you wouldn't think so. Democratic states may have done away with emperors and kings, but they have hardly dispensed with gross inequalities in wealth, rank, and power.

However, humanity hasn't always lived this way. For about 98 percent of our existence as a species (and for four million years before then), our ancestors lived in small, largely nomadic hunting-and-gathering bands containing about 30 to 50 people apiece. It was in this social context that human nature evolved. It has been only about ten thousand years since people began to settle down into villages, some of which eventually grew into cities. And it has been only in the last two thousand years that the majority of people in the world have not lived in hunting-and-gathering societies. This brief period of time is not nearly sufficient for noticeable evolution to have taken place. Thus, the few remaining foraging societies are the closest analogues we have to the "natural" state of humanity.

To judge from surviving examples of hunting-and-gathering bands and villages, our kind got along quite well for the greater part of prehistory without so much as a paramount chief. In fact, for tens of thousands of years, life went on without kings, queens, prime ministers, presidents, parliaments, congresses, cabinets, governors, and mayors—not to mention the police officers, sheriffs, marshals, generals, lawyers, bailiffs, judges, district attorneys, court clerks, patrol cars, paddy wagons, jails, and penitentiaries that help keep them in power. How in the world did our ancestors ever manage to leave home without them?

Small populations provide part of the answer. With 50 people per band or 150 per village, everybody knew everybody else intimately. People gave with the expectation of taking and took with the expectation of giving. Because chance played a great role in the capture of animals, collection of wild foodstuffs, and success of rudimentary forms of agriculture, the individuals who had the luck of the catch on one day needed a handout on the next. So the best way for them to provide for their inevitable rainy day was to be generous. As expressed by anthropologist Richard Gould, "The greater the amount of risk, the greater the extent of sharing." Reciprocity is a small society's bank.

In reciprocal exchange, people do not specify how much or exactly what they expect to get back or when they expect to get it. That would besmirch the quality of that transaction and make it similar to mere barter or to buying and selling. The distinction lingers on in societies dominated by other forms of exchange, even capitalist ones. For we do carry out a give-and-take among close kin and friends that is informal, uncalculating, and imbued with a spirit of generosity. Teenagers do not pay cash for their meals at home or for the use of the family car, wives do not bill their husbands for cooking a meal, and friends give each other birthday gifts and Christmas presents. But much of this is marred by the expectation that our generosity will be acknowledged with expression of thanks.

Where reciprocity really prevails in daily life, etiquette requires that generosity be taken for granted. As Robert Dentan discovered during his fieldwork among the Semai of Central Malaysia, no one ever says "thank you" for the meat received from another hunter. Having struggled all day to lug the carcass of a pig home through the jungle heat, the hunter allows his prize to be cut up into exactly equal portions, which he then gives away to the entire group. Dentan explains that to express gratitude for the portion received indicates that you are the kind of ungenerous person who calculates how much you give and take: "In this context, saying 'thank you' is very rude, for it suggests, first, that one has calculated the amount of a gift and, second, that one did not expect the donor to be so generous." To call attention to one's generosity is to indicate that others are in debt to you and that you expect them to repay you. It is repugnant to egalitarian peoples even to suggest that they have been treated generously.

Canadian anthropologist Richard Lee tells how, through a revealing incident, he learned about this aspect of reciprocity. To please the !Kung, the "bush-men" of the Kalahari desert, he decided to buy a large ox and have it slaughtered as a present. After days of searching Bantu agricultural villages for the largest and fattest ox in the region, he acquired what appeared to be a perfect specimen. But his friends took him aside and assured him that he had been duped into buying an absolutely worthless animal. "Of course, we will eat it," they said, "but it won't fill us up—we will eat and go home to bed with stomachs rumbling." Yet, when Lee's ox was slaughtered, it turned out to be covered with a thick layer of fat. Later, his friends explained why they had said his gift was valueless, even though they knew better than he what lay under the animal's skin.

"Yes, when a young man kills much meat he comes to think of himself as a chief or a big man, and he thinks of the rest of us as his servants or inferiors. We can't accept this. We refuse one who boasts, for someday his pride will make him kill somebody. So we always speak of his meat as worthless. This way we cool his heart and make him gentle."

Lee watched small groups of men and women returning home every evening with the animals and wild fruits and plants that they had killed or collected. They shared everything equally, even with campmates who had stayed behind and spent the day sleeping or taking care of their tools and weapons.

"Not only do families pool that day's production, but the entire camp— residents and visitors alike—shares equally in the total quantity of food available," Lee observed. "The evening meal of any one family is made up of portions of food from each of the other families resident. There is a constant flow of nuts, berries, roots, and melons from one family fire-place to another, until each person has received an equitable portion. The following morning a different combination of foragers moves out of camp, and when they return late in the day, the distribution of foodstuffs is repeated."

In small, prestate societies, it was in everybody's best interest to maintain each other's freedom of access to the natural habitat. Suppose a !Kung with a lust for power were to get up and tell his campmates, "From now on, all this land and everything on it belongs to me. I'll let you use it but only with my permission and on the condition that I get first choice of anything you capture, collect, or grow." His campmates, thinking that he had certainly gone crazy, would pack up their few belongings, take a long walk, make a new camp, and resume their usual life of egalitarian reciprocity. The man who would be king would be left by himself to exercise a useless sovereignty.

The Headman: Leadership, Not Power

To the extent that political leadership exists at all among band-and-village societies, it is exercised by individuals called headmen. These headmen, however, lack the power to compel others to obey their orders. How can a leader be powerless and still lead?

The political power of genuine rulers depends on their ability to expel or exterminate disobedient individuals and groups. When a headman gives a command, however, he has no certain physical means of punishing those who disobey. So, if he wants to stay in "office," he gives few commands. Among the Eskimo, for instance, a group will follow an outstanding hunter and defer to his opinion with respect to choice of hunting spots. But in all other matters, the leader's opinion carries no more weight than any other man's. Similarly, among the !Kung, each band has its recognized leaders, most of whom are males. These men speak out more than others and are listened to with a bit more deference. But they have no formal authority and can only persuade, never command. When Lee asked the !Kung whether they had headmen—meaning powerful chiefs—they told him, "Of course we have headmen! In fact, we are all headmen. Each one of us is headman over himself."

Headmanship can be a frustrating and irksome job. Among Indian groups such as the Mehinacu of Brazil's Zingu National Park, headmen behave something like zealous scoutmasters on overnight cookouts. The first one up in the morning, the headman tries to rouse his companions by standing in the middle of the village plaza and shouting to them. If something needs to be done, it is the headman who starts doing it, and it is the headman who works harder than anyone else. He sets an example not only for hard work but also for generosity: After a fishing or hunting expedition, he gives away more of his catch than anyone else does. In trading with other groups, he must be careful not to keep the best items for himself.

In the evening, the headman stands in the center of the plaza and exhorts his people to be good. He calls upon them to control their sexual appetites, work hard in their gardens, and take frequent baths in the river. He tells them not to sleep during the day or bear grudges against each other.

Coping with Freeloaders

During the reign of reciprocal exchange and egalitarian headmen, no individual, family, or group smaller than the band or village itself could control access to natural resources. Rivers, lakes, beaches, oceans, plants and animals, the soil and subsoil were all communal property.

Among the !Kung, a core of people born in a particular territory say that they "own" the water holes and hunting rights, but this has no effect on the people who happen to be visiting and living with them at any given time. Since !Kung from neighboring bands are related through marriage, they often visit each other for months at a time and have free use of whatever resources they need without having to ask permission. Though people from distant bands must make a request to use another band's territory, the "owners" seldom refuse them.

The absence of private possession in land and other vital resources means that a form of communism probably existed among prehistoric hunting and collecting bands and small villages. Perhaps I should emphasize that this did not rule out the existence of private property. People in simple band-and-village societies own personal effects such as weapons, clothing, containers, ornaments, and tools. But why should anyone want to steal such objects? People who have a bush camp and move about a lot have no use for extra possessions. And since the group is small enough that everybody knows everybody else, stolen items cannot be used anonymously. If you want something, better to ask for it openly, since by the rules of reciprocity such requests cannot be denied.

I don't want to create the impression that life within egalitarian band-and-village societies unfolded entirely without disputes over possessions. As in every social group, nonconformists and malcontents tried to use the system for their own advantage. Inevitably there were freeloaders, individuals who consistently took more than they gave and lay back in their hammocks while others did the work. Despite the absence of a criminal justice system, such behavior eventually was punished. A widespread belief among band-and-village peoples attributes death and misfortune to the malevolent conspiracy of sorcerers. The task of identifying these evildoers falls to a group's shamans, who remain responsive to public opinion during their divinatory trances. Well-liked individuals who enjoy strong support from their families need not fear the shaman. But quarrelsome, stingy people who do not give as well as take had better watch out.

From Headman to Big Man

Reciprocity was not the only form of exchange practiced by egalitarian band-and-village peoples. Our kind long ago found other ways to give and take. Among them the form of exchange known as redistribution played a crucial role in creating distinctions of rank during the evolution of chiefdoms and states.

Redistribution occurs when people turn over food and other valuables to a prestigious figure such as a headman, to be pooled, divided into separate portions, and given out again. The primordial form of redistribution was probably keyed to seasonal hunts and harvests, when more food than usual became available.

True to their calling, headmen-redistributors not only work harder than their followers but also give more generously and reserve smaller and less desirable portions for themselves than for anyone else. Initially, therefore, redistribution strictly reinforced the political and economic equality associated with reciprocal exchange. The redistributors were compensated purely with admiration and in proportion to their success in giving bigger feasts, in personally contributing more than anybody else, and in asking little or nothing for their effort, all of which initially seemed an innocent extension of the basic principle of reciprocity.

But how little our ancestors understood what they were getting themselves into! For if it is a good thing to have a headman give feasts, why not have several headmen give feasts? Or, better yet, why not let success in organizing and giving feasts be the measure of one's legitimacy as a headman? Soon, where conditions permit, there are several would-be headmen vying with each other to hold the most lavish feasts and redistribute the most food and other valuables. In this fashion there evolved the nemesis that Richard Lee's !Kung informants had warned about: the youth who wants to be a "big man."

A classic anthropological study of big men was carried out by Douglas Oliver among the Siuai, a village people who live on the South Pacific island of Bougainville, in the Solomon Islands. In the Siuai language, big men were known as *mumis*. Every Siuai boy's highest ambition was to become a *mumi*. He began by getting married, working hard, and restricting his own consumption of meats and coconuts. His wife and parents, impressed with the seriousness of his intentions, vowed to help him prepare for his first feast. Soon his circle of supporters widened and he began to construct a clubhouse in which his male followers could lounge about and guests could be entertained and fed. He gave a feast at the consecration of the clubhouse; if this was a success, the circle of people willing to work for him grew larger still, and he began to hear himself spoken of as a mumi. Larger and larger feasts meant that the mumi's demands on his supporters became more irksome. Although they grumbled about how hard they had to work, they remained loyal as long as their mumi continued to maintain and increase his renown as a "great provider."

Finally the time came for the new mumi to challenge the older ones. He did this at a *muminai* feast, where both sides kept a tally of all the pigs, coconut pies, and sago-almond puddings given away by the host mumi and his followers to the guest mumi and his followers. If the guests could not reciprocate with a feast as lavish as that of the challengers, their mumi suffered a great social humiliation, and his fall from mumihood was immediate.

At the end of a successful feast, the greatest of mumis still faced a lifetime of personal toil and dependence on the moods and inclinations of his followers. Mumihood did not confer the power to coerce others into doing one's bidding, nor did it elevate one's standard of living above anyone else's. In fact, because giving things away was the essence of mumihood, great mumis consumed less meat and other delicacies than ordinary men. Among the Kaoka, another Solomon Islands group, there is the saying, "The giver of the feast takes the bones and the stale cakes; the meat and the fat go to the others." At one great feast attended by 1,100 people, the host mumi, whose name was Soni, gave away thirty-two pigs and a large quantity of sago-almond puddings. Soni himself and some of his closest followers went hungry. "We shall eat Soni's renown," they said.

From Big Man to Chief

The slide (or ascent?) toward social stratification gained momentum wherever extra food produced by the inspired diligence of redistributors could be stored while awaiting muminai feasts, potlatches, and other occasions of redistribution. The more concentrated and abundant the harvest and the less perishable the crop, the greater its potential for endowing the big man with power. Though others would possess some stored-up foods of their own, the redistributor's stores would be the largest. In times of scarcity, people would come to him, expecting to be fed; in return, he could call upon those who had special skills to make cloth, pots, canoes, or a fine house for his own use. Eventually, the redistributor no longer needed to work in the fields to gain and surpass bigman status. Management of the harvest surpluses, a portion of which continued to be given to him for use in communal feasts and other communal projects (such as trading expeditions and warfare), was sufficient to validate his status. And, increasingly, people viewed this status as an office, a sacred trust, passed on from one generation to the next according to the rules of hereditary succession. His dominion was no longer a small, autonomous village but a large political community. The big man had become a chief.

Returning to the South Pacific and the Trobriand Islands, one can catch a glimpse of how these pieces of encroaching stratification fell into place. The Trobrianders had hereditary chiefs who held sway over more than a dozen villages containing several thousand people. Only chiefs could wear certain shell ornaments as the insignia of high rank, and it was forbidden for commoners to stand or sit in a position that put a chief's head at a lower elevation. British anthropologist Bronislaw Malinowski tells of seeing all the people present in the village of Bwoytalu drop from their verandas "as if blown down by a hurricane" at the sound of a drawn-out cry warning that an important chief was approaching.

Yams were the Trobrianders' staff of life; the chiefs validated their status by storing and redistributing copious quantities of them acquired through donations from their brothers-in-law at harvest time. Similar "gifts" were received by husbands who were commoners, but chiefs were polygymous and, having as many as a dozen wives, received many more yams than anyone else. Chiefs placed their yam supply on display racks specifically built for this purpose next to their houses. Commoners did the same, but a chief's yam racks towered over all the others.

This same pattern recurs, with minor variations, on several continents. Striking parallels were seen, for example, twelve thousand miles away from the Trobrianders, among chiefdoms that flourished throughout the southeastern region of the United States—specifically among the Cherokee, former inhabitants of Tennessee, as described by the eighteenth-century naturalist William Bartram.

At the center of the principal Cherokee settlements stood a large circular house where a council of chiefs discussed issues involving their villages and where redistributive feasts were held. The council of chiefs had a paramount who was the principal figure in the Cherokee redistributive network. At the harvest time a large crib, identified as the "chiefs granary," was erected in each field. "To this," explained Bartram, "each family carries and deposits a certain quantity according to his ability or inclination, or none at all if he so chooses." The chief's granaries functioned as a public treasury in case of crop failure, a source of food for strangers or travelers, and as military store. Although every citizen enjoyed free access to the store, commoners had to acknowledge that it really belonged to the supreme chief, who had "an exclusive right and ability... to distribute comfort and blessings to the necessitous."

Supported by voluntary donations, chiefs could now enjoy lifestyles that set them increasingly apart from their followers. They could build bigger and finer houses for themselves, eat and dress more sumptuously, and enjoy the sexual favors and personal services of several wives. Despite these harbingers, people in chiefdoms voluntarily invested unprecedented amounts of labor on behalf of communal projects. They dug moats, threw up defensive earthen embankments, and erected great log palisades around their villages. They heaped up small mountains of rubble and soil to form platforms and mounds on top of which they built temples and big houses for their chief. Working in teams and using nothing but levers and rollers, they moved rocks weighing fifty tons or more and set them in precise lines and perfect circles, forming sacred precincts for communal rituals marking the change of seasons.

If this seems remarkable, remember that donated labor created the mega-lithic alignments of Stonehenge and Carnac, put up the great statues on Easter Island, shaped the huge stone heads of the Olmec in Vera Cruz, dotted Polynesia with ritual precincts set on great stone platforms, and filled the Ohio, Tennessee, and Mississippi valleys with hundreds of large mounds. Not until it was too late did people realize that their beautiful chiefs were about to keep the meat and fat for themselves while giving nothing but bones and stale cakes to their followers.

In the End

As we know, chiefdoms would eventually evolve into states, states into empires. From peaceful origins, humans created and mounted a wild beast that ate continents. Now that beast has taken us to the brink of global annihilation.

Will nature's experiment with mind and culture end in nuclear war? No one knows the answer. But I believe it is essential that we understand our past before we can create the best possible future. Once we are clear about the roots of human nature, for example, we can refute, once and for all, the notion that it is a biological imperative for our kind to form hierarchical groups. An observer viewing human life shortly after cultural takeoff would easily have concluded that our species was destined to be irredeemably egalitarian except for distinctions of sex and age. That someday the world would be divided into aristocrats and commoners, masters and slaves, billionaires and homeless beggars would have seemed wholly contrary to human nature as evidenced in the affairs of every human society then on Earth.

Of course, we can no more reverse the course of thousands of years of cultural evolution than our egalitarian ancestors could have designed and built the space shuttle. Yet, in striving for the preservation of mind and culture on Earth, it is vital that we recognize the significance of cultural takeoff and the great difference between biological and cultural evolution. We must rid ourselves of the notion that we are an innately aggressive species for whom war is inevitable. We must reject as unscientific claims that there are superior and inferior races and that the hierarchical divisions within and between societies are the consequences of natural selection rather than of a long process of cultural evolution, We must struggle to gain control over cultural selection through objective studies of the human condition and the recurrent process of history. Not only a more just society, but our very survival as a species may depend on it.

Review Questions

1. What is the difference among headmen, big men, and chiefs according to Harris?

2. What does Harris see as the connection between forms of leadership and modes of economic exchange? How does this connection work?

3. Harris makes a distinction between biological evolution and cultural evolution. What is the distinction and how does he apply it to types of leadership?

CHAPTER ELEVEN

The Founding Indian Fathers

Jack Weatherford

As we saw in the last article, the members of small societies could make political decisions without the presence of complex, hierarchical political organization. But as societies have grown both in population and territory, the complexity of political institutions has grown with them. Chieftainships gave way to kingdoms and then states. The regulation of trade; the distribution of goods, services, and wealth; and relations between states including warfare demanded the formation of more complex political systems. Political hierarchies evolved, usually led by hereditary, often divine, rulers supported by ruling elites and a large number of bureaucrats. Although rulers could often depend on their birthright and supernatural power to claim political legitimacy, coercion was also an important tool for the maintenance of power. Large-scale societies, it seemed, could not institutionalize the democratic processes that characterized small societies. Yet the colonists who founded the United States did manage to do so.

Many Americans believe that U.S. democracy stems directly from the ideas of Athenian philosophers. In this article, Jack Weatherford argues for another, unrecognized, political model also used by our founding fathers to shape governmental structure, the League of the Iroquois and some other features of American Indian political process and organization. Indian influence, he argues, found its way into colonial thinking through such individuals as Benjamin Franklin, who had extensive contact with native peoples. Weatherford describes how Indian, especially Iroquoian, political structure served as a model that helped to produce a democratic federal structure incorporating states with substantial local power, and that later, contact with Indians as colonists moved west continued to shape U.S. political organization. It is no accident, he claims, that a basic political institution in the United States is called by the Algonquin name, caucus.

―――――――――

Every day of the school year, troops of children march across the lawn of the United States Capitol perched atop the District of Columbia's highest elevation. The building dominates the Washington skyline, a model of classical symmetry and precision. Two giant wings of precisely equal proportion reach out from a Roman dome that surveys the city of Washington. If reduced to a ruin, the forest of Greek columns decorating the building would appear to be as much at home in Rome or Naples as in Athens or Corinth. The building revels in its Old World heritage.

Indian schoolchildren walking through the halls of Congress would rarely see a hint that the building sits in America overlooking the Potomac River and not along the shores of the Mediterranean Sea. The building copies European, primarily classical, styles, and its halls proudly display pictures, friezes, and busts of famous political thinkers from Hammurabi and Solomon to Rousseau and Voltaire. In the hallways stand statues of American politicians posing in Greek tunics and Roman togas as though they were Roman senators or Athenian orators. Greek busts of the vice-presidents of the United States line the halls of the Senate, lending them the aura of a classical cemetery.

The children pass under doorways that bear weighty engravings and quotations from European documents such as the Magna Carta interspersed with quotes from the United States Declaration of Independence or Constitution. The building and its appointments proudly proclaim their part in the great march of European progress and civilization. They portray the blessed dove of democracy hatching in Athens and then taking wing for a torturous flight of two millennia, pausing only momentarily over Republican Rome, the field of Runnymede, and the desk of Voltaire before finally alighting to rest permanently and securely in the virgin land of America.

A child standing squarely in the middle of the Capitol beneath the great dome sees a painted band circling the upper wall representing the history of America. In that work, the Indians appear as just one more dangerous obstacle, like the wild animals, the Appalachian Mountains, the Mississippi River, and the western deserts, that blocked the progress of European civilization and technology in the white man's march across America. The most peaceful picture with an Indian theme in the rotunda shows the baptism of Pocahontas, daughter of the Indian leader Powhatan. Surrounded by Europeans and dressed in English clothes, she symbolically renounces the savage life of the Indians for the civilization of the British.

The lesson in this august setting presents itself forcefully on every visitor. The United States government derives from European precedents, and the Americans gave civilization to the Indians. Nothing in the Capitol hints that contemporary Americans owe the slightest debt to the Indians for teaching us about democratic institutions.

Despite these civic myths surrounding the creation of American government, America's settlers from Europe knew little of democracy. The English came from a nation ruled by monarchs who claimed that God conferred their right to rule and even allowed them to wage wars of extinction against the Irish. Colonists also fled to America from France, which was wandering aimlessly through history under the extravagances of a succession of kings named Louis, most of whom pursued debauched and extravagant reigns that oppressed, exploited, and at times even starved their subjects.

Despite the ideal government sketched by Plato in *The Republic*, and the different constitutions analyzed by Aristotle in his *Politics*, the Old World offered America few democratic models for government. Democratic government had no fortress in the Old World. Despite the democratic rhetoric that came into fashion in eighteenth-century Europe, no such systems existed there at that time. The monarchy and the aristocracy of England were engaged in a protracted struggle that would eventually lead to the supremacy of Parliament (and a closely limited electoral franchise until the reforms of the nineteenth century). France had not yet begun its experiments with participatory democracy. The Founding Fathers of the United States judiciously assembled bits and pieces of many different systems to invent a completely new one. In fashioning the new system, they even borrowed some distinctive elements from the American Indians.

The Founding Fathers faced a major problem when it came time to invent the United States. They represented, under the Articles of Confederation, thirteen separate and sovereign states. How could one country be made from all thirteen without each one yielding its own power?

Reportedly, the first person to propose a union of all the colonies and to propose a federal model for it was the Iroquois chief Canassatego, speaking at an Indian-British assembly in Pennsylvania in July 1744. He complained that the Indians found it difficult to deal with so many different colonial administrations, each with its own policy. It would make life easier for everyone involved if the colonists could have a union which allowed them to speak with one voice. He not only proposed that the colonies unify themselves, but told them how they might do it. He suggested that they do as his people had done and form a union like the League of the Iroquois.

Hiawatha and Deganwidah founded the League of the Iroquois sometime between A.D. 1000 and 1450 under a constitution they called the *Kaianerekowa* or Great Law of Peace. When the Europeans arrived in America, the league constituted the most extensive and important political unit north of the Aztec civilization. From earliest contact the Iroquois intrigued the Europeans, and they were the subject of many amazed reports. Benjamin Franklin, however, seems to have been the first to take their system as a potentially important model by which the settlers might be able to fashion a new government.

Benjamin Franklin first became acquainted with the operation of Indian political organization in his capacity as official printer for the colony of Pennsylvania. His job included publication of the records and speeches of the various Indian assemblies and treaty negotiations, but following his instinctive curiosity, he broadened this into a study of Indian culture and institutions. Because of his expertise and interest in Indian matters, the colonial government of Pennsylvania offered him his first diplomatic assignment as their Indian commissioner. He held this post during the 1750s and became intimately familiar with the intricacies of Indian political culture and in particular with the League of the Iroquois. After this taste of Indian diplomacy, Franklin became a lifelong champion of the Indian political structure and advocated its use by the Americans. During this time he also refined his political techniques of persuasion, compromise, and slow consensus building that proved so important to his later negotiations as the ambassador to France and as a delegate to the Constitutional Convention.

Echoing the original proposal of Canassatego, Franklin advocated that the new American government incorporate many of the same features as the government of the Iroquois. Speaking to the Albany Congress in 1754, Franklin called on the delegates of the various English colonies to unite and emulate the Iroquois League, a call that was not heeded until the Constitution was written three decades later. Even though the Founding Fathers finally adopted some of the essential features of the Iroquois League, they never followed it in quite the detail advocated by Franklin.

The Iroquois League united five principal Indian nations—the Mohawk, Onondaga, Seneca, Oneida, and Cayuga. Each of these nations had a council composed of delegates called sachems who were elected by the tribes of that nation. The Seneca Nation elected eight sachems to its council, the Mohawk and Oneida nations each had councils of nine sachems, the Cayuga Nation had a council of ten, and the Onondaga Nation had a council of fourteen. Each of these nations governed its own territory, and its own council met to decide the issues of public policy for each one. But these councils exercised jurisdiction over the internal concerns of that one nation only; in this regard they exercised powers somewhat like the individual governments of the colonies.

In addition to the individual councils of each separate nation, the sachems formed a grand Council of the League in which all fifty sachems of the six nations sat together to discuss issues of common concern. The sachems represented their individual nations, but at the same time they represented the whole League of the Iroquois, thereby making the decisions of the council the law for all five nations. In this council each sachem had equal authority and privileges, with his power dependent on his oratorical power to persuade. The council met in the autumn of at least one year in five in a longhouse in the Onondaga Nation; if needed they could be called into session at other times as well. Their power extended to all matters of common concern among the member nations. In the words of Lewis Henry Morgan, America's first modern anthropologist, the council "declared war and made peace, sent and received embassies, entered into treaties of alliance, regulated the affairs of subjugated nations, received new members into the League, extended its protection over feeble tribes, in a word, took all needful measures to promote their prosperity, and enlarge their dominion."[1]

Through this government the nations of the Iroquois controlled territory from New England to the Mississippi River, and they built a league that endured for centuries. Unlike European governments, the league blended the sovereignty of several nations into one government. This model of several sovereign units united into one government presented precisely the solution to the problem confronting the writers of the United States Constitution. Today we call this a "federal" system in which each state retains power over internal affairs and the national government regulates affairs common to all. Henry Steele Commager later wrote of this crucial time that even "if Americans did not actually invent federalism, they were able to take out an historical patent on it."[2] The Indians invented it even though the United States patented it.

Another student of the Iroquois political organization was Charles Thomson, the perpetual secretary of the Continental Congress. He

---

1   Lewis Henry Morgan, League of the Iroquois (Rochester: Sage, 1851), pp. 66-67.
2   Henry Steele Commager. The Empire of Reason: How Europe Imagined and America Realized the Enlightenment (Garden City, NY: Anchor), p. 207.

spent so much energy studying the Indians and their way of life that the Delaware Nation adopted him as a full member. Following Thomas Jefferson's request, Thomson wrote at length on Indian social and political institutions for inclusion in an appendix to Jefferson's *Notes on the State of Virginia*. According to his description of Indian political tradition, each Indian town built a council house for making local decisions and for electing delegates to the tribal council. The tribal council in turn elected delegates to the national council. Even though Thomson wrote this several years before the Constitutional Convention, this description reads like a blueprint for the United States Constitution, especially when we remember that the Constitution allowed the state legislatures (rather than the general populace) to elect senators. Thomson stresses that the sachems or political leaders do not acquire their positions by heredity but by election, and he adds that because outsiders can be naturalized into the Indian nation, even they can be elected to such offices.

The Americans followed the model of the Iroquois League not only in broad outline but also in many of the specific provisions of their *Kaianerekowa*. According to the *Kaianerekowa*, the sachems were not chiefs, a position frequently associated with leadership in war. As a lawmaker, the sachem could never go to war in his official capacity as a sachem. "If disposed to take the warpath, he laid aside his civil office, for the time being, and became a common warrior."[3] This followed the tradition in many Indian tribes that relied upon separate leaders for peace and for war. The colonists followed this model too in eventually separating civilian authorities from military ones. Members of Congress, judges, and other officials could not also act as military leaders without giving up their elected office; similarly, military leaders could not be elected to political office without first resigning their military position. This contrasted with British traditions; church and military leaders frequently served as members of the House of Lords and frequently played major political roles in the House of Commons as well. Similarly, this inability to separate the civil government and the military has doomed many of the imitators of American democracy, particularly in Africa and Latin America.

If the conduct of any sachem appeared improper to the populace or if he lost the confidence of his electorate, the women of his clan impeached him and expelled him by official action, whereupon the women then choose a new sachem. This concept of impeachment ran counter to European tradition, in which the monarch ruled

---

3   Morgan, p. 72.

until death, even if he became insane or incapacitated, as in the case of George III. The Americans followed the Iroquois precedent of always providing for ways to remove leaders when necessary, but the Founding Fathers saw no reason to follow the example of the Iroquois in granting women the right to vote or any other major role in the political structure.

One of the most important characteristics of the Iroquois League permitted it to expand as needed; the council could vote to admit new members. This proved to be an important feature of the system after the Tuscarora Indians of North Carolina faced attack in 1712 by the army of Colonel John Barnwell and again in 1713 by the army of Colonel James Moore. Having thoroughly defeated the Tuscaroras, the Carolina colonists demanded reparations from the Indians to pay the colonists' expenses incurred in the war. Because the Indians had no money to pay, the colonists seized four hundred of them and sold them into slavery at the rate of ten pounds sterling apiece. The surviving Tuscaroras fled North Carolina to seek refuge among the Iroquois. In 1714 the Tuscaroras applied for formal membership in the league, and the Iroquois admitted them in 1722 as the Sixth Nation. Similarly the league later incorporated other decimated groups such as the Erie, but the league did not allow for an entity such as a colony, which had played such an important part in European governments since the times of the ancient Greeks.

In a radical break with Old World tradition, the emerging government of the United States emulated this Iroquois tradition of admitting new states as members rather than keeping them as colonies. The west became a series of territories and then states, but the United States treated each new territory as a future partner rather than as a colony. The new government codified this Indian practice into American law through the Congressional Resolution of 1780, the Land Ordinances of 1784 and 1785, and the Northwest Ordinance, together with similar provisions written directly into the Constitution. No direct proof links these laws with the Iroquois, but it seems likely to be more than mere coincidence that both the Iroquois and the United States governments enacted such similar procedures.

Although the Iroquois recognized no supreme leader in their system analogous to the president of the United States, the framers of the Constitution deliberately or inadvertently imitated the Great Council in establishing the electoral college system to select a president. Each state legislature selected a group of electors equal in number to that state's combined total of senators and representatives. Like the sachems, each elector then had one vote in the electoral college.

In the two centuries since the Constitution went into effect, some aspects of the system have changed. The voters rather than the state legislatures now elect both the electoral college and the senators through popular vote, but the system preserves the general features of the League of the Iroquois.

Upon election to the council, the new sachem "lost" his name and thenceforth other sachems called him by the title of his office. In much the same way, proceedings of the United States Senate do not permit the use of names such as "Senator Kennedy" or "Rudy Boschwitz." Instead the senators must be addressed by their office title as "the Senior Senator from Massachusetts" or "the Junior Senator from Minnesota." Other titles such as "Majority Leader," "Mr. Chairman," or "Mr. President" may be used, but all personal names remain strictly taboo.

Another imitation of the Iroquois came in the simple practice of allowing only one person to speak at a time in political meetings. This contrasts with the British tradition of noisy interruptions of one another as the members of Parliament shout out agreement or disagreement with the speaker. Europeans were accustomed to shouting down any speaker who displeased them; in some cases they might even stone him or inflict worse damage.

The Iroquois permitted no interruptions or shouting. They even imposed a short period of silence at the end of each oration in case the speaker had forgotten some point or wished to elaborate or change something he had said. Even though the American Congress and legislatures did not adopt the practice of silence at the end, they did allow speakers "to revise and extend" the written record after speaking.

The purpose of debate in Indian councils was to persuade and educate, not to confront. Unlike European parliaments, where opposing factions battle out an issue in the public arena, the council of the Indians sought to reach an agreement through compromise. This important difference in nuance led Bruce Burton to observe in his study of American law that "American democracy owes its distinctive character of debate and compromise to the principles and structures of American Indian civil government."[4] Still today, this difference separates the operation of the United States Congress and the state legislatures from their European counterparts. American legislative bodies are composed primarily of individuals forming shifting factions

---

4   Bruce A. Burton, "Iroquois Confederate Law and the Origins of the U.S. Constitution," Northeast Indian Quarterly, Fall 1986, p. 4.

from one issue to another, whereas the legislative bodies of Europe operate through opposing political parties that control the votes of individual representatives.

In keeping with Iroquois tradition, Franklin proposed that since the sachems did not own land or receive any financial compensation for their work, the officials of the United States should not be paid. They should perform their work as a sacred trust freely given to the communal welfare. Even though the Founding Fathers did not incorporate this, they did work to prevent property qualifications for holding office and for exercising the right to vote. They also tended to limit salaries paid to officeholders to a minimum to cover basic expenses of life rather than making public office a sinecure or a route to wealth. . . .

From Hollywood films and adventure novels Americans often conclude that strong chiefs usually commanded the Indian tribes. More often, however, as in the case of the Iroquois, a council ruled, and any person called the "head" of the tribe usually occupied a largely honorary position of respect rather than power. Chiefs mostly played ceremonial and religious roles rather than political or economic ones. Unlike the words "caucus" and "powwow," which are Indian-derived and indicative of Indian political traditions, the word "chief is an English word of French origin that British officials tried to force onto Indian tribes in order that they might have someone with whom to trade and sign treaties.

In Massachusetts the British tried to make one leader into *King* Philip. The British imputed monarchy to the Indian system when no such institution existed. Thus while the English settlers learned from the Indians how to speak and act in group councils, they simultaneously pushed the Indians toward a monarchical and thus less democratic system. . . .

In almost every North American tribe, clan, or nation for which we have detailed political information, the supreme authority rested in a group rather than in an individual. It took many generations of close interaction between colonists and Indians before the principles of group decision-making replaced the European traditions of relying on a single supreme authority. The importance of these Indian councils and groups shows clearly in the English lack of words to explain such a process.

One of the most important political institutions borrowed from the Indians was the caucus. Even though the word appears to be proper Latin and some law students with a semester of Latin occasionally decline the plural as *cauci*, the word comes from the Algonquian languages. The caucus permits informal discussion of an issue without necessitating a yea or nay vote on any particular question. This agreed with the traditional Indian way of talking through an issue or of making a powwow; it made political decisions less divisive and combative. The caucus became a mainstay of American democracy both in the Congress and in political and community groups all over the country. The caucus evolved into such an important aspect of American politics that the political parties adopted it to nominate their presidential candidates. In time this evolved into the political convention, which still functions as an important part of contemporary American politics but is largely absent from European politics. . . .

Even after the founding of the United States, the Indians continued to play a significant role in the evolution of democracy because of their sustained interactions with Americans on the frontier. The frontiersmen constantly reinvented democracy and channeled it into the eastern establishment of the United States.

Time and again the people of the frontier rebelled against the entrenched and conservative values of an ever more staid coastal elite. As the frontier gradually moved westward, the settlements on the edge sent such rebels as Henry Clay, Andrew Jackson, David Crockett, and Abraham Lincoln back to reinvest the spirit of democracy into the political institutions of the east. Some of these men, such as Sam Houston, lived for long periods with Indians. Houston spent so much time with the Cherokee that they adopted him into their nation about 1829. The influence of the Cherokees stayed with him throughout his tenure as president of Texas from 1836 to 1838 and again from 1841 to 1844. Throughout his life he maintained close working relations with a variety of Indian nations and a strong commitment to liberty.

Even Alexis de Tocqueville, who denigrated the achievements of the Indians, noticed that the settlers on the frontier "mix the ideas and customs of savage life with the civilization of their fathers." In general he found this reprehensible, for it made their "passions more intense" and "their religious morality less authoritative,"[5] but these traits certainly may be interpreted by others as among the virtues of a democratic people.

Most democratic and egalitarian reforms of the past two hundred years in America originated on the frontier and not in the settled cities of the east. The frontier states dropped property and religious requirements for voters. They extended the franchise to women, and in

---

5   Alexis de Tocqueville, *Democracy in America 2*, vols, in Phillips Bradley (ed.)
      (New York: Random House, 1945), p. 334.

1916 Montana elected Jeannette Rankin as the first woman in Congress four years before the Nineteenth Amendment to the Constitution gave women the right to vote. The western states started the public election of senators in place of selection by the legislature. They also pioneered the use of primary elections and electoral recalls of unpopular officers. Even today they have more elective offices, such as judges; such offices in the east are usually filled by appointment by the governor or the legislature. This strong bias toward the electoral process and equal votes for all has been reinforced repeatedly by the people who have had the closest and the longest connections with the Indians on the frontier. . . .

Washington, D.C., has never recognized the role of the Indians in the writing of the United States Constitution or in the creation of political institutions that seem so uniquely American. But an inadvertent memorial does exist. An older woman from Israel pointed this out to me one spring day as I cut across the lawn of the United States Capitol, where I then worked for Senator John Glenn. She stopped me, and in a husky voice asked me who was the Indian woman atop the Capitol dome. Suddenly looking at it through her eyes, I too saw the figure as an Indian even though I knew that it was not.

When the United States government embarked on an expansion of the Capitol in the middle of the nineteenth century, the architects proposed to cap the dome with a symbol of freedom. They chose for this a nineteen-foot bronze statue of a Roman woman who would stand on the pinnacle of the Capitol. Sculptor Thomas Crawford crowned the woman with a Phrygian cap, which in Roman history had been the sign of the freed slave. At that time Jefferson Davis, the future president of the Confederate States of America, still served as the secretary of war for the United States, and he objected strongly to what he interpreted as an antisouthern and antislavery symbol. He compelled Crawford to cap her with something less antagonistic to southern politicians. Crawford designed a helmet covered with a crown of feathers, but in putting this headdress on the figure, her whole appearance changed. Now instead of looking like a classical Greek or Roman, she looked like an Indian.

She still stands today on the pseudoclassical Capitol overlooking the city of Washington. The Washington Monument rises to the same height, but no other building has been allowed to rise higher than she. Even though no one intended her to be an Indian, she now reigns as the nearest thing to a monument that Washington ever built to honor the Indians who contributed to the building of a federal union based on democracy.

Review Questions

1. Weatherford argues that American Indian political structure served as a model for the U.S Constitution. What evidence does he cite to support his assertion?

2. As Weatherford described, what were the main structural features of the League of the Iroquois?

3. What organizational features characteristic of the Iriquoi are reflected in the U.S. Constitution devised by the founding fathers?

4. What life experiences enabled some colonial leaders as opposed to others to bring information about Indian political structure to those who framed the U.S. Constitution?

5. How did the western movement of American settlers affect the development of democracy in the United States? Why?

6

KINSHIP: DESCENT SYSTEMS

CHAPTER TWELVE

Kinship and Family

Social life is essential to human existence. We remain in the company of other people from the day we are born to the time of our death. People teach us to speak. They show us how to relate to our surroundings. They give us the help and the support we need to achieve personal security and mental well-being. Alone, we are relatively frail, defenseless primates; in groups we are astonishingly adaptive and powerful. Yet despite these advantages, well-organized human societies are difficult to achieve. Some species manage to produce social organization genetically. But people are not like bees or ants. We lack the genetically coded directions for behavior that make these insects successful social animals. Although we seem to inherit a general need for social approval, we also harbor individual interests and ambitions that can block or destroy close social ties. To overcome these divisive tendencies, human groups organize around several principles designed to foster cooperation and group loyalty. Kinship is among the strongest of these.

We may define **kinship** as the complex system of culturally defined social relationships based on marriage (the principle of **affinity**) and birth (the principle of **consanguinity**). The study of kinship involves consideration of such principles as descent, kinship status and roles, family and other kinship groups, marriage, and residence. In fact, kinship has been such an important organizing factor in many of the societies studied by anthropologists that it is one of the most elaborate areas of the discipline. What are some of the important concepts?

First is descent. **Descent** is based on the notion of a common heritage. It is a cultural rule tying together people on the basis of reputed common ancestry. Descent functions to guide inheritance, group loyalty, and, above all, the formation of families and extended kinship groups.

There are three main rules of descent. One is **patrilineal descent,** which links relatives through males only. In patrilineal systems, females are part of their father's line, but their children descend from the husbands. **Matrilineal descent** links relatives through females only. Males belong to their mother's line; the children of males descend from the wives. **Bilateral descent** links a person to kin through both males and females simultaneously. Americans are said to have bilateral descent, whereas most of the people in India, Japan, and China are patrilineal. Such groups as the Apache and Trobriand Islanders are matrilineal.

Descent often defines groups called, not surprisingly, **descent groups.** One of these is the **lineage,** a localized group that is based on unilineal (patrilineal or matrilineal) descent and that usually has some corporate powers. In the Marshall Islands, for example, the matriline holds rights to land, which, in turn, it allots to its members. Lineages in India sometimes hold rights to land but are a more important arena for other kinds of decisions such as marriage. Lineage mates must be consulted about the advisability, timing, and arrangements for weddings.

Clans are composed of lineages. Clan members believe they are all descended from a common ancestor, but because clans are larger, members cannot trace their genealogical relationships to everyone in the group. In some societies, clans may be linked together in even larger groups called **phratries.** Because phratries are usually large, the feeling of common descent they offer is weaker.

Ramages, or cognatic kin groups, are based on bilateral descent. They often resemble lineages in size and function but provide more recruiting flexibility. An individual can choose membership from among several ramages where he or she has relatives.

Another important kinship group is the family. This unit is more difficult to define than we may think, because people have found so many different ways to organize "familylike" groups. Here we will follow anthropologist George P. Murdock's approach and define the **family** as a kin group consisting of at least one married couple sharing the same residence with their children and performing sexual, reproductive, economic, and educational functions. A **nuclear family** consists of a single married couple and their children. An **extended family** consists of two or more married couples and their children. Extended families have a quality all their own and are often found in societies where family performance and honor are paramount to the reputation of individual family members. Extended families are most commonly based on patrilineal descent. Women marry into such families and must establish themselves among the line members and other women who live there.

Marriage, the socially approved union of two people, is a second major principle of kinship. The regulation of marriage takes elaborate forms from one society to the next. Marriage may be **exogamous,** meaning marriage outside any particular named group, or **endogamous,** indicating the opposite. Bhil tribals of India, for example, are clan and village exogamous (they should marry outside these groups), but tribal endogamous (they should marry other Bhils).

Marriage may also be **monogamous,** where it is preferred that only one woman should be married to one man at a time, or **polygamous,** meaning that one person may be married to more than one person simultaneously. There are two kinds of polygamy, **polygyny,** the marriage of one man with more than one woman simultaneously, and **polyandry,** the marriage of one woman with more than one man.

Many anthropologists view marriage as a system of alliances between families and descent lines. Viewed in these terms, rules such as endogamy and exogamy can be explained as devices to link or internally strengthen various kinship groups. The **incest taboo,** a legal rule that prohibits sexual intercourse or marriage between particular classes of kin, is often explained as a way to extend alliances between kin groups.

Finally, the regulation of marriage falls to the parents and close relatives of eligible young people in many societies. These elders concern themselves with more than wedding preparations; they must also see to it that young people marry appropriately, which means they consider the reputation of prospective spouses and their families' economic strength and social rank.

The selections in Part Five illustrate several aspects of kinship systems. In the first article, Nancy Scheper-Hughes looks at the relationship that poor Brazilian mothers have with their infants. Because babies die so often, mothers must delay forming attachments to them until their children show that they can survive. The second article, by David McCurdy, looks at the way kinship organizes life for the inhabitants of a Rajasthani Bhil village. Arranging a marriage requires use and consideration of clans, lineages, families, and weddings. Despite its origin in peasant society, the Indian kinship system is proving useful as people try to cope with a modernizing society. The third article, by Melvyn Goldstein, describes a rare form of marriage—polyandry—and shows why, despite other choices, Tibetan brothers often choose to share a single wife among them. Finally, Margery Wolf looks at the structure of the Taiwanese extended family from the point of view of the women who constitute it. It is only by establishing her own uterine family that a woman can gain power within the patrilineal group.

Key Terms

affinity
bilateral descent
clan
consanguinity
descent
descent groups
endogamy
exogamy
extended family
family
incest taboo
kinship

lineage
marriage
matrilineal descent
monogamy
nuclear family
patrilineal descent
phratry
polyandry
polygamy
polygyny
ramage

CHAPTER THIRTEEN

Family and Kinship in Village India

David W. McCurdy

Anyone who reads older ethnographic accounts of different cultures will inevitably run across terms such as clan, lineage, avunculocal, levirate, extended family, polyandry, cross-cousin, and Crow terminology. All these terms and many more were created by anthropologists to describe categories, groups, social arrangements, and roles associated with the complex kinship systems that characterized so many of the groups they studied. The importance of kinship for one of these societies, that found in an Indian village, is the topic of this article by David McCurdy. He argues that kinship forms the core social groups and associations in rural India in a system well adapted to family-centered land-holding and small-scale farming. He concludes by pointing out that Indians have used their close family ties to adapt to life in the emerging cash-labor-oriented modernizing world.

On a hot afternoon in May, 1962, I sat talking with three Bhil men in the village of Ratakote, located in southern Rajasthan, India.[1] We spoke about the results of recent national elections, their worry over a cattle disease that was afflicting the village herds, and predictions about when

---

1   Ratakote is a Bhil tribal village located 21 miles southwest of Udaipur, Rajasthan, in the Aravalli hills. I did ethnographic research in the village from 1961 to 1963, and again in 1985, 1991, and 1994 for shorter periods of time.

the monsoon rains would start. But our longest discussion concerned kin—the terms used to refer to them, the responsibilities they had toward one another, and the importance of marrying them off properly. It was toward the end of this conversation that one of the men, Kanji, said, "Now sāb (Bhili for sāhib), you are finally asking about a good thing. This is what we want you to tell people about us when you go back to America."

As I thought about it later, I was struck by how different this social outlook was from mine. I doubt that I or any of my friends in the United States would say something like this. Americans do have kin. We have parents, although our parents may not always live together, and we often know other relatives, some of whom are likely to play important parts in our lives. We grow up in families and we often create new ones if we have children. But we also live in a social network of other people whom we meet at work or encounter in various "outside" social settings, and these people can be of equal or even greater importance to us than kin. Our social worlds include such non-kin structures as companies and other work organizations, schools, neighborhoods, churches and other religious groups, and voluntary associations, including recreational groups and social clubs. We are not likely to worry much about our obligations to relatives with the notable exceptions of our children and grandchildren (middle-class American parents are notoriously child-centered), and more grudgingly, our aging parents. We are not supposed to "live off" relatives or lean too heavily on them.

Not so in Ratakote. Ratakote's society, like many agrarian villages around the world, is kinship-centered. Villagers anchor themselves in their families. They spend great energy on creating and maintaining their kinship system. This actually is not so surprising. Elaborate kinship systems work well in agrarian societies where families tend to be corporate units and where peoples' social horizons are often limited to the distance they can walk in a day. For the same reasons, families in the United States were also stronger in the past when more of them owned farms and neighborhood businesses.

What may come as a surprise, however, is how resilient and strong Indian kinship systems such as Ratakote's have been in the face of recent economic changes, especially the growth of wage labor. Let us look more closely at the Bhil kinship system, especially at arranged marriage, to illustrate these ideas.

Arranging a Marriage

If there is anything that my American students have trouble understanding about India, it is arranged marriage. They can not imagine sitting passively by while their parents advertise their charms and evaluate emerging nuptial candidates. The thought of living—to say nothing of having sex with—a total stranger seems out of the question to them. In our country, personal independence takes precedence over loyalty to family.

Not so in India. There, arranged marriage is the norm, and most young people, as well as their elders, accept and support the custom. (They often find it sexually exciting, too.) There are many reasons why this is so, but one stands out for discussion here. Marriage constructs alliances between families, lineages, and clans. The resulting kinship network is a pivotal structure in Indian society. It confers social strength and security. People's personal reputations depend on the quality and number of their allied kin. There is little question in their minds about who should arrange marriages. The decision is too important to leave up to inexperienced and impressionable young people.

As an aside I should note that young Indians play a greater part in the process than they used to. Middle-class boys often visit the families of prospective brides, where they manage to briefly "interview" them. They also tap into their kinship network to find out personal information about prospects. Young women also seek out information about prospective grooms. Bhils are no exception. They often conspire to meet those to whom they have been betrothed, usually at a fair or other public event where their contact is likely to go unnoticed. If they don't like each other, they will begin to pressure their parents to back out of the arrangement.

The importance of arranging a marriage was brought home to me several times during fieldwork in Ratakote, but one instance stands out most clearly. When I arrived in the swvillage for a short stay in 1985, Kanji had just concluded marriage arrangements for his daughter, Rupani.[2] What he told me about the process underscored the important role kinship plays in the life of the village.

Kanji started by saying that he and his wife first discussed Rupani's marriage the previous year when the girl first menstruated. She seemed too young for such a union then so they had waited nine months before committing to the marriage process. Even then, Rupani was still only 15 years old. Kanji explained that everyone preferred early marriage for their children because young people were likely to become sexually active as they grew older and might fall in love and elope, preempting the arrangement process altogether. Now they figured that

---

2   Kanji and Rupani are not real people. Their experiences are a composite of several life histories.

the time had come, and they began a series of steps to find a suitable spouse that would eventually involve most of their kin.

The first step was to consult the members of Kanji's *lineage*. Lineage is an anthropological term, not one used by Bhils. But Bhils share membership in local groups of relatives that meet the anthropological definition. Lineages (in this case patrilineages) include closely related men who are all descended from a known ancestor. Kanji's lineage consists of his two married brothers, three married sons of his deceased father's brother (his father is also dead), and his own married son when the latter is home. All are the descendants of his grandfather who had migrated to Ratakote many years earlier. He had talked with all of them informally about the possibility of his daughter's marriage before this. Now he called them together for formal approval.

The approval of lineage mates is necessary because they are essential to the marriage process. Each one of them will help spread the word to other villages that Rupani is available for marriage. They will loan money to Kanji for wedding expenses, and when it comes time for the wedding ceremony, they will provide much of the labor needed to prepare food and arrange required activities. Each family belonging to the lineage will host a special meal for the bride (the groom is similarly entertained in his village) during the wedding period, and one or two will help her make offerings to their lineal ancestors. The groom will also experience this ritual.

The lineage also has functions not directly related to marriage. It has the right to redistribute the land of deceased childless, male members, and it provides its members with political support. It sees to memorial feasts for deceased members. Its members may cooperatively plow and sow fields together and combine their animals for herding.

With lineage approval in hand, Kanji announced Rupani's eligibility in other villages. (Bhils are village exogamous, meaning they prefer to marry spouses from other communities.) Kanji and his lineage mates went about this by paying visits to feminal relatives in other villages. These are kin of the women, now living in Ratakote, who have married into his family. They also include the daughters of his family line who have married and gone to live in other villages, along with their husbands and husbands' kin.

Once the word has been spread, news of prospective candidates begins to filter in. It may arrive with feminal kin from other villages when they visit Ratakote. Or it may come from neighbors who are acting as go-betweens in Ratakote for kin who live in other villages and who seek partners for their children. Either way, a process of evaluation starts. Does the family of the suggested boy or girl have a good reputation? Are they hospitable to their in-laws? Do they meet their obligations to others? What is the reputation of the boy or girl they are offering in marriage? Is he or she tall or short, light or dark, robust or frail, cheerful or complaining, hardworking or lazy? What about their level of education? Does the family have sufficient land and animals? Have they treated other sons- and daughters-in-law well?

The most fundamental question to ask, however, is whether the prospective spouse is from the right clan. In anthropology, the term *clan* refers to an aggregate of people who all believe they are descended from a common ancestor. In Ratakote this group is called an *arak*. Araks are named and the names are used as surnames when Bhils identify themselves. Kanji comes from the pargi arak and is thus known as Kanji Pargi. There is Lalu Bodar, Naraji Katara, Dita Hira-vat, Nathu Airi—all men named for one of the 36 araks found in Ratakote. Women also belong to their father's clan, but unlike many American women who adopt their husband's surname at marriage, they keep their arak name all their lives.

Araks are based on a rule of patrilineal descent. This means that their members trace ancestry through males only. (Matrilineal descent traces the line through females only, and bilateral descent, which is found in U.S. society, includes both sexes.) Patrilineal descent not only defines arak membership, it governs inheritance. (Sons inherit equally from their fathers in Ratakote; daughters do not inherit despite a national law giving them that right.) It says that the children of divorced parents stay with the father's family. It bolsters the authority of men over their wives and children. It supports the rule of patrilocality. It even defines the village view of conception. Men plant the "seeds" that grow into children; women provide the fields in which the seeds germinate and grow.

The arak symbolizes patrilineal descent. It is not an organized group, although the members of an arak worship the same mother goddess no matter where they live. Instead it is an identity, an indicator that tells people who their lineal blood relatives are. There are pargis in hundreds of other Bhil villages. Most are strangers to Kanji but if he meets pargis elsewhere, he knows they share a common blood heritage with him.

It is this sense of common heritage that affects marriage. Bhils, like most Indians, believe that clan (arak) mates are close relatives even though they may be strangers. Marriage with them is forbidden. To make sure incest is impossible, it is also forbidden to marry anyone from your mother's arak or your father's mother's arak, to say nothing of anyone else you know you are related to.

This point was driven home to me on another occasion when a neighbor of Kanji's, Kamalaji Kharadi, who was sitting smoking with several other men, asked me which arak I belonged to. Instead of letting it go at "McCurdy," I said that I didn't have an arak. I explained that Americans didn't have a kinship group similar to this, and that was why I had to ask questions about kinship.

My listeners didn't believe me. After all, I must have a father and you get your arak automatically from him. It is a matter of birth and all people are born. They looked at each other as if to say, "We wonder why he won't tell us what his arak is?", then tried again to get me to answer. My second denial led them to ask, "OK, then what is your wife's arak?" (If you can't get at it one way, then try another.) I answered that she didn't have an arak either. This caused a mild sensation. "Then how do you know if you have not married your own relative?", they asked, secretly, I think, delighted by the scandalous prospect.

The third step that occurred during the arrangement of Rupani's marriage came after the family had settled on a prospective groom. This step is the betrothal, and it took place when the groom's father and some of his lineage mates and neighbors paid a formal visit to Kanji's house. When they arrive, Kanji must offer his guests a formal meal, usually slaughtering a goat and distilling some liquor for the occasion. The bride, her face covered by her sari, will be brought out for a brief viewing, as well. But most of the time will be spent making arrangements—when will the actual wedding take place?; who will check the couple's horoscopes for fit?; how much will the bride price (also called bride wealth by many anthropologists) be?

Bride price (dapa) deserves special comment. It is usually a standard sum of money (about 700 rupees in 1985), although it may also include silver ornaments or other valuables. The dapa is given by the grooms father and his line to the parents of the bride. Bhils view this exchange as a compensation for the loss of the bride's services to her family. It also pays for a shift in her loyalty.

The exchange points up an important strain on families in patrilineal societies, the transfer of a woman from her natal family and line to those of her husband. This transfer includes not only her person, but her loyalty, labor, and children. Although she always will belong to her father's arak, she is now part of her husband's family, not his.

This problem is especially troublesome in India because of the close ties formed there by a girl and her parents. Parents know their daughter will leave when she marries, and they know that in her husband's house and village, she will be at a disadvantage. She will be alone, and out of respect for his parents her husband may not favor her wishes, at least in public. Because of this, they tend to give her extra freedom and support. In addition, they recognize the strain she will be under when she first goes to live with her new husband and his family. To ease her transition, they permit her to visit her parents frequently for a year or two. They also may try to marry her into a village where other women from Ratakote have married, so that she has some kin or at least supporters.

After her marriage, a woman's parents and especially her brothers find it hard not to care about her welfare. Their potential interest presents a built-in structural conflict that could strain relations between the two families if nothing were done about it.

A solution to this problem is to make the marriage into an exchange, and bride price is one result. Bride price also helps to dramatize the change in loyalty and obligation accompanying the bride's entrance into her new family.

Bhils have also devised a number of wedding rituals to dramatize the bride's shift in family membership. The bride must cry to symbolize that she is leaving her home. The groom ritually storms the bride's house at the beginning of the final ceremony. He does so like a conquering hero, drawing his sword to strike a ceremonial arch placed over the entrance while simultaneously stepping on a small fire (he wears a slipper to protect his foot), ritually violating the household's sacred hearth. At the end of the wedding, the groom, with some friends, engages in a mock battle with the bride's brothers and other young men, and symbolically abducts her. The meaning of this ritual is a dramatic equivalent of a father "giving away the bride" at American weddings.

One additional way of managing possible tension between in-laws is the application of respect behavior. The parents of the bride must always treat those of the groom and their relatives with respect. They must not joke in their presence, and they must use respectful language and defer to the groom's parents in normal conversation. In keeping with the strong patrilineal system, a groom may not accept important gifts from his wife's family except on ritual occasions, such as weddings, when exchange is expected. A groom may help support his own father, but he should not do so with his in-laws. That is up to their sons.

Bride price exchange also sets in motion a life-long process of mutual hospitality between the two families. Once the marriage has taken place, the families will become part of each other's feminal kin. They will exchange gifts on some ritual occasions, open their houses to each other, and, of course, help one another make future marriages.

The Future of Indian Kinship

On our last trip to India in 1994, my wife and I learned that Rupani had delivered three children since her wedding. Kanji had visited them a few months before we arrived, and he said that Rupani was happy and that he had wonderful grandchildren. But he also mentioned that her husband now spent most of his time in the nearby city of Udaipur working in construction there. He sent money home, but his absence left Rupani to run the house and raise the children by herself, although she did so with the assistance of his parents and lineage mates.

Rupani's case is not unusual. Every morning 70 or 80 men board one of the 20 or so busses that travel the road, now paved, that runs through Ratakote to the city. There they wait to be recruited by contractors for day labor at a low wage. If they are successful, gain special skills, or make good connections, they may get more permanent, better-paying jobs and live for weeks at a time in the city.

The reason they have to take this kind of work is simple. Ratakote has more than doubled in population since 1962. (The village had a population of 1,184 in 1963. By 1994 an estimate put the number at about 2,600.) There is not enough land for everyone to farm nor can the land produce enough to feed the growing population, even in abundant years. Work in the city is the answer, especially for householders whose land is not irrigated like Kanji's.

Cash labor has a potential to break down the kinship system that Bhils value so highly. It frees men and women from economic dependence on the family (since they make their own money working for someone else). It takes up time, too, making it difficult for them to attend the leisurely eleven-day weddings of relatives or meet other obligations to kin that require their presence. With cash labor, one's reputation is likely to hinge less on family than on work. For some, work means moving the family altogether. Devaji Katara, one of Kanji's neighbors, has a son who has moved with his wife and children to the Central Indian city of Indore. He has a good factory job there, and the move has kept them together. By doing so, however, he and they are largely removed from the kinship loop.

Despite these structural changes, kinship in Ratakote and for India as a whole remains exceptionally strong. Even though they may live farther away, Bhil sons and daughters still visit their families regularly. They send money home, and they try to attend weddings. They talk about their kin, too, and surprisingly, they continue the long process of arranging marriage for their children.

Perhaps one reason for kinship's vitality is the use to which kinship is put by many Indians. The people of Ratakote and other

Indians have never given up teaching their children to respect their elders and subordinate their interests to those of the family. Family loyalty is still a paramount value. They use this loyalty to help each other economically. Family members hire each other in business. They take one another in during hard times. They offer hospitality to each other. Unlike Americans who feel guilty about accepting one-sided help from relatives, Indians look to the future. Giving aid now may pay off with a job or a favor later. Even if it doesn't, it is the proper thing to do.

Instead of breaking up the kinship network, work that takes men and families away from the village has simply stretched it out. An Indian student I know has found relatives in every American city he has visited. He knows of kin in Europe and southeast Asia too. Anywhere he goes he is likely to have relatives to stay with and to help him. When he settles down he will be expected to return the favor. Another Indian acquaintance, who went to graduate school in the United States and who continues to work here, has sent his father thousands of dollars to help with the building of a house. This act, which would surprise many Americans, seems perfectly normal to him.

Kanji is not disturbed by the economic changes that are overtaking the quiet agricultural pace of Ratakote. I last left him standing in front of his house with a grandson in his arms. His son, who had left the village in 1982 to be a "wiper" on a truck, returned to run the farm. He will be able to meet the family's obligation to lineage and feminal kin. For Kanji, traditional rules of inheritance have pulled a son and, for the moment at least, a grandson, back into the bosom of the family where they belong.

Review Questions

1. What are the main ways that kinship organizes Bhil society in Ratakote, according to McCurdy?

2. What is meant by the terms *clan, lineage, family, patrilineal descent, patrilocal residence, alliance, and feminal kin group?* Give examples of each.

3. Why do Bhil parents feel that marriage is too important a matter to be left up to their children?

4. What attributes do Bhil parents look for in a prospective bride or groom? How do young people try to influence the marriage partner their parents choose for them?

5.   Although the U.S. kinship system seems limited by comparison
     to India's, many argue that it is more important than most of us
     think. Can you think of ways this might be true?

CHAPTER FOURTEEN

Uterine Families and the Women's Community

Margery Wolf

The size and organization of extended families vary from one society to the next, but extended families often share some important attributes. They are most often based on a rule of patrilineal descent. For men, the patrilineal family extends in an unbroken line of ancestors and descendants. Membership is permanent; loyalty assured. For women, the patrilineal family is temporary. Born into one family and married into another, women discover that their happiness and interests depend on bearing children to create their own uterine family. This and the importance of a local women's group are the subjects of this article by Margery Wolf in her discussion of Taiwanese family life.

Few women in China experience the continuity that is typical of the lives of the menfolk. A woman can and, if she is ever to have any economic security, must provide the links in the male chain of descent, but she will never appear in anyone's genealogy as that all-important name connecting the past to the future. If she dies before she is married, her tablet will not appear on her father's altar; although she was a temporary member of his household, she was not a member of his family. A man is born into his family and remains a member of it throughout his life and even after his death. He is identified with the family from birth, and every action concerning him, up to and including his death, is in the context of that group. Whatever other uncertainties may trouble his life, his place in the line of ancestors provides a permanent setting. There is no such secure setting for a woman. She will abruptly leave the household into which she is born, either as an infant or as an adult bride, and enter another whose members treat her with suspicion or even hostility.

A man defines his family as a large group that includes the dead, and not-yet-born, and the living members of his household. But how does a woman define her family? This is not a question that China specialists often consider, but from their treatment of the family in general, it would seem that a woman's family is identical with that of the senior male in the household in which she lives. Although I have never asked, I imagine a Taiwanese man would define a woman's family in very much those same terms. Women, I think, would give quite a different answer. They do not have an unchanging place, assigned at birth, in any group, and their view of the family reflects this.

When she is a child, a woman's family is defined for her by her mother and to some extent by her grandmother. No matter how fond of his daughter the father may be, she is only a temporary member of his household and useless to his family—he cannot even marry her to one of his sons as he could an adopted daughter. Her irrelevance to her father's family in turn affects the daughter's attitude toward it. It is of no particular interest to her, and the need to maintain its continuity has little meaning for her beyond the fact that this continuity matters a great deal to some of the people she loves. As a child she probably accepts to some degree her grandmother's orientation toward the family: the household, that is, those people who live together and eat together, including perhaps one or more of her father's married brothers and their children. But the group that has the most meaning for her and with which she will have the most lasting ties is the smaller, more cohesive unit centering on her mother, that is, the uterine family—her mother and her mother's children. Father is important to the group, just as grandmother is important to some of the children, but he is not quite a member of it, and for some uterine families he may even be "the enemy." As the girl grows up and her grandmother dies and a brother or two marries, she discovers that her mother's definition of the family is becoming less exclusive and may even include such outsiders as her brother's new wife. Without knowing precisely when it happened, she finds that her brother's interests and goals have shifted in a direction she cannot follow. Her mother does not push her aside, but when the mother speaks of the future, she speaks in terms of her son's future. Although the mother sees her uterine family as adding new members and another generation, her daughter sees it as dissolving, leaving her with strong particular relationships, but with no group to which she has permanent loyalties and obligations.

When a young woman marries, her formal ties with the household of her father are severed. In one of the rituals of the wedding ceremony the bride's father or brothers symbolically inform her by means of spilt water that she, like the water, may never return, and when her wedding sedan chair passes over the threshold of her fathers house, the doors are slammed shut behind her. If she is ill-treated by her husband's family, her father's family may intervene, but unless her parents are willing to bring her home and support her for the rest of her life (and most parents are not), there is little they can do beyond shaming the other family. This is usually enough.

As long as her mother is alive, the daughter will continue her contacts with her father's household by as many visits as her new situation allows. If she lives nearby she may visit every few days, and no matter where she lives she must at least be allowed to return at New Year. After her mother dies her visits may become perfunctory, but her relations with at least one member of her uterine family, the group that centered on her mother, remain strong. Her brother plays an important ritual role throughout her life. She may gradually lose contact with her sisters as she and they become more involved with their own children, but her relations with her brother continue. When her sons marry, he is the guest of honor at the wedding feasts, and when her daughters marry he must give a small banquet in their honor. If her sons wish to divide their father's estate, it is their mother's brother who is called on to supervise. And when she dies, the coffin cannot be closed until her brother determines to his own satisfaction that she died a natural death and that her husband's family did everything possible to prevent it.

With the ritual slam of her father's door on her wedding day, a young woman finds herself quite literally without a family. She enters the household of her husband—a man who in an earlier time, say fifty years ago, she would never have met and who even today, in modern rural Taiwan, she is unlikely to know very well. She is an outsider, and for Chinese an outsider is always an object of deep suspicion. Her husband and her father-in-law do not see her as a member of their family. But they do see her as essential to it; they have gone to great expense to bring her into their household for the purpose of bearing a new generation for their family. Her mother-in-law, who was mainly responsible for negotiating the terms of her entry, may harbor some resentment over the hard bargaining, but she is nonetheless eager to see another generation added to *her* uterine family. A mother-in-law often has the same kind of ambivalence toward her daughter-in-law as she has toward her husband—the younger woman seems a member of her family at times and merely a member of the household at others. The new bride may find that her husband's sister is hostile or at best condescending, both attitudes reflecting the daughter's distress at an outsider who seems to be making her way right into the heart of the family.

Chinese children are taught by proverb, by example, and by experience that the family is the source of their security, and relatives the only people who can be depended on. Ostracism from the family is one of the harshest sanctions that can be imposed on erring youth. One of the reasons mainlanders as individuals are considered so untrustworthy on Taiwan is the fact that they are not subject to the controls of (and therefore have no fear of ostracism from) their families. If a timid new bride is considered an object of suspicion and potentially dangerous because she is a stranger, think how uneasy her own first few months must be surrounded by strangers. Her irrelevance to her father's family may result in her having little reverence for descent lines, but she has warm memories of the security of the family her mother created. If she is ever to return to this certainty and sense of belonging, a woman must create her own uterine family by bearing children, a goal that happily corresponds to the goals of the family into which she has married. She may gradually create a tolerable niche for herself in the household of her mother-in-law, but her family will not be formed until she herself forms it of her own children and grandchildren. In most cases, by the time she adds grandchildren, the uterine family and the household will almost completely overlap, and there will be another daughter-in-law struggling with loneliness and beginning a new uterine family.

The ambiguity of a man's position in relation to the uterine families accounts for much of the hostility between mother-in-law and daughter-in-law. There is no question in the mind of the older woman but that her son is her family. The daughter-in-law might be content with this situation once her sons are old enough to represent her interests in the household and in areas strictly under men's control, but until then, she is dependent on her husband. If she were to be completely absorbed into her mother-in-law's family—a rare occurrence unless she is a *simpua*—there would be little or no conflict; but under most circumstances she must rely on her husband, her mother-in-law's son, as her spokesman, and here is where the trouble begins. Since it is usually events within the household that she wishes to affect, and the household more or less overlaps with her mother-in-law's uterine family, even a minor foray by the younger woman suggests to the older one an all-out attack on everything she has worked so hard to build in the years of her own loneliness and insecurity. The birth of grandchildren further complicates their relations, for the one sees them as new members for her family and the other as desperately needed recruits to her own small circle of security.

In summary, my thesis contends . . . that because we have heretofore focused on men when examining the Chinese family—a reasonable approach to a patrilineal system—we have missed not only some of the system's subtleties but also its near-fatal weaknesses. With a male focus we see the Chinese family as a line of descent, bulging to encompass all the members of a man's household and spreading out through his descendants. With a female focus, however, we see the Chinese family not as a continuous line stretching between the vague horizons of past and future, but as a contemporary group that comes into existence out of one woman's need and is held together insofar as she has the strength to do so, or, for that matter, the need to do so. After her death the uterine family survives only in the mind of her son and is symbolized by the special attention he gives her earthly remains and her ancestral tablet. The rites themselves are demanded by the ideology of the patriliny, but the meaning they hold for most sons is formed in the uterine family. The uterine family has no ideology, no formal structure, and no public existence. It is built out of sentiments and loyalties that die with its members, but it is no less real for all that. The descent lines of men are born and nourished in the uterine families of women, and it is here that a male ideology that excludes women makes its accommodations with reality.

Women in rural Taiwan do not live their lives in the walled courtyards of their husband's households. If they did, they might be as powerless as their stereotype. It is in their relations in the outside world (and for women in rural Taiwan that world consists almost entirely of the village) that women develop sufficient backing to maintain some independence under their powerful mothers-in-law and even occasionally to bring the men's world to terms. A successful venture into the men's world is no small feat when one recalls that the men of a village were born there and are often related to one another, whereas the women are unlikely to have either the ties of childhood or the ties of kinship to unite them. All the same, the needs, shared interests, and common problems of women are reflected in every village in a loosely knit society that can when needed be called on to exercise considerable influence.

Women carry on as many of their activities as possible outside the house. They wash clothes on the riverbank, clean and pare vegetables at a communal pump, mend under a tree that is a known meeting place, and stop to rest on a bench or group of stones with other women. There is a continual moving back and forth between kitchens, and conversations are carried on from open doorways through the long, hot afternoons of summer. The shy young girl who enters the village as a bride is examined as frankly and suspiciously by the women as an animal that is up for sale. If she is deferential to her elders, does not criticize or compare her new world unfavorably with the one she has left, the older residents will gradually accept her presence on the edge of their conversations and stop changing the topic to general subjects when she brings the family laundry to scrub on the rocks near them. As the young bride meets other girls in her position, she makes allies for the future, but she must also develop relationships with the older women. She learns to use considerable discretion in making and receiving confidences, for a girl who gossips freely about the affairs of her husband's household may find herself labeled a troublemaker. On the other hand, a girl who is too reticent may find herself always on the outside of the group, or worse yet, accused of snobbery. I described in *The House of Lim* the plight of Lim Chui-ieng, who had little village backing in her troubles with her husband and his family as the result of her arrogance toward the women's community. In Peihotien the young wife of the storekeeper's son suffered a similar lack of support. Warned by her husband's parents not to be too "easy" with the other villagers lest they try to buy things on credit, she obeyed to the point of being considered unfriendly by the women of the village. When she began to have serious troubles with her husband and eventually his family, there was no one in the village she could turn to for solace, advice, and, most important, peacemaking.

Once a young bride has established herself as a member of the women's community, she has also established for herself a certain amount of protection. If the members of her husband's family step beyond the limits of propriety in their treatment of her—such as refusing to allow her to return to her natal home for her brother's wedding or beating her without serious justification—she can complain to a woman friend, preferably older, while they are washing vegetables at the communal pump. The story will quickly spread to the other women, and one of them will take it on herself to check the facts with another member of the girl's household. For a few days the matter will be thoroughly discussed whenever a few women gather. In a young wife's first few years in the community, she can expect to have her mother-in-law's side of any disagreement given fuller weight than her own—her mother-in-law has, after all, been a part of the community a lot longer.

However, the discussion itself will serve to curb many offenses. Even if the older woman knows that public opinion is falling to her side, she will still be somewhat more judicious about refusing her daughter-in-law's next request. Still, the daughter-in-law who hopes to make use of the village forum to depose her mother-in-law or at least gain herself special privilege will discover just how important the prerogatives of age and length of residence are. Although the women can serve as a powerful protective force for their defenseless younger members, they are also a very conservative force in the village.

Taiwanese women can and do make use of their collective power to lose face for their menfolk in order to influence decisions that are ostensibly not theirs to make. Although young women may have little or no influence over their husbands and would not dare express an unsolicited opinion (and perhaps not even a solicited one) to their fathers-in-law, older women who have raised their sons properly retain considerable influence over their sons' actions, even in activities exclusive to men. Further, older women who have displayed years of good judgment are regularly consulted by their husbands about major as well as minor economic and social projects. But even men who think themselves free to ignore the opinions of their women are never free of their own concept, face. It is much easier to lose face than to have face. We once asked a male friend in Peihotien just what "having face" amounted to. He replied, "When no one is talking about a family, you can say it has face." This is precisely where women wield their power. When a man behaves in a way that they consider wrong, they talk about him—not only among themselves, but to their sons and husbands. No one "tells him how to mind his own business," but it becomes abundantly clear that he is losing face and by continuing in this manner may bring shame to the family of his ancestors and descendants. Few men will risk that.

The rules that a Taiwanese man must learn and obey to be a successful member of his society are well developed, clear, and relatively easy to stay within. A Taiwanese woman must also learn the rules, but if she is to be a successful woman, she must learn not to stay within them, but to *appear* to stay within them; to manipulate them, but not to appear to be manipulating them; to teach them to her children, but not to depend on her children for her protection. A truly successful Taiwanese woman is a rugged individualist who has learned to depend largely on herself while appearing to lean on her father, her husband, and her son. The contrast between the terrified young bride and the loud, confident, often lewd old woman who has outlived her mother-in-law and her husband reflects the tests met and passed by not strictly following the rules and by making purposeful use of those who must. The Chinese male's conception of women as "narrow-hearted" and socially inept may well be his vague recognition of this facet of women's power and technique.

The women's subculture in rural Taiwan is, I believe, below the level of consciousness. Mothers do not tell their about-to-be-married daughters how to establish themselves in village society so that they may have some protection from an oppressive family situation, nor do they warn them to gather their children into an exclusive circle under their own control. But girls grow up in village society and see their mothers and sisters-in-law settling their differences to keep them from a public airing or presenting them for the women's community to judge. Their mothers have created around them the meaningful unit in their father's households, and when they are desperately lonely and unhappy in the households of their husbands, what they long for is what they have lost. . . . [Some] areas in the subculture of women . . . mesh perfectly into the main culture of the society. The two cultures are not symbiotic because they are not sufficiently independent of one another, but neither do they share identical goals or necessarily use the same means to reach the goals they do share. Outside the village the women's subculture seems not to exist. The uterine family also has no public existence, and appears almost as a response to the traditional family organized in terms of a male ideology.

Review Questions

1. According to Wolf, what is a uterine family, and what relatives are likely to be members?

2. Why is the uterine family important to Chinese women who live in their husband's patrilineal extended families?

3. What is the relationship between a woman's uterine family and her power within her husband's family?

4. Why might the existence of the uterine family contribute to the division of extended families into smaller constituent parts?

5. How do you think a Chinese woman's desire to have a uterine family affects attempts to limit the Chinese population?

7

KINSHIP: MARRIAGE

CHAPTER FIFTEEN

Mother's Love: Death without Weeping

Nancy Scheper-Hughes

Kinship systems are based on marriage and birth. Both, anthropologists assume, create ties that can link kin into close, cooperative, enduring structures. What happens to such ties, however, in the face of severe hardship imposed by grinding poverty and urban migration? Can we continue to assume, for example, that there will be a close bond between mother and child? This is the question pursued by Nancy Scheper-Hughes in the following article about the mother-infant relationship among poor women in a Brazilian shantytown. The author became interested in the question following a "baby die-off" in the town of Bom Jesus in 1965. She noticed that mothers seemed to take these events casually. After twenty-five years of research in the Alto do Cruzeiro shantytown there, she has come to see such indifference as a cultural response to high rates of infant death due to poverty and malnutrition. Mothers, and surrounding social institutions such as the Catholic church, expect babies to die easily. Mothers concentrate their support on babies who are "fighters" and let themselves grow attached to their children only when they are reasonably sure that the offspring will survive. The article also provides an excellent illustration of what happens to kinship systems in the face of poverty and social dislocation. Such conditions may easily result in the formation of woman-headed families and in a lack of the extended kinship networks so often found in more stable, rural societies.

In a current epilogue to this article, Scheper-Hughes notes that political changes in Brazil since the 1980s have led to improved health for mothers and babies. Mothers have fewer babies and no longer give up on offspring who in the past would have seemed destined to die. Unfortunately, the rise of drugs and gangs along with vigilante death squads have become a major threat to survival and social life in Bom Jesus.

> *I have seen death without weeping*
> *The destiny of the Northeast is death*
> *Cattle they kill*
> *To the people they do something worse*
> *—Anonymous Brazilian singer (1965)*

"Why do the church bells ring so often?" I asked Nailza de Arruda soon after I moved into a corner of her tiny mud-walled hut near the top of the shantytown called the Alto do Cruzeiro (Crucifix Hill). I was then a Peace Corps volunteer and a community development/health worker. It was the dry and blazing hot summer of 1965, the months following the military coup in Brazil, and save for the rusty, clanging bells of N.S. das Dores Church, an eerie quiet had settled over the market town that I call Bom Jesus da Mata. Beneath the quiet, however, there was chaos and panic. "It's nothing," replied Nailza, "just another little angel gone to heaven."

Nailza had sent more than her share of little angels to heaven, and sometimes at night I could hear her engaged in a muffled but passionate discourse with one of them, two-year-old Joana. Joana's photograph, taken as she lay propped up in her tiny cardboard coffin, her eyes open, hung on a wall next to one of Nailza and Ze Antonio taken on the day they eloped.

Nailza could barely remember the other infants and babies who came and went in close succession. Most had died unnamed and were hastily baptized in their coffins. Few lived more than a month or two. Only Joana, properly baptized in church at the close of her first year and placed under the protection of a powerful saint, Joan of Arc, had been expected to live. And Nailza had dangerously allowed herself to love the little girl.

In addressing the dead child, Nailza's voice would range from tearful imploring to angry recrimination: "Why did you leave me? Was your patron saint so greedy that she could not allow me one child on this earth?" Ze Antonio advised me to ignore Nailza's odd behavior, which he understood as a kind of madness that, like the birth and death of children, came and went. Indeed, the premature birth of a stillborn son some months later "cured" Nailza of her "inappropriate" grief, and the day came when she removed Joana's photo and carefully packed it away.

More than fifteen years elapsed before I returned to the Alto do Cruzeiro, and it was anthropology that provided the vehicle of my return. Since 1982 I have returned several times in order to pursue a problem that first attracted my attention in the 1960s. My involvement with the people of the Alto do Cruzeiro now spans a quarter of a century and three generations of parenting in a community where mothers and daughters are often simultaneously pregnant.

The Alto do Cruzeiro is one of three shantytowns surrounding the large market town of Bom Jesus in the sugar plantation zone of Pernambuco in Northeast Brazil, one of the many zones of neglect that have emerged in the shadow of the now tarnished economic miracle of Brazil. For the women and children of the Alto do Cruzeiro the only miracle is that some of them have managed to stay alive at all.

The Northeast is a region of vast proportions (approximately twice the size of Texas) and of equally vast social and developmental problems. The nine states that make up the region are the poorest in the country and are representative of the Third World within a dynamic and rapidly industrializing nation. Despite waves of migrations from the interior to the teeming shantytowns of coastal cities, the majority still live in rural areas on farms and ranches, sugar plantations and mills.

Life expectancy in the Northeast is only forty years, largely because of the appallingly high rate of infant and child mortality. Approximately one million children in Brazil under the age of five die each year. The children of the Northeast, especially those born in shantytowns on the periphery of urban life, are at a very high risk of death. In these areas, children are born without the traditional protection of breast-feeding, subsistence gardens, stable marriages, and multiple adult caretakers that exists in the interior. In the hillside shantytowns that spring up around cities or, in this case, interior market towns, marriages are brittle, single parenting is the norm, and women are frequently forced into the shadow economy of domestic work in the homes of the rich or into unprotected and oftentimes "scab" wage labor on the surrounding sugar plantations, where they clear land for planting and weed for a pittance, sometimes less than a dollar a day. The women of the Alto may not bring their babies with them into the homes of the wealthy, where the often-sick infants are considered sources of contamination, and they cannot carry the little ones to the riverbanks where they wash clothes because the river is heavily infested with schistosomes and other deadly parasites.

Nor can they carry their young children to the plantations, which are often several miles away. At wages of a dollar a day, the women of the Alto cannot hire baby sitters. Older children who are not in school will sometimes serve as somewhat indifferent caretakers. But any child not in school is also expected to find wage work. In most cases, babies are simply left at home alone, the door securely fastened. And so many also die alone and unattended.

Bom Jesus da Mata, centrally located in the plantation zone of Pernam-buco, is within commuting distance of several sugar plantations and mills. Consequently, Bom Jesus has been a magnet for rural workers forced off their small subsistence plots by large landowners wanting to use every available piece of land for sugar cultivation. Initially, the rural migrants to Bom Jesus were squatters who were given tacit approval by the mayor to put up temporary straw huts on each of the three hills overlooking the town. The Alto do Cruzeiro is the oldest, the largest, and the poorest of the shantytowns. Over the past three decades many of the original migrants have become permanent residents, and the primitive and temporary straw huts have been replaced by small homes (usually of two rooms) made of wattle and daub, sometimes covered with plaster. The more affluent residents use bricks and tiles. In most Alto homes, dangerous kerosene lamps have been replaced by light bulbs. The once tattered rural garb, often fashioned from used sugar sacking, has likewise been replaced by store-bought clothes, often castoffs from a wealthy *patrão* (boss). The trappings are modern, but the hunger, sickness, and death that they conceal are traditional, deeply rooted in a history of feudalism, exploitation, and institutionalized dependency.

My research agenda never wavered. The questions I addressed first crystallized during a veritable "die-off" of Alto babies during a severe drought in 1965. The food and water shortages and the political and economic chaos occasioned by the military coup were reflected in the handwritten entries of births and deaths in the dusty, yellowed pages of the ledger books kept at the public registry office in Bom Jesus. More than 350 babies died in the Alto during 1965 alone—this from a shantytown population of little more than 5,000. But that wasn't what surprised me. There were reasons enough for the deaths in the miserable conditions of shantytown life. What puzzled me was the seeming indifference of Alto women to the death of their infants, and their willingness to attribute to their own tiny offspring an aversion to life that made their death seem wholly natural, indeed all but anticipated.

Although I found that it was possible, and hardly difficult, to rescue infants and toddlers from death by diarrhea and dehydration with a simple sugar, salt, and water solution (even bottled Coca-Cola worked fine), it was more difficult to enlist a mother herself in the rescue of a child she perceived as ill-fated for life or better off dead, or to convince her to take back into her threatened and besieged home a baby she had already come to think of as an angel rather than as a son or daughter.

I learned that the high expectancy of death, and the ability to face child death with stoicism and equanimity, produced patterns of nurturing that differentiated between those infants thought of as thrivers and survivors and those thought of as born already "wanting to die." The survivors were nurtured, while stigmatized, doomed infants were left to die, as mothers say, *a mingua*, "of neglect." Mothers stepped back and allowed nature to take its course. This pattern, which I call mortal selective neglect, is called passive infanticide by anthropologist Marvin Harris. The Alto situation, although culturally specific in the form that it takes, is not unique to Third World shantytown communities and may have its correlates in our own impoverished urban communities in some cases of "failure to thrive" infants.

I use as an example the story of Zezinho, the thirteen-month-old toddler of one of my neighbors, Lourdes. I became involved with Zezinho when I was called in to help Lourdes in the delivery of another child, this one a fair and robust little tyke with a lusty cry. I noted that while Lourdes showed great interest in the newborn, she totally ignored Zezinho who, wasted and severely malnourished, was curled up in a fetal position on a piece of urine-and-feces-soaked cardboard placed under his mother's hammock. Eyes open and vacant, mouth slack, the little boy seemed doomed.

When I carried Zezinho up to the community day-care center at the top of the hill, the Alto women who took turns caring for one another's children (in order to free themselves for part-time work in the cane fields or washing clothes) laughed at my efforts to save Ze, agreeing with Lourdes that here was a baby without a ghost of a chance. Leave him alone, they cautioned. It makes no sense to fight with death. But I did do battle with Ze, and after several weeks of force-feeding (malnourished babies lose their interest in food), Ze began to succumb to my ministrations. He acquired some flesh across his taut chest bones, learned to sit up, and even tried to smile. When he seemed well enough, I returned him to Lourdes in her miserable scrap-material lean-to, but not without guilt about what I had done. I wondered whether returning Ze was at all fair to Lourdes and to his little brother. But I was busy and washed my hands of the matter. And Lourdes did seem more interested in Ze now that he was looking more human.

When I returned in 1982, there was Lourdes among the women who formed my sample of Alto mothers—still struggling to put together some semblance of life for a now grown Ze and her five other surviving children. Much was made of my reunion with Ze in 1982, and everyone enjoyed retelling the story of Ze's rescue and of how his mother had given him up for dead. Ze would laugh the loudest when told how I had had to force-feed him like a fiesta turkey. There was no hint of guilt on the part of Lourdes and no resentment on the part of Ze. In fact, when questioned in private as to who was the best friend he ever had in life, Ze took a long drag on his cigarette and answered without a trace of irony, "Why my mother, of course!" "But of course," I replied.

Part of learning how to mother in the Alto do Cruzeiro is learning when to let go of a child who shows that it "wants" to die or that it has no "knack" or no "taste" for life. Another part is learning when it is safe to let oneself love a child. Frequent child death remains a powerful shaper of maternal thinking and practice. In the absence of firm expectation that a child will survive, mother love as we conceptualize it (whether in popular terms or in the psychobiological notion of maternal bonding) is attenuated and delayed with consequences for infant survival. In an environment already precarious to young life, the emotional detachment of mothers toward some of their babies contributes even further to the spiral of high mortality-high fertility in a kind of macabre lock-step dance of death.

The average woman of the Alto experiences 9.5 pregnancies, 3.5 child deaths, and 1.5 stillbirths. Seventy percent of all child deaths in the Alto occur in the first six months of life, and 82 percent by the end of the first year. Of all deaths in the community each year, about 45 percent are of children under the age of five.

Women of the Alto distinguish between child deaths understood as natural (caused by diarrhea and communicable diseases) and those resulting from sorcery the evil eye, or other magical or supernatural afflictions. They also recognize a large category of infant deaths seen as fated and inevitable. These hopeless cases are classified by mothers under the folk terminology "child sickness" or "child attack." Women say that there are at least fourteen different types of hopeless child sickness, but most can be subsumed under two categories—chronic and acute. The chronic cases refer to infants who are born small and wasted. They are deathly pale, mothers say, as well as weak and passive. They demonstrate no vital force, no liveliness. They do not suck vigorously; they hardly cry. Such babies can be this way at birth or they can be born sound but soon show no resistance, no "fight" against the common crises of infancy: diarrhea, respiratory infections, tropical fevers.

The acute cases are those doomed infants who die suddenly and violently. They are taken by stealth overnight, often following convulsions that bring on head banging, shaking, grimacing, and shrieking. Women say it is horrible to look at such a baby. If the infant begins to foam at the mouth or gnash its teeth or go rigid with its eyes turned back inside its head, there is absolutely no hope. The infant is "put aside"—left alone—often on the floor in a back room, and allowed to die. These symptoms (which accompany high fevers, dehydration, third-stage malnutrition, and encephalitis) are equated by Alto women with madness, epilepsy, and worst of all, rabies, which is greatly feared and highly stigmatized.

Most of the infants presented to me as suffering from chronic child sickness were tiny, wasted famine victims, while those labeled as victims of acute child attack seemed to be infants suffering from the deliriums of high fever or the convulsions that can accompany electrolyte imbalance in dehydrated babies.

Local midwives and traditional healers, praying women, as they are called, advise Alto women on when to allow a baby to die. One midwife explained: "If I can see that a baby was born unfortuitously, I tell the mother that she need not wash the infant or give it a cleansing tea. I tell her just to dust the infant with baby powder and wait for it to die." Allowing nature to take its course is not seen as sinful by these often very devout Catholic women. Rather, it is understood as cooperating with God's plan.

Often I have been asked how consciously women of the Alto behave in this regard. I would have to say that consciousness is always shifting between allowed and disallowed levels of awareness. For example, I was awakened early one morning in 1987 by two neighborhood children who had been sent to fetch me to a hastily organized wake for a two-month-old infant whose mother I had unsuccessfully urged to breast-feed. The infant was being sustained on sugar water, which the mother referred to as *soro* (serum), using a medical term for the infant's starvation regime in light of his chronic diarrhea. I had cautioned the mother that an infant could not live on *soro* forever.

The two girls urged me to console the young mother by telling her that it was "too bad" that her infant was so weak that Jesus had to take him. They were coaching me in proper Alto etiquette. I agreed, of course, but asked, "And what do *you* think?" Xoxa, the eleven-year-old, looked down at her dusty flip-flops and blurted out, "Oh, Dona Nanci, that baby never got enough to eat, but you must never say that!" And so the death of hungry babies remains one of the best kept secrets of life in Bom Jesus da Mata.

Most victims are waked quickly and with a minimum of ceremony. No tears are shed, and the neighborhood children form a tiny procession, carrying the baby to the town graveyard where it will join a multitude of others. Although a few fresh flowers may be scattered over the tiny grave, no stone or wooden cross will mark the place, and the same spot will be reused within a few months' time. The mother will never visit the grave, which soon becomes an anonymous one.

What, then, can be said of these women? What emotions, what sentiments motivate them? How are they able to do what, in fact, must be done? What does mother love mean in this inhospitable context? Are grief, mourning, and melancholia present, although deeply repressed? If so, where shall we look for them? And if not, how are we to understand the moral visions and moral sensibilities that guide their actions?

I have been criticized more than once for presenting an unflattering portrait of poor Brazilian women, women who are, after all, themselves the victims of severe social and institutional neglect. I have described these women as allowing some of their children to die, as if this were an unnatural and inhuman act rather than, as I would assert, the way any one of us might act, reasonably and rationally, under similarly desperate conditions. Perhaps I have not emphasized enough the real pathogens in this environment of high risk: poverty, deprivation, sexism, chronic hunger, and economic exploitation. If mother love is, as many psychologists and some feminists believe, a seemingly natural and universal maternal script, what does it mean to women for whom scarcity, loss, sickness, and deprivation have made that love frantic and robbed them of their grief, seeming to turn their hearts to stone?

Throughout much of human history—as in a great deal of the impoverished Third World today—women have had to give birth and to nurture children under ecological conditions and social arrangements hostile to child survival, as well as to their own well-being. Under circumstances of high childhood mortality, patterns of selective neglect and passive infanticide may be seen as active survival strategies.

They also seem to be fairly common practices historically and across cultures. In societies characterized by high childhood mortality and by a correspondingly high (replacement) fertility, cultural practices of infant and child care tend to be organized primarily around survival goals. But what this means is a pragmatic recognition that not all of one's children can be expected to live. The nervousness about child survival in areas of northeast Brazil, northern India, or Bangladesh, where a 30 percent or 40 percent mortality rate in the first years of life is common, can lead to forms of delayed attachment and a casual or benign neglect that serves to weed out the worst bets so as to enhance the life chances of healthier siblings, including those yet to be born. Practices similar to those that I am describing have been recorded for parts of Africa, India, and Central America.

Life in the Alto do Cruzeiro resembles nothing so much as a battlefield or an emergency room in an overcrowded inner-city public hospital. Consequently, morality is guided by a kind of "lifeboat ethics," the morality of triage. The seemingly studied indifference toward the suffering of some of their infants, conveyed in such sayings as "little critters have no feelings," is understandable in light of these women's obligation to carry on with their reproductive and nurturing lives.

In their slowness to anthropomorphize and personalize their infants, everything is mobilized so as to prevent maternal overattachment and, therefore, grief at death. The bereaved mother is told not to cry, that her tears will dampen the wings of her little angel so that she cannot fly up to her heavenly home. Grief at the death of an angel is not only inappropriate, it is a symptom of madness and of a profound lack of faith.

Infant death becomes routine in an environment in which death is anticipated and bets are hedged. While the routinization of death in the context of shantytown life is not hard to understand, and quite possible to empathize with, its routinization in the formal institutions of public life in Bom Jesus is not as easy to accept uncritically. Here the social production of indifference takes on a different, even a malevolent, cast.

In a society where triplicates of every form are required for the most banal events (registering a car, for example), the registration of infant and child death is informal, incomplete, and rapid. It requires no documentation, takes less than five minutes, and demands no witnesses other than office clerks. No questions are asked concerning the circumstances of the death, and the cause of death is left blank, unquestioned and unexamined. A neighbor, grandmother, older sibling, or common-law husband may register the death. Since most infants die at home, there is no question of a medical record.

From the registry office, the parent proceeds to the town hall, where the mayor will give him or her a voucher for a free baby coffin. The full-time municipal coffinmaker cannot tell you exactly how many baby coffins are dispatched each week. It varies, he says, with the seasons. There are more needed during the drought months and during the big festivals of Carnaval and Christmas and São Joao's Day because people are too busy, he supposes, to take their babies to the clinic. Record keeping is sloppy.

Similarly, there is a failure on the part of city-employed doctors working at two free clinics to recognize the malnutrition of babies who are weighed, measured, and immunized without comment and as if they were not, in fact, anemic, stunted, fussy, and irritated starvation babies. At best the mothers are told to pick up free vitamins or a health "tonic" at the municipal chambers. At worst, clinic personnel will give tranquilizers and sleeping pills to quiet the hungry cries of "sick-to-death" Alto babies.

The church, too, contributes to the routinization of, and indifference toward, child death. Traditionally, the local Catholic church taught patience and resignation to domestic tragedies that were said to reveal the imponderable workings of God's will. If an infant died suddenly, it was because a particular saint had claimed the child. The infant would be an angel in the service of his or her heavenly patron. It would be wrong, a sign of a lack of faith, to weep for a child with such good fortune. The infant funeral was, in the past, an event celebrated with joy. Today however, under the new regime of "liberation theology," the bells of N.S. das Dores parish church no longer peal for the death of Alto babies, and no priest accompanies the procession of angels to the cemetery where their bodies are disposed of casually and without ceremony. Children bury children in Bom Jesus da Mata. In this most Catholic of communities, the coffin is handed to the disabled and irritable municipal gravedigger, who often chides the children for one reason or another. It may be that the coffin is larger than expected and the gravedigger can find no appropriate space. The children do not wait for the gravedigger to complete his task. No prayers are recited and no sign of the cross made as the tiny coffin goes into its shallow grave.

When I asked the local priest, Padre Marcos, about the lack of church ceremony surrounding infant and childhood death today in Bom Jesus, he replied: "In the old days, child death was richly celebrated. But those were the baroque customs of a conservative church that wallowed in death and misery. The new church is a church of hope and joy. We no longer celebrate the death of child angels. We try to tell mothers that Jesus doesn't want all the dead babies they send him." Similarly, the new church has changed its baptismal customs, now often refusing to baptize dying babies brought to the back door of a church or rectory. The mothers are scolded by the church attendants and told to go home and take care of their sick babies. Baptism, they are told, is for the living; it is not to be confused with the sacrament of extreme unction, which is the anointing of the dying. And so it appears to the women of the Alto that even the church has turned away from them, denying the traditional comfort of folk Catholicism.

The contemporary Catholic church is caught in the clutches of a double bind. The new theology of liberation imagines a kingdom of God on earth based on justice and equality, a world without hunger, sickness, or childhood mortality. At the same time, the church has not changed its official position on sexuality and reproduction, including its sanctions against birth control, abortion, and sterilization. The padre of Bom Jesus da Mata recognizes this contradiction intuitively, although he shies away from discussions on the topic, saying that he prefers to leave questions of family planning to the discretion and the "good consciences" of his impoverished parishioners. But this, of course, sidesteps the extent to which those good consciences have been shaped by traditional church teachings in Bom Jesus, especially by his recent predecessors. Hence, we can begin to see that the seeming indifference of Alto mothers toward the death of some of their infants is but a pale reflection of the official indifference of church and state to the plight of poor women and children.

Nonetheless, the women of Bom Jesus are survivors. One woman, Biu, told me her life history, returning again and again to the themes of child death, her first husband's suicide, abandonment by her father and later by her second husband, and all the other losses and disappointments she had suffered in her long forty-five years. She concluded with great force, reflecting on the days of Carnaval '88 that were fast approaching:

No, Dona Nanci, I won't cry, and I won't waste my life thinking about it from morning to night.. . . Can I argue with God for the state that I'm in? No! And so I'll dance and I'll jump and I'll play Carnaval! And yes, I'll laugh and people will wonder at a *pobre* like me who can have such a good time.

And no one did blame Biu for dancing in the streets during the four days of Carnaval—not even on Ash Wednesday, the day following Carnaval '88 when we all assembled hurriedly to assist in the burial of Mercea, Bius beloved *casula,* her last-born daughter who had died at home of pneumonia during the festivities. The rest of the family barely had time to change out of their costumes. Severino, the child's uncle and godfather, sprinkled holy water over the little angel while he prayed: "Mercea, I don't know whether you were called, taken, or thrown out of this world. But look down at us from your heavenly home with tenderness, with pity, and with mercy." So be it.

Brief Epilogue

Many students write after reading this article asking me whether the situation has changed in the Alto do Cruzeiro. Is life better or worse for mothers and newborn babies? One of the advantages of long-term ethnographic research is seeing history in the making. I began my engagements with the people of the Alto in 1964 at the start of twenty years of military rule, a ruthless regime that produced deep impoverishment among those living in urban *favelas* and in rural areas. The scarcities and insecurities of that era contributed to the death of infants and small babies. By the time I completed my study of mother love and child death in the early 1990s Brazil was well on its way to democratization which ushered in many important changes, most notably a free, public, national health care system (SUS) which guaranteed poor women adequate pre- and post-natal care.

The decade of the 1990s witnessed what population experts call the demographic or epidemiologic transition. As both births and infant deaths declined, mothers began to treat their infants as potentially capable of survival and the old stance of maternal "watchful waiting" accompanied by "letting go" of infants thought of as having no "taste" or "talent" for life, was replaced by a maternal ethos of "holding on" and "holding dear" each infant. Today, young women of the Alto can expect to give birth to three or fewer babies and to see all of them live to adolescence. Many factors produced this reproductive transition: the 'modernization' of Catholic beliefs about infant death; the under-the-counter availability of Cytotec, a risky "morning after" pill; the implementation under the national health care system (Serviço Único de Saúde) of local 'health agents' who went door to door in poor communities, identifying and rescuing vulnerable infants, toddlers and old people. The primary cause of the decline in infant mortality on the Alto do Cruzeiro, however, was the "simple" installation of water pipes reaching virtually all the homes in the shantytown with sufficient, clean water. Water = life! It is painful to consider how "culture," "belief," and even "maternal sentiments" follow basic changes in the material conditions— and therefore the possibilities—of everyday life.

Motherhood is not only a social and a cultural construction, but a constellation of embodied practices responding to the requirements and limitations of the political and economic conditions that determine the resilience or vulnerability of infants and their mothers. Today, new problems have beset the people of the Alto do Cruzeiro. Since the publication of "Death without Weeping" drugs and gangs have made their ugly mark on the community and death squads have sprung up to impose a kind of vigilante justice. These anti-social features of life in "Bom Jesus" take some of the pleasure away, as one sees the young men of the Alto who survived that dangerous first year of life, felled by bullets and knife wounds at the hands of gang leaders, *bandidos*, and local police in almost equal measure.

Review Questions

1. What did Scheper-Hughes notice about mothers' reactions during the baby die-off of 1965 in Bom Jesus, Brazil?

2. How do poor Brazilian mothers react to their infants' illnesses and death? How do other institutions, such as the church, clinic, and civil authorities respond? Give examples.

3. How does Scheper-Hughes explain the apparent indifference of mothers to the death of their infants?

4. What does the indifference of mothers to the deaths of their children say about basic human nature, especially the mother-child bond?

CHAPTER SIXTEEN

Polyandry: When Brothers Take a Wife

Melvyn C. Goldstein

Many of the world's societies permit polygamy, the marriage of an individual to more than one spouse. The most common form of polygamy is polygyny, an arrangement in which a man marries more than one wife. Polygyny may exist for many reasons, not the least of which is its relationship to the substantial economic contributions of women. But there is a second kind of polygamy called polyandry, organized around the marriage of a woman to more than one husband, and its causes may seem less clear. In this article, Melvyn Goldstein describes the fraternal polyandry practiced by Tibetans living in Northern Nepal and seeks to explain why, despite having a choice of marriage forms including monogamy and polygyny, men and women often choose this rare form of marriage. He argues that, by marrying a single wife, a group of brothers can more easily preserve their family resources, whereas monogamous or polygynous marriage usually costs a man his inheritance and requires him to make a fresh start.

Eager to reach home. Dorje drives his yaks hard over the seventeen-thousand-foot mountain pass, stopping only once to rest. He and his two older brothers, Pema and Sonam, are jointly marrying a woman from the next village in a few weeks, and he has to help with the preparations.

Dorje, Pema, and Sonam are Tibetans living in Limi, a two-hundred-square-mile area in the northwest corner of Nepal, across the border from Tibet. The form of marriage they are about to enter—fraternal polyandry in anthropological parlance—is one of the world's rarest forms of marriage but is not uncommon in Tibetan society, where it has been practiced from time immemorial. For many Tibetan social strata, it traditionally represented the ideal form of marriage and family.

The mechanics of fraternal polyandry are simple. Two, three, four, or more brothers jointly take a wife, who leaves her home to come and live with them. Traditionally, marriage was arranged by parents, with children, particularly females, having little or no say. This is changing somewhat nowadays, but it is still unusual for children to marry without their parents' consent. Marriage ceremonies vary by income and region and range from all the brothers sitting together as grooms to only the eldest one formally doing so. The age of the brothers plays an important role in determining this: very young brothers almost never participate in actual marriage ceremonies, although they typically join the marriage when they reach their midteens.

The eldest brother is normally dominant in terms of authority, that is, in managing the household, but all the brothers share the work and participate as sexual partners. Tibetan males and females do not find the sexual aspect of sharing a spouse the least bit unusual, repulsive, or scandalous, and the norm is for the wife to treat all the brothers the same.

Offspring are treated similarly. There is no attempt to link children biologically to particular brothers, and a brother shows no favoritism toward his child even if he knows he is the real father because, for example, his other brothers were away at the time the wife became pregnant. The children, in turn, consider all of the brothers as their fathers and treat them equally, even if they also know who is their real father. In some regions children use the term "father" for the eldest brother and "father's brother" for the others, while in other areas they call all the brothers by one term, modifying this by the use of "elder" and "younger."

Unlike our own society, where monogamy is the only form of marriage permitted, Tibetan society allows a variety of marriage types, including monogamy, fraternal polyandry, and polygyny. Fraternal polyandry and monogamy are the most common forms of marriage, while polygyny typically occurs in cases where the first wife is barren. The widespread practice of fraternal polyandry, therefore, is not the outcome of a law requiring brothers to marry jointly. There is choice, and in fact, divorce traditionally was relatively simple in Tibetan society. If a brother in a polyandrous marriage became dissatisfied and wanted to separate, he simply left the main house and set up his own household. In such cases, all the children stayed in the main household with the remaining brother(s), even if the departing brother was known to be the real father of one or more of the children.

The Tibetans' own explanation for choosing fraternal polyandry is materialistic. For example, when I asked Dorje why he decided to marry with his two brothers rather than take his own wife, he thought for a moment, then said it prevented the division of his family's farm (and animals) and thus facilitated all of them achieving a higher standard of living. And when I later asked Dorje's bride whether it wasn't difficult for her to cope with three brothers as husbands, she laughed and echoed the rationale of avoiding fragmentation of the family and land, adding that she expected to be better off economically, since she would have three husbands working for her and her children.

Exotic as it may seem to Westerners, Tibetan fraternal polyandry is thus in many ways analogous to the way primogeniture functioned in nineteenth-century England. Primogeniture dictated that the eldest son inherited the family estate, while younger sons had to leave home and seek their own employment—for example, in the military or the clergy. Primogeniture maintained family estates intact over generations by permitting only one heir per generation. Fraternal polyandry also accomplishes this but does so by keeping all the brothers together with just one wife so that there is only one *set* of heirs per generation.

While Tibetans believe that in this way fraternal polyandry reduces the risk of family fission, monogamous marriages among brothers need not necessarily precipitate the division of the family estate: brothers could continue to live together, and the family land could continue to be worked jointly. When I asked Tibetans about this, however, they invariably responded that such joint families are unstable because each wife is primarily oriented to her own children and interested in their success and well-being over that of the children of the other wives. For example, if the youngest brother's wife had three sons while the eldest brother's wife had only one daughter, the wife of the youngest brother might begin to demand more resources for her children since, as males, they represent the future of the family. Thus the children from different wives in the same generation are competing sets of heirs, and this makes such families inherently unstable. Tibetans perceive that conflict will spread from the wives to their husbands and consider this likely to cause family fission. Consequently, it is almost never done.

Although Tibetans see an economic advantage to fraternal polyandry, they do not value the sharing of a wife as an end in itself. On the contrary, they articulate a number of problems inherent in the practice. For example, because authority is customarily exercised by the eldest brother, his younger male siblings have to subordinate themselves with little hope of changing their status within the family. When these younger brother are aggressive and individualistic, tensions and difficulties often occur despite there being only one set of heirs.

In addition, tension and conflict may arise in polyandrous families because of sexual favoritism. The bride normally sleeps with the eldest brother, and the two have the responsibility to see to it that the other males have opportunities for sexual access. Since the Tibetan subsistence economy requires males to travel a lot, the temporary absence of one or more brothers facilitates this, but there are also other rotation practices. The cultural ideal unambiguously calls for the wife to show equal affection and sexuality to each of the brothers (and vice versa), but deviations from this ideal occur, especially when there is a sizable difference in age between the partners in the marriage.

Dorje's family represents just such a potential situation. He is fifteen years old and his two older brothers are twenty-five and twenty-two years old. The new bride is twenty-three years old, eight years Dorje's senior. Sometimes such a bride finds the youngest husband immature and adolescent and does not treat him with equal affection; alternatively, she may find his youth attractive and lavish special attention on him. Apart from that consideration, when a younger male like Dorje grows up, he may consider his wife "ancient" and prefer the company of a woman his own age or younger. Consequently, although men and women do not find the idea of sharing a bride or a bridegroom repulsive, individual likes and dislikes can cause familial discord.

Two reasons have commonly been offered for the perpetuation of fraternal polyandry in Tibet: that Tibetans practice female infanticide and therefore have to marry polyandrously, owing to a shortage of females; and that Tibet, lying at extremely high altitudes, is so barren and bleak that Tibetans would starve without resort to this mechanism. A Jesuit who lived in Tibet during the eighteenth century articulated this second view: "One reason for this most odious custom is the sterility of the soil, and the small amount of land that can be cultivated owing to the lack of water. The crops may suffice if the brothers all live together, but if they form separate families they would be reduced to beggary."

Both explanations are wrong, however. Not only has there never been institutionalized female infanticide in Tibet, but Tibetan society gives females considerable rights, including inheriting the family estate in the absence of brothers. In such cases, the woman takes a bridegroom who comes to live in her family and adopts her family's name and identity. Moreover, there is no demographic evidence of a shortage of females. In Limi, for example, there were (in 1974) sixty females and fifty-three males in the fifteen- to thirty-five-year age category, and many adult females were unmarried.

The second reason is incorrect because the climate in Tibet is extremely harsh, and ecological factors do play a major role in perpetuating polyandry, but polyandry is not a means of preventing starvation. It is characteristic, not of the poorest segments of the society, but rather of the peasant landowning families.

In the old society, the landless poor could not realistically aspire to prosperity, but they did not fear starvation. There was a persistent labor shortage throughout Tibet, and very poor families with little or no land and few animals could subsist through agricultural labor, tenant farming, craft occupations such as carpentry, or by working as servants. Although the per-person family income could increase somewhat if brothers married polyandrously and pooled their wages, in the absence of inheritable land, the advantage of fraternal polyandry was not generally sufficient to prevent them from setting up their own households. A more skilled or energetic younger brother could do as well or better alone, since he would completely control his income and would not have to share it with his siblings. Consequently, while there was and is some polyandry among the poor, it is much less frequent and more prone to result in divorce and family fission.

An alternative reason for the persistence of fraternal polyandry is that it reduces population growth (and thereby reduces the pressure on resources) by relegating some females to lifetime spinsterhood (see Figure 1). Fraternal polyandrous marriages in Limi (in 1974) averaged 2.35 men per woman, and not surprisingly, 31 percent of the females of child-bearing age (twenty to forty-nine) were unmarried. These spinsters either continued to live at home, set up their own households, or worked as servants for other families. They could also become Buddhist nuns. Being unmarried is not synonymous with exclusion from the reproductive pool. Discreet extramarital relationships are tolerated, and actually half of the adult unmarried women in Limi had one or more children. They raised these children as single mothers, working for wages or weaving cloth and blankets for sale. As a group, however, the unmarried women had far fewer offspring than the married women, averaging only 0.7 children per woman, compared with 3.3 for married women, whether polyandrous, monogamous, or polygynous. When polyandry helps regulate population, this function of polyandry is not consciously perceived by Tibetans and is not the reason they consistently choose it.

If neither a shortage of females nor the fear of starvation perpetuates fraternal polyandry, what motivates brothers, particularly younger brothers, to opt for this system of marriage? From the perspective of the younger brother in a landholding family, the main incentive is the attainment or maintenance of the good life. With polyandry, he can expect a more secure and higher standard of living, with access not only to his family's land and animals but also to its inherited collection of clothes, jewelry, rugs, saddles, and horses. In addition, he will experience less work pressure and much greater security because all responsibility does not fall on one "father." For Tibetan brothers, the question is whether to trade off the greater personal freedom inherent in monogamy for the real or potential economic security, affluence, and social prestige associated with life in a larger, labor-rich polyandrous family.

A brother thinking of separating from his polyandrous marriage and taking his own wife would face various disadvantages. Although in the majority of Tibetan regions all brothers theoretically have rights to their family's estate, in reality, Tibetans are reluctant to divide their land into small fragments. Generally, a younger brother who insists on leaving the family will receive only a small plot of land, if that. Because of its power and wealth, the rest of the family usually can block any attempt of the younger brother to increase his share of land through litigation. Moreover, a younger brother may not even get a house and cannot expect to receive much above the minimum in terms of movable possessions, such as furniture, pots, and pans. Thus a brother contemplating going it on his own must plan on achieving economic security and the good life not through inheritance but through his own work.

The obvious solution for younger brothers—creating new fields from virgin land—is generally not a feasible option. Most Tibetan populations live at high altitudes (above 12,000 feet), where arable land is extremely scarce. For example, in Dorje's village, agriculture ranges only from about 12,900 feet, the lowest point in the area, to 13,300 feet. Above that altitude, early frost and snow destroy the staple barley crop. Furthermore, because of the low rainfall caused by the Himalayan rain shadow, many areas in Tibet and northern Nepal that are within the appropriate altitude range for agriculture have no reliable sources of irrigation. In the end, although there is plenty of unused land in such areas, most of it is either too high or too arid.

Even where unused land capable of being farmed exists, clearing the land and building the substantial terraces necessary for irrigation constitute a great undertaking. Each plot has to be completely dug out to a depth of two to two and a half feet so that the large rocks and boulders can be removed. At best, a man might be able to bring a few new fields under cultivation in the first years after separating from his brothers, but he could not expect to acquire substantial amounts of arable land this way.

In addition, because of the limited farmland, the Tibetan subsistence economy characteristically includes a strong emphasis on

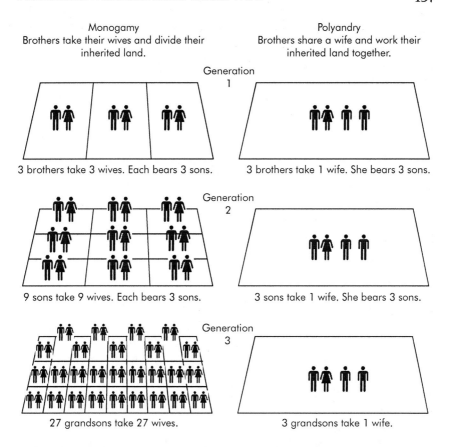

Monogamy
Brothers take their wives and divide their inherited land.

Polyandry
Brothers share a wife and work their inherited land together.

Generation 1

3 brothers take 3 wives. Each bears 3 sons.

3 brothers take 1 wife. She bears 3 sons.

Generation 2

9 sons take 9 wives. Each bears 3 sons.

3 sons take 1 wife. She bears 3 sons.

Generation 3

27 grandsons take 27 wives.

3 grandsons take 1 wife.

FIGURE 1 Family Planning in Tibet

An economic rationale for fraternal polyandry is outlined in the diagram above, which emphasizes only the male offspring in each generation. If every wife is assumed to bear three sons, a family splitting up into monogamous households would rapidly multiply and fragment the family land. In this case, a rule of inheritance, such as primogeniture, could retain the family land intact, but only at the cost of creating many landless male offspring. In contrast, the family practicing fraternal polyandry maintains a steady ratio of persons to land.

animal husbandry. Tibetan farmers regularly maintain cattle, yaks, goats, and sheep, grazing them in the areas too high for agriculture. These herds produce wool, milk, cheese, butter, meat, and skins. To obtain these resources, however, shepherds must accompany the animals on a daily basis. When first setting up a monogamous household, a younger brother like Dorje would find it difficult to both farm and manage animals.

In traditional Tibetan society, there was an even more critical factor that operated to perpetuate fraternal polyandry—a form of hereditary servitude somewhat analogous to serfdom in Europe. Peasants were tied to large estates held by aristocrats, monasteries, and the Lhasa government. They were allowed the use of some farmland to produce their own subsistence but were required to provide taxes in kind and corvée (free labor) to their lords. The corvée was a substantial hardship, since a peasant household was in many cases required to furnish the lord with one laborer daily for most of the year and more on specific occasions such as the harvest. This enforced labor, along with the lack of new land and the ecological pressure to pursue both agriculture and animal husbandry, made polyandrous families particularly beneficial. The polyandrous family allowed an internal division of adult labor, maximizing economic advantage. For example, while the wife worked the family fields, one brother could perform the lord's corvée, another could look after the animals, and a third could engage in trade.

Although social scientists often discount other people's explanations of why they do things, in the case of Tibetan fraternal polyandry, such explanations are very close to the truth. The custom, however, is very sensitive to changes in its political and economic milieu and, not surprisingly, is in decline in most Tibetan areas. Made less important by the elimination of the traditional serf-based economy, it is disparaged by the dominant non-Tibetan leaders of India, China, and Nepal. New opportunities for economic and social mobility in these countries, such as the tourist trade and government employment, are also eroding the rationale for polyandry, and so it may vanish within the next generation.

Review Questions

1. What is fraternal polyandry, and how does this form of marriage manage potential conflict over sex, children, and inheritance?

2. Why do many Tibetans choose polyandry over monogamous or polygynous marriage?

3. According to Tibetans, what are some of the disadvantages of polyandry?

4. What is wrong with the theory that Tibetan polyandry is caused either by a shortage of women due to infanticide or is a way to prevent famine by limiting population and land pressure?

5. Why might Tibetan polyandry disappear under modern conditions?

8

RACE, ETHNICITY
AND NATIONALITY

CHAPTER SEVENTEEN

Mixed Blood

Jeffrey M. Fish

Many Americans believe that people can be divided into races. For them, races are biologically defined groups. Anthropologists, on the other hand, have long argued that U.S. racial groups are American cultural constructions; they represent the way Americans classify people rather than a genetically determined reality. In this article, Jeffrey Fish demonstrates the cultural basis of race by comparing how races are defined in the United States and Brazil. In America, a person's race is determined not by how he or she looks, but by his or her heritage. A person will be classified as black, for example, if one of his or her parents is classified that way no matter what the person looks like. In Brazil, on the other hand, people are classified into a series of tipos on the basis of how they look. The same couple may have children classified into three or four different tipos based on a number of physical markers such as skin color and nose shape. As a result, Fish's daughter, who has brown skin and whose mother is black, can change her race from black in the United States to moreno (brunette), a category just behind branca (blond) in Brazil, by simply taking a plane there.

Last year my daughter, who had been living in Rio de Janeiro, and her Brazilian boyfriend paid a visit to my cross-cultural psychology class. They had agreed to be interviewed about Brazilian culture. At one point in the interview I asked her, "Are you black?" She said, "Yes." I then asked him the question, and he said "No".

"How can that be?" I asked. "He's darker than she is."

Psychologists have begun talking about race again. They think that it may be useful in explaining the biological bases of behavior. For example, following publication of *The Bell Curve*, there has been renewed debate about whether black-white group differences in scores on IQ tests reflect racial differences in intelligence. (Because this article is about race, it will mainly use racial terms, like black and white, rather than cultural terms, like African-American and European-American.)

The problem with debates like the one over race and IQ is that psychologists on both sides of the controversy make a totally unwarranted assumption: that there is a biological entity called "race." If there were such an entity, then it would at least be possible that differences in behavior between "races" might be biologically based.

Before considering the controversy, however, it is reasonable to step back and ask ourselves "What is race?" If, as happens to be the case, race is not a biologically meaningful concept, then looking for biologically based racial differences in behavior is simply a waste of time.

The question "What is race?" can be divided into two more limited ones. The answers to both questions have long been known by anthropologists, but seem not to have reached other social or behavioral scientists, let alone the public at large. And both answers differ strikingly from what we Americans think of as race.

The first question is "How can we understand the variation in physical appearance among human beings?" It is interesting to discover that Americans (including researchers, who should know better) view only a part of the variation as "racial," while other equally evident variability is not so viewed.

The second question is "How can we understand the kinds of racial classifications applied to differences in physical appearance among human beings?" Surprisingly, different cultures label these physical differences in different ways. Far from describing biological entities, American racial categories are merely one of numerous, very culture-specific schemes for reducing uncertainty about how people should respond to other people. The fact that Americans believe that Asians, blacks, Hispanics, and whites constitute biological entities called races is a matter of cultural interest rather than scientific substance. It tells us something about American culture—but nothing at all about the human species.

The short answer to the question "What is race?" is: There is no such thing. Race is a myth. And our racial classification scheme is loaded with pure fantasy.

Let's start with human physical variation. Human beings are a species, which means that people from anywhere on the planet can mate with others from anywhere else and produce fertile offspring. (Horses and donkeys are two different species because, even though they can mate with each other, their offspring—mules—are sterile.)

Our species evolved in Africa from earlier forms and eventually spread out around the planet. Over time, human populations that were geographically separated from one another came to differ in physical appearance. They came by these differences through three major pathways: mutation, natural selection, and genetic drift. Since genetic mutations occur randomly, different mutations occur and accumulate over time in geographically separated populations. Also, as we have known since Darwin, different geographical environments select for different physical traits that confer a survival advantage. But the largest proportion of variability among populations may well result from purely random factors; this random change in the frequencies of already existing genes is known as genetic drift.

If an earthquake or disease kills off a large segment of a population, those who survive to reproduce are likely to differ from the original population in many ways. Similarly, if a group divides and a subgroup moves away, the two groups will, by chance, differ in the frequency of various genes. Even the mere fact of physical separation will, over time, lead two equivalent populations to differ in the frequency of genes. These randomly acquired population differences will accumulate over successive generations along with any others due to mutation or natural selection.

A number of differences in physical appearance among populations around the globe appear to have adaptive value. For example, people in the tropics of Africa and South America came to have dark skins, presumably, through natural selection, as protection against the sun. In cold areas, like northern Europe or northern North America, which are dark for long periods of time, and where people covered their bodies for warmth, people came to have light skins—light skins make maximum use of sunlight to produce vitamin D.

The indigenous peoples of the New World arrived about 15,000 years ago, during the last ice age, following game across the Bering Strait. (The sea level was low enough to create a land bridge because so much water was in the form of ice.) Thus, the dark-skinned Indians of the South American tropics are descended from light-skinned ancestors, similar in appearance to the Eskimo. In other words, even though skin color is the most salient feature thought by Americans to be an indicator of race—and race is assumed to have great time depth—it is subject to relatively rapid evolutionary change.

Meanwhile, the extra ("epicanthic") fold of eyelid skin, which Americans also view as racial, and which evolved in Asian populations to protect the eye against the cold, continues to exist among South American native peoples because its presence (unlike a light skin) offers no reproductive disadvantage. Hence, skin color and eyelid form, which Americans think of as traits of different races, occur together or separately in different populations.

Like skin color, there are other physical differences that also appear to have evolved through natural selection—but which Americans do not think of as racial. Take, for example, body shape. Some populations in very cold climates, like the Eskimo, developed rounded bodies. This is because the more spherical an object is, the less surface area it has to radiate heat. In contrast, some populations in very hot climates, like the Masai, developed lanky bodies. Like the tubular pipes of an old-fashioned radiator, the high ratio of surface area to volume allows people to radiate a lot of heat.

In terms of American's way of thinking about race, lanky people and rounded people are simply two kinds of whites or blacks. But it is equally reasonable to view light-skinned people and dark-skinned people as two kinds of "lankys" or "roundeds." In other words, our categories for racial classification of people arbitrarily include certain dimensions (light versus dark skin) and exclude others (rounded versus elongated bodies).

There is no biological basis for classifying race according to skin color instead of body form—or according to any other variable, for that matter. All that exists is variability in what people look like—and the arbitrary and culturally specific ways different societies classify that variability. There is nothing left over that can be called race. This is why race is a myth.

Skin color and body form do not vary together: Not all dark-skinned people are lanky; similarly, light-skinned people may be lanky or rounded. The same can be said of the facial features Americans think of as racial—eye color, nose width (actually, the ratio of width to length), lip thickness ("evertedness"), hair form, and hair color. They do not vary together either. If they did, then a "totally white" person would have very light skin color, straight blond hair, blue eyes, a narrow nose, and thin lips; a "totally black" person would have very dark skin color, black tight curly hair, dark brown eyes, a broad nose, and thick lips; those in between would have—to a correlated degree—wavy light brown hair, light brown eyes, and intermediate nose and lip forms.

While people of mixed European and African ancestry who look like this do exist, they are the exception rather than the rule. Anyone who wants to can make up a chart of facial features (choose a location with a diverse population, say, the New York City subway) and verify that there are people with all possible admixtures of facial features. One might see someone with tight curly blond hair, light skin, blue eyes, broad nose, and thick lips—whose features are half "black" and half "white." That is, each of the persons facial features occupies one end or the other of a supposedly racial continuum, with no intermediary forms (like wavy light brown hair). Such people are living proof that supposedly racial features do not vary together.

Since the human species has spent most of its existence in Africa, different populations in Africa have been separated from each other longer than East Asians or Northern Europeans have been separated from each other or from Africans. As a result, there is remarkable physical variation among the peoples of Africa, which goes unrecognized by Americans who view them all as belonging to the same race.

In contrast to the very tall Masai, the diminutive stature of the very short Pygmies may have evolved as an advantage in moving rapidly through tangled forest vegetation. The Bushmen of the Kalahari desert have very large ("steatopygous") buttocks, presumably to store body fat in one place for times of food scarcity, while leaving the rest of the body uninsulated to radiate heat. They also have "peppercorn" hair. Hair in separated tufts, like tight curly hair, leaves space to radiate the heat that rises through the body to the scalp; straight hair lies flat and holds in body heat, like a cap. By viewing Africans as constituting a single race, Americans ignore their greater physical variability, while assigning racial significance to lesser differences between them.

Although it is true that most inhabitants of northern Europe, east Asia, and central Africa look like Americans' conceptions of one or another of the three purported races, most inhabitants of south Asia, southwest Asia, north Africa, and the Pacific islands do not. Thus, the 19th century view of the human species as comprised of Caucasoid, Mongoloid, and Negroid races, still held by many Americans, is based on a partial and unrepresentative view of human variability. In other words, what is now known about human physical variation does not correspond to what Americans think of as race.

In contrast to the question of the actual physical variation among human beings, there is the question of how people classify that variation. Scientists classify things in scientific taxonomies—chemists' periodic table of the elements, biologists' classification of life forms into kingdoms, phyla, and so forth.

In every culture, people also classify things along culture-specific dimensions of meaning. For example, paper clips and staples are understood by Americans as paper fasteners, and nails are not, even though, in terms of their physical properties, all three consist of differently shaped pieces of metal wire. The physical variation in pieces of metal wire can be seen as analogous to human physical variation; and the categories of cultural meaning, like paper fasteners versus wood fasteners, can be seen as analogous to races. Anthropologists refer to these kinds of classifications as folk taxonomies.

Consider the avocado—is it a fruit or a vegetable? Americans insist it is a vegetable. We eat it in salads with oil and vinegar. Brazilians, on the other hand, would say it is a fruit. They eat it for dessert with lemon juice and sugar.

How can we explain this difference in classification?

The avocado is an edible plant, and the American and Brazilian folk taxonomies, while containing cognate terms, classify some edible plants differently. The avocado does not change. It is the same biological entity, but its folk classification changes, depending on who's doing the classifying.

Human beings are also biological entities. Just as we can ask if an avocado is a fruit or a vegetable, we can ask if a person is white or black. And when we ask race questions, the answers we get come from folk taxonomies, not scientific ones. Terms like "white" or "black" applied to people—or "vegetable" or "fruit" applied to avocados—do not give us biological information about people or avocados. Rather, they exemplify how cultural groups (Brazilians or Americans) classify people and avocados.

Americans believe in "blood," a folk term for the quality presumed to be carried by members of so-called races. And the way offspring—regardless of their physical appearance—always inherit the less prestigious racial category of mixed parentage is called "hypo-descent" by anthropologists. A sentence thoroughly intelligible to most Americans might be, "Since Mary's father is white and her mother is black, Mary is black because she has black 'blood.'" American researchers who think they are studying racial differences in behavior would, like other Americans, classify Mary as black—although she has just as much white "blood."

According to hypo-descent, the various purported racial categories are arranged in a hierarchy along a single dimension, from the most prestigious ("white"), through intermediary forms ("Asian"), to the least prestigious ("black"). And when a couple come from two different categories, all their children (the "descent" in "hypo-descent") are classified as belonging to the less prestigious category (thus, the "hypo"). Hence, all the offspring of one "white" parent and one "black" parent—regardless of the children's physical appearance—are called "black" in the United States.

The American folk concept of "blood" does not behave like genes. Genes are units which cannot be subdivided. When several genes jointly determine a trait, chance decides which ones come from each parent. For example, if eight genes determine a trait, a child gets four from each parent. If a mother and a father each have the hypothetical genes BBBBWWWW, then a child could be born with any combination of B and W genes, from BBBBBBBB to WWWWWWWW. In contrast, the folk concept "blood" behaves like a uniform and continuous entity. It can be divided in two indefinitely—for example, quadroons and octoroons are said to be people who have one-quarter and one-eighth black "blood," respectively. Oddly, because of hypo-descent, Americans consider people with one-eighth black "blood" to be black rather than white, despite their having seven-eighths white "blood."

Hypo-descent, or "blood," is not informative about the physical appearance of people. For example, when two parents called black in the United States have a number of children, the children are likely to vary in physical appearance. In the case of skin color, they might vary from lighter than the lighter parent to darker than the darker parent. However, they would all receive the same racial classification—black— regardless of their skin color.

All that hypo-descent tells you is that, when someone is classified as something other than white (e.g., Asian), at least one of his or her parents is classified in the same way, and that neither parent has a less prestigious classification (e.g., black). That is, hypo-descent is informative about ancestry—specifically, parental classification—rather than physical appearance.

There are many strange consequences of our folk taxonomy. For example, someone who inherited no genes that produce "African"- appearing physical features would still be considered black if he or she has a parent classified as black. The category "passing for white" includes many such people. Americans have the curious belief that people who look white but have a parent classified as black are "really" black in some biological sense, and are being deceptive if they present themselves as white. Such examples make it clear that race is a social rather than a physical classification.

From infancy, human beings learn to recognize very subtle differences in the faces of those around them. Black babies see a wider variety of black faces than white faces, and white babies see a wider variety of white faces than black faces. Because they are exposed only to a limited range of human variation, adult members of each "race" come to see their own group as containing much wider variation than others. Thus, because of this perceptual learning, blacks see greater physical variation among themselves than among whites, while whites see the opposite. In this case, however, there is a clear answer to the question of which group contains greater physical variability. Blacks are correct.

Why is this the case?

Take a moment. Think of yourself as an amateur anthropologist and try to step out of American culture, however briefly.

It is often difficult to get white people to accept what at first appears to contradict the evidence they can see clearly with their own eyes—but which is really the result of a history of perceptual learning. However, the reason that blacks view themselves as more varied is not that their vision is more accurate. Rather, it is that blacks too have a long—but different—history of perceptual learning from that of whites (and also that they have been observers of a larger range of human variation).

The fact of greater physical variation among blacks than whites in America goes back to the principle of hypo-descent, which classifies all people with one black parent and one white parent as black. If they were all considered white, then there would be more physical variation among whites. Someone with one-eighth white "blood" and seven-eighths black "blood" would be considered white; anyone with any white ancestry would be considered white. In other words, what appears to be a difference in biological variability is really a difference in cultural classification.

Perhaps the clearest way to understand that the American folk taxonomy of race is merely one of many—arbitrary and unscientific like all the others— is to contrast it with a very different one, that of Brazil. The Portuguese word that in the Brazilian folk taxonomy corresponds to the American "race" is *"tipo."* *Tipo*, a cognate of the English word "type," is a descriptive term that serves as a kind of shorthand for a series of physical features. Because people's physical features vary separately from one another, there are an awful lot of tipos in Brazil.

Since tipos are descriptive terms, they vary regionally in Brazil—in part reflecting regional differences in the development of colloquial Portuguese, but in part because the physical variation they describe is different in different regions. The Brazilian situation is so complex I will limit my delineation of tipos to some of the main ones used in the city of Salvador, Bahia, to describe people whose physical appearance is understood to be made up of African and European features. (I will use the female terms throughout; in nearly all cases the male term simply changes the last letter from *a* to *o*.)

Proceeding along a dimension from the "whitest" to the "blackest" tipos, a *loura* is whiter-than-white, with straight blond hair, blue or green eyes, light skin color, narrow nose, and thin lips. Brazilians who come to the United States think that a *loura* means a "blond" and are surprised to find that the American term refers to hair color only. A *branca* has light skin color, eyes of any color, hair of any color or form except tight curly, a nose that is not broad, and lips that are not thick. *Branca* translates as "white," though Brazilians of this tipo who come to the United States—especially those from elite families—are often dismayed to find that they are not considered white here, and, even worse, are viewed as Hispanic despite the fact that they speak Portuguese.

A *morena* has brown or black hair that is wavy or curly but not tight curly, tan skin, a nose that is not narrow, and lips that are not thin. Brazilians who come to the United States think that a *morena* is a "brunette," and are surprised to find that brunettes are considered white but *morenas* are not. Americans have difficulty classifying *morenas*, many of whom are of Latin American origin: Are they black or Hispanic? (One might also observe that *morenas* have trouble with Americans, for not just accepting their appearance as a given, but asking instead "Where do you come from?" "What language did you speak at home?" "What was your maiden name?" or even, more crudely, "What *are* you?")

A *mulata* looks like a *morena,* except with tight curly hair and a slightly darker range of hair colors and skin colors. A *preta* looks like a *mulata,* except with dark brown skin, broad nose, and thick lips. To Americans, *mulatas* and *pretas* are both black, and if forced to distinguish between them would refer to them as light-skinned blacks and dark-skinned blacks, respectively.

If Brazilians were forced to divide the range of tipos, from *loura* to *preta,* into "kinds of whites" and "kinds of blacks" (a distinction they do not ordinarily make), they would draw the line between *morenas* and *mulatas;* whereas Americans, if offered only visual information, would draw the line between *brancas* and *morenas.*

The proliferation of tipos, and the difference in the white-black dividing line, do not, however, exhaust the differences between Brazilian and American folk taxonomies. There are tipos in the Afro-European domain that are considered to be neither black nor white—an idea that is difficult for Americans visiting Brazil to comprehend. A person with tight curly blond (or red) hair, light skin, blue (or green) eyes, broad nose, and thick lips, is a *sarará.* The opposite features—straight black hair, dark skin, brown eyes, narrow nose, and thin lips—are those of a *cabo verde. Sarará* and *cabo verde* are both tipos that are considered by Brazilians in Salvador, Bahia, to be neither black nor white.

When I interviewed my American daughter and her Brazilian boyfriend, she said she was black because her mother is black (even though I am white). That is, from her American perspective, she has "black blood"—though she is a *morena* in Brazil. Her boyfriend said that he was not black because, viewing himself in terms of Brazilian tipos, he is a *mulato* (not a *preto).*

There are many differences between the Brazilian and American folk taxonomies of race. The American system tells you about how people's parents are classified but not what they look like. The Brazilian system tells you what they look like but not about their parents. When two parents of intermediate appearance have many children in the United States, the children are all of one race; in Brazil they are of many tipos.

Americans believe that race is an immutable biological given, but people (like my daughter and her boyfriend) can change their race by getting on a plane and going from the United States to Brazil—just as, if they take an avocado with them, it changes from a vegetable into a fruit. In both cases, what changes is not the physical appearance of the person or avocado, but the way they are classified.

I have focused on the Brazilian system to make clear how profoundly folk taxonomies of race vary from one place to another. But the Brazilian system is just one of many. Haiti's folk taxonomy, for example, includes elements of both ancestry and physical appearance, and even includes the amazing term (for foreigners of African appearance) *un blanc noir*—literally, "a black white." In the classic study *Patterns of Race in the Americas,* anthropologist Marvin Harris gives a good introduction to the ways in which the conquests by differing European powers of differing New World peoples and ecologies combined with differing patterns of slavery to produce a variety of folk taxonomies. Folk taxonomies of race can be found in many—though by no means all—cultures in other parts of the world as well.

The American concept of race does not correspond to the ways in which human physical appearance varies. Further, the American view of race ("hypo-descent") is just one among many folk taxonomies, [none] of which correspond to the facts of human physical variation. This is why race is a myth and why races as conceived by Americans (and others) do not exist. It is also why differences in behavior between "races" cannot be explained by biological differences between them.

When examining the origins of IQ scores (or other behavior), psychologists sometimes use the term "heritability"—a statistical concept that is not based on observations of genes or chromosomes. It is important to understand that questions about heritability of IQ have nothing to do with racial differences in IQ. "Heritability" refers only to the relative ranking of individuals *within* a population, under given environmental conditions, and not to differences *between* populations. Thus, among the population of American whites, it may be that those with high IQs tend to have higher-IQ children than do those with low IQs. Similarly, among American blacks, it may be that those with high IQs also tend to have higher-IQ children.

In both cases, it is possible that the link between the IQs of parents and children may exist for reasons that are not entirely environmental. This heritability of IQ *within* the two populations, even if it exists, would in no way contradict the average social advantages of American whites as a group compared to the average social disadvantages of American blacks as a group. Such differences in social environments can easily account for any differences in the average test scores *between* the two groups. Thus, the heritability of IQ *within* each group is irrelevant to understanding differences *between* the groups.

Beyond this, though, studies of differences in behavior between "populations" of whites and blacks, which seek to find biological causes rather than only social ones, make a serious logical error. They assume that blacks and whites are populations in some biological sense, as sub-units of the human species. (Most likely, the researchers make this assumption because they are American and approach race in terms of the American folk taxonomy.)

In fact, though, the groups are sorted by a purely social rule for statistical purposes. This can easily be demonstrated by asking researchers how they know that the white subjects are really white and the black subjects are really black. There is no biological answer to this question, because race as a biological category does not exist. All that researchers can say is, "The tester classified them based on their physical appearance," or "Their school records listed their race," or otherwise give a social rather than biological answer.

So when American researchers study racial differences in behavior, in search of biological rather than social causes for differences between socially defined groups, they are wasting their time. Computers are wonderful machines, but we have learned about "garbage in/garbage out." Applying complex computations to bad data yields worthless results. In the same way, the most elegant experimental designs and statistical analyses, applied flawlessly to biologically meaningless racial categories, can only produce a very expensive waste of time.

As immigrants of varied physical appearance come to the United States from countries with racial folk taxonomies different from our own, they are often perplexed and dismayed to find that the ways they classify themselves and others are irrelevant to the American reality. Brazilians, Haitians, and others may find themselves labeled by strange, apparently inappropriate, even pejorative terms, and grouped together with people who are different from and unreceptive to them. This can cause psychological complications (a Brazilian immigrant—who views himself as white—being treated by an American therapist who assumes that he is not).

Immigration has increased, especially from geographical regions whose people do not resemble American images of blacks, whites, or Asians. Intermarriage is also increasing, as the stigma associated with it diminishes. These two trends are augmenting the physical diversity among those who marry each other—and, as a result, among their children. The American folk taxonomy of race (purportedly comprised of stable biological entities) is beginning to change to accommodate this new reality. After all, what race is someone whose four grandparents are black, white, Asian, and Hispanic?

Currently, the most rapidly growing census category is "Other," as increasing numbers of people fail to fit available options. Changes in the census categories every 10 years reflect the government's attempts to grapple with the changing self-identifications of Americans—even as statisticians try to maintain the same categories over time in order to make demographic comparisons. Perhaps they will invent one or more "multiracial" categories, to accommodate the wide range of people whose existence defies current classification. Perhaps they will drop the term "race" altogether. Already some institutions are including an option to "check as many as apply," when asking individuals to classify themselves on a list of racial and ethnic terms.

Thinking in terms of physical appearance and folk taxonomies helps to clarify the emotionally charged but confused topics of race. Understanding that different cultures have different folk taxonomies suggests that we respond to the question "What race is that person?" not by "Black" or "White," but by "Where?" and "When?"

Review Questions

1. What is Jeffrey Fish's main point about the way Americans define race?

2. What is the difference between the way race is defined in the United States and in Brazil? List the Brazilian folk taxonomy of *tipos* and how to translate *tipos* into U.S. racial categories.

3. What evidence challenges the view that races are biologically defined types? What evidence would have to exist to prove that the human species is genetically divided into races?

4. Why does Fish feel it is important to understand that race as
    Americans define it does not represent a biological reality?

9
GENDER

CHAPTER EIGHTEEN

Heading Home: Women, Work, and Identity in America

Dianna Shandy and Karine Moe

Young, successfully employed college-educated women face a dilemma when they decide to have children. Can they continue to work full-time with the same intensity that up to then has brought them occupational success, or will they have to cut back? What will adjustments required by motherhood and family do to their occupational identity and ability to compete on an equal basis with men? In this article, Dianna Shandy and Karine Moe discuss these and other questions concerning women's work and place in the home once they have children. Basing their comments on extensive interviews and focus groups as well as labor statistics, they argue that younger professional women, pushed by the stress of trying to do everything and pulled by the pleasure of being with their children, are beginning to choose home over work once they have a family. Despite doing so, they can often continue to hold their past occupational identity in the minds of those who know them.

Jennifer, a tall, well-dressed woman in her mid-thirties, fingers the stem of her wine glass and braces herself for the question she will get a dozen times that night at a cocktail party her husband is holding for his clients: *"And what do you do?"*

This question, which most of us might write off as "small talk," is anything but trivial. It reflects the importance we attribute to one's occupation as the primary source of our public social identity. So normally when we answer the what-do-you-do question, we identity ourselves by our occupation. We might say things such as, "I am a college professor at Metro State," or "I'm a wealth management consultant over at Grant and Smith Securities."

Although most North Americans don't like to admit there is a class system (we prefer to believe we accept people for "who they are"), we actually, and often without thinking, rank each other on the basis of our occupational identity. For example, Jennifer's husband is president of an advertising company with both local and regional accounts. The clients at his cocktail party tend to be presidents, vice presidents, or division managers who work for the companies his firm promotes. They represent a more affluent class of people than, say, firefighters, fast-food restaurant managers, or administrative assistants although some of these jobs, such as firefighting, confer prestige.

Occupational identity conveys more than just one's class, however. It implies relative status between individuals. When men and women work at the same jobs, their work signifies that they are approximately equal. This assertion not only gains credence from observations of contemporary U.S. society, but from anthropological fieldwork and cross-cultural comparison. Take a well-known study by Ernestine Friedl, for example.[1] She points out that decades of ethnographic research in a variety of the world's societies have caused many anthropologists to conclude that males inherit a predisposition to dominate females everywhere. Friedl argues against this position by citing evidence about gender relations in four contrasting hunting and gathering societies. She asserts that control of publicly (beyond the family) shared resources, especially animal protein, determines the degree to which females are equal to males. First, she notes that among the Washo Indians (a foraging group that lived in the Sierra Nevada Mountains of southern California) both men and women foraged for edible plants and both caught rabbits and other small animals as a source of protein. The result was relative gender equality. Men and women were not segregated in daily activities. Both sexes could take lovers, dissolve marriages, and make decisions for the group. The Hadza of Tanzania, she points out, also display relative gender equality largely because men and women forage separately and work to meet their own individual needs for food.

On the other hand, the Tiwi living on islands off the North coast of Australia show a more typical hunter/gatherer pattern. The men hunt

---

1   Ernestine Friedl, "Society and Sex Roles," *Human Nature*, April 1978.

and the women gather, and the male control of meat (protein), which is shared publicly by the whole group, results in domination over women. Men hunt and control the public distribution of meat; women gather only for family needs.

Finally, in the fourth case represented by the Inuit of the Arctic, males provide virtually all the food by hunting seals, walruses, whales, and fish. As a result, Inuit women are "used, abused, and traded," as Friedl puts it. Friedl also notes that gender inequality continues in many agriculturally based societies where men control most of the food that is publicly exchanged. Anthropologists Jane Collier and Michelle Rosaldo have also argued that while women's roles as gatherers contributed significantly to the food supply, these contributions were symbolically less important than the men's hunting activities.[2]

Friedl's argument appears to inform what is happening to U.S. women. Women have increasingly gained power and equality as they hold jobs once reserved for men. This has long been a goal for women in our society, and women in America now wield governmental and corporate power at levels never before seen in the history of this country. Women now have unprecedented access to education, jobs, and income.

And that's not all. A large part of the growth in the post-World War II U.S. economy can be attributed to the dramatic increase in the labor force participation by women, especially those who are married. And this participation extends to management and leadership positions and the ownership of one-third of all U.S. businesses that employ a quarter of the workforce.

Going hand in hand with this surge in women's contributions to economic productivity is the fact that women are at least as well educated as men. Women make up a full 58% of the nation's college students and are, overall, the majority in graduate and professional schools. They are hired in equal numbers by the country's most prestigious law firms. The majority of veterinarians and accountants are women. Women physicians will soon dominate certain sub-specialties within medicine.

In addition, while the number of women in the labor force has increased over the last few decades, fewer males have sought work. Labor economists note that if current trends continue, by 2020 only 70% of men will participate in the U.S. labor force, and by 2050, their participation will decline to 66%.

---

2   Jane F. Collier and Michelle Z. Rosaldo, "Politics and Gender in Simple Societies," in Sherry B. Ortner and Harriet S. Whitehead (eds.), *On Sexual Meanings: The Cultural Construction of Gender and Sexuality* (Cambridge: Cambridge University Press, 1981).

To be sure, there continues to be a wage gap between males and females for the labor force as a whole. However, when you look at specific niches within the population a different picture emerges. Without children, men and women pursue their careers neck in neck in terms of pay when they work similar jobs for similar hours. In fact, the gender wage gap for childless people between the ages of 27 and 33 is practically zero. Does this all mean that gender bias is absent in the world of work in America today? No. However, while gender discrimination at work continues, women have seen substantial gains in job equality over the past three or four decades.

Returning Home

And this brings us back to Jennifer's unease about the what-do-you-do question. Despite the statistics presented above, she, like an increasing number of young, married women with children, decided to give up her career for life as an at-home mother. She did so despite the fact that her personal history fit the trend toward job equality and the growing public influence of women. She graduated from a prestigous eastern college with honors and gained her degree as an attorney at a "top 10" law school. She obtained a high-paying job in a firm specializing in mergers and acquisitions where she was in line to become a partner. Then something happened that changed her promising career: she had one, then two children. Now, as an at-home mom, she grapples with the issue of identity in settings like business cocktail parties where occupational achievement outranks motherhood as an acceptable identity.

Jennifers decision to leave her career is not unique. A study of well-educated women that we have been conducting reveals that a growing number of young, professional women are leaving work to become "at-home moms." As we have discovered, this attorney turned at-home mother is emblematic of a growing number of American women today. In fact, the full-time labor force participation of married women with professional degrees and children under 18 fell from nearly two-thirds to just over a half between 1998 and 2005. From a labor market perspective, this is a significant and remarkable shift, with dramatic ramifications for economic growth. Having gained a foothold in formerly male-dominated positions, it becomes paradoxical that many highly educated, accomplished women are leaving their careers, often as a consequence of becoming mothers. This article is about why we think this is happening and at least partly how women are managing to do this without losing status.

Who Drops Out

To better understand this conundrum, we (an anthropologist and a labor economist) joined forces to look at national trends and learn more through interviews and focus groups about what kinds of women leave work. We discovered from national labor force participation data that a surprising number of college-educated, especially professional, women were opting out of the labor force. From here we designed interviews and focus groups with women who were making or had made the decision to leave their jobs in order to stay home with their children, as well as those who were continuing to juggle home and office.

The first thing we discovered was that age counts. We learned that women in their twenties and thirties seemed to approach childbirth, child rearing, and employment differently than their mothers and grandmothers. This older generation, the so-called Baby Boomers (women in their late forties to early sixties) were the first large wave of women to compete for prominent positions in the labor force. They entered work with high expectations and demonstrated ability, and like today's younger women, soon found that work conflicted with marriage and the need to raise children. Overall their response has been to try to manage both work and family by attempting to adjust to both, although with varying degrees of success. Nonetheless, these women were pioneering in their ability to anticipate and overcome obstacles and thereby created occupational opportunities for their daughters.

The second thing we discovered was that daughters of Baby Boomers (women in their early thirties to mid-forties and usually labeled Gen Xers or Millennials) benefited from the pioneering work of their mother's generation; however, they were the most likely to report having been "blindsided" by the realities of juggling career and children. Angie, a mother of two children in her mid-thirties with an MBA typifies this group. When she considered her own expectations for combining work with motherhood she said: "I thought women could do it all but just that my [own] mother did not do it well."

The third thing we discovered was that Millennials, married and well-educated women with young children, seemed to be far more pragmatic than older women about the conflict between work and family. Accordingly, they were also the most creative in the strategies they had devised to manage this conflict. They were still gunning for top spots educationally, but they reported being more mindful about how they would negotiate career and family. We found that women in their twenties and early thirties were more likely than older women to have reduced their responsibilities at work for family reasons. For some this meant selecting a career that was more flexible and amenable to the demands of child rearing. Others were planning to have careers and children sequentially. Still others intended to have children first and move into a career at some undefined future point when their children were older. But as we have noted above, many, faced with the need and desire to raise children, have left work behind, at least for the time being.

Finally, we should note that men rarely drop out of work to become at-home dads. Among married couples, when one parent leaves the labor force, 97 times out of 100 it is the woman who does so. The phenomenon of at-home dads is a growing trend, but when you look at the bigger picture of labor force participation, the number of men who do this is quite small. In this case couples bend to traditional gender roles—mom quits her job and dad presses even harder in his.

Before we go any further, we should note that by virtue of our focus on college-educated women for both our surveys and our interviews, we are *de facto* conducting a study of elite women. We realize that the notion of having a so-called "choice" not to work is available only to a narrow slice of American women, while many others need two incomes to keep their household afloat. In this respect our study does not tell the story of all women.

However, we argue that it is important to focus on college-educated and therefore relatively elite women because their experiences shape the lives of all American women. These women represent the potential leaders, the voices for change. If we don't have a critical mass of women executives, how can we expect the culture of companies to change? How can we expect laws to keep pace with women's lives if they aren't represented in Washington? Therefore, while at first glance middle- and upper-middle-class mothers are targeted most directly by our analysis, we believe the implications of our argument affect all women in America.

Why Do Women "Opt Out"?

So why do women "opt out" now when they have unprecedented access to education, jobs, and income, and potentially suffer the loss of their occupational identity? One suggested answer focuses solely on generation. It says that members of the younger generation, both men and women, are more likely to exit the work force than their elders. Although we don't deny the importance of generation, we feel gender has to be part of the explanation too. In our research, we have grappled with the intersection of gender and generation to understand the outflow of professional women from the labor force. And we agree that younger women approach issues of work and family differently than older women. However, it is important to acknowledge that while gender and generation vie with one another for explanatory power, gender is crucial to what is happening here. Indeed, we believe that gender is more important than generation as a way to understand current intersections of gender, work, and identity in America today.

So if it is not just a generational difference, what are the gender-related factors that bear on women's decision to return home?

What "Pushes" Women to Go Home?

There are several things that "push" women to leave the workforce. Let's look at a few of them.

The 100-Hour Couple

One of the most intriguing explanations for why women leave the workforce is the phenomenon of the 100-hour couple. Let's consider Valerie's situation. Valerie was an English and Political Science double major in college. A child of a single mother who single-handedly supported and raised five children, Valerie attended a state university and worked her way through school. She went on to attend law school and to work as a real estate attorney. She married her husband, also an attorney, who worked in banking. By the time they had their second child, their careers were at a zenith, with Valerie and her husband each working an average of 75-hours a week. To meet their work obligations, they had a full-time and a part-time nanny. When they discovered they needed yet a third nanny to help out because of work obligations that increasingly spilled over into evenings and weekends, they decided to re-evaluate their situation. They concluded that one of them had to reduce hours at work or quit his or her job altogether. They recognized that they could live on either Valerie's or her husband's salary alone, although her husband's income was significantly larger than hers. Therefore, for financial as well as for other less tangible reasons that could not be tallied on a spreadsheet, Valerie decided to leave her job and to stay home with their children. Valerie described her decision in the following way:

> If we were financially able, one of us needed to quit our jobs. What was the point of having kids if we weren't spending time with them? Strangers were raising my children—65 hours per week of child care. Deciding to quit my job and stay home with my children was the right thing to do.

Valerie's case illustrates some key points. As women's educational qualifications rise, so too have their occupational aspirations and their chance for marriage with economically successful men. It's not surprising that well-educated women gravitate toward high-powered, high-paying jobs and marry elite men who have done the same. Whereas previous generations saw a surplus of professional men relative to women, the educational gap has closed. Instead of the CEO marrying his secretary or the doctor marrying his nurse, the CEO is marrying the CFO and the doctor is marrying the doctor. With this larger pool of well-educated, well-employed women, we have transitioned to high-powered couples resulting in a rapid and significant increase in the percent of high earning couples that together work over 100 hours per week.

In Valerie's case, she and her husband surpassed 150-hour workweeks, but when we look across a larger sample of families, 100 hours is a threshold for couples who make a decision for one, and as pointed out it is usually the woman, to alter their work situation.

The Second Shift

Another factor pushing women out of the workforce is what sociologist Arlie Hochschild calls the second shift. Here she gives life to the old adage, "A man may work from sun to sun, but a woman's work is never done." The second shift refers to the work women do to maintain and sustain the household in addition to their paid employment. The second shift is commonly seen as a significant stressor for women across socioeconomic groups. It is well documented that women shoulder a disproportionate percentage of housework. For example, one study reports that women do an average of 27 hours of housework a week, compared to 16 hours a week for men. Important here is that while women have made significant gains in the workplace itself, the sexual division of labor at home endures. A recent trend to hire household help is opening possibilities to redefine this aspect of women's lives, but even when families hire people to watch their children or clean their homes, women tend to take on the burden of managing the work that is done in the home and caring for the children.

Although it might strike many as a significant luxury to be able to afford to pay someone to clean their homes and watch their children, in our interviews we found that hiring and supervising staff to care for the home and the children placed additional stress on women and was cited by them as part of the decision to quit their jobs. Women also mentioned moral and ethical concerns. Is it "right and fair," to hire women who often have to leave their own children behind to work these jobs? Then, too, was it advisable to hire nannies with lower educational levels to care for their children, and how does one manage the inevitabilities of sick children and/or sick child care providers?

The women we interviewed did not just describe trying to balance the needs of their children and their jobs, but also the reality of their responsibility to manage their homes. For many the solution was to stay home full-time.

The Glass Ceiling

Women mentioned a third factor that caused them to consider resigning their jobs. They talked about encountering a "glass ceiling" at work, one that is a form of discrimination that limits a woman's advancement. They felt they were being blocked from moving upward in the institution because of some tacit or unwritten set of norms about women, especially married women with children. The women we interviewed were frustrated by seeing their counterparts without children (or with a spouse at home caring for their children and managing the household) advance more swiftly in their careers then they did. It seemed unfair since these co-workers did not have to take parental leave to care for children and were more available to work longer hours. One woman lamented that her peers who had not taken time off for children were now vice presidents sitting in corner offices.

One way to look at this is that women quit their jobs not because of their families but because the pressures and inflexibility of their work situations actually leave them no way to maintain both. This is why many women we spoke with take issue with the term "opting out." Work conditions permitting, some of the women we interviewed would have preferred to "opt in," albeit on terms that better allowed them to both keep their jobs and raise their children.

When we raised the possibility during a focus group of reducing their hours at the job while still remaining employed, one advertising executive summarized the opinion of many of her counterparts when she said, "Part time is just a joke." Another woman with an MBA said, "My boss was reluctant to let me go part time at all. When I cut my hours my boss said he'd pay me less per hour. After three months of fighting and going several levels above him [in the company], I was able to keep my same hourly wage."

We should point out that when viewed cross-culturally different countries manage the intersection of parenting and labor force participation in other ways. The United States, when compared to other industrialized countries, rarely accommodates the need for parents to have and care for children. One woman we interviewed who ironically worked for a children's museum took 12 weeks of unpaid leave when her first child was born. The only thing the museum guaranteed was that she would get her job back when she returned from leave. In its Feburary 1, 2007 issue, *USA Today* reported that the United States and Australia are the only industrialized countries that fail to provide paid leave for new mothers, although there are exceptions in some U.S. states. Australian mothers have it better, however, with one year of job-protected leave. The U.S. Family and Medical Leave Act provides for 12 weeks of job-protected leave, but it only covers those who work for larger companies. Out of 168 nations in a Harvard University study, 163 had some form of paid maternity leave, putting the United States at the end of the list in company with Lesotho, Papua New Guinea, and Swaziland.[3]

Factors That "Pull" Women Home

Beyond understanding some of the reasons women are "pushed" out of the work force, it is also important to understand what "pulls" them there.

Being with Their Children

One of the reasons women gave us for why they liked being "at-home" revolved around being with their children. Take for example the case of Carol. Carol loves being home with her three kids—all in school now—and is thankful that she is able to do this. She loves spending time with the kids, talking to them, being the one they turn to with their questions. And, she likes the freedom and flexibility. Last summer she drove across the country with her children to visit her mom for a month. Having the latitude to make this trip was especially meaningful to her when her mother died the following winter after a long battle with cancer.

Sara introduces a long list of activities her children participate in by saying that Ryan and Aidan "get a lot of mommy time." She notes that she is able to do this because she has "a flexible enough schedule. I can just cart them wherever they need to go." She goes on to describe visits to grandparents in New Mexico and Florida. "When we go we stay for a week. So, before I quit working at General Mills I would max

---

3   "The Work, Family, and Equality Index: How Does the United States Measure Up?" by Jody, Heymann, Alison Earle, and Jeffrey Hayes, published by The Project on Global Working Families, Boston, MA and Montreal, Quebec. The information is on their website: http://www.mcgill.ca/files/ ihsp/WFFIFinal2007.pdf.

out my vacation." Having control over their time tended to be a central concern for many of these women.

Lower Stress

Many women seek to pursue a less hectic life. One woman's husband credits her with running "a great back office" such that the family spends their weekends together playing and not running errands. Most were tired of the "juggle and struggle" they encountered when they were still working. They had had to negotiate with their spouses over when, where, who, and how to cover child care. Another woman pointed out that staying at home "made my husband's life easier" and that "he enjoys his children more because he is not worrying about the day-to-day." And women freely point out that this arrangement also allows them to get their needs met by allowing them "time for themselves."

Sense of Responsibility

Women also discussed the moral importance and timing of their decision to head home. One attorney noted, "Conventional wisdom says we need to be there because we have infants. In hindsight, it's absolutely flipped. Now that the kids are getting older, it's more important for me to be there." Another bond trader noted that it was easier to hire someone to care for her children when they were "cute naughty" as toddlers, but now that they were not so cute as misbehaving adolescents she felt the need to be more in charge of her kids' care.

Nostalgia

We also found that many women are pulled home by a longing to reproduce what for them was a pleasant upbringing. Some had at-home mothers who were there for them with amenities such as milk and cookies after school. On the other hand, some felt the need to redress the rejection they felt as latchkey kids when mothers were not there for them.

Group Support

Finally, it seems to be increasingly easier for young women to leave work as other like-minded women make the same choice. In one veterinarian turned at-home mom's words, "I run with a pack of smart women." The result is the formation of social networks of women with their children providing a sense of support, occasions for conversation about domestic matters, and opportunities for their children to play together. Although it's not fun to be an ex-veterinarian who stays home by herself with her kids, it is easier to do so when all your friends are doing it too.

Financial Costs

What happens when women give up their paychecks? As one woman aptly noted, "The paycheck gives you a tangible sense of value." Other women we interviewed described how their husband's work time, as the sole income earner, expands as his home effort decreases. Still other women lament the loss of what they called the "fuck you money," or the financial independence their own earnings afforded them and that potentially allowed them to leave their marriage if they ever felt they needed to. Still others argue that their power did not change because their husbands appreciated their efforts at home. The threat that they might return to work and thus destroy the comfortable support system they provided moderates\d the increased power that a husband might otherwise enjoy. But it is clear that by leaving work and a paycheck, divorce or the death of a husband will likely have a greater impact on their lives.

Returning to Work

A lot has been written about the difficulty of re-entering the workforce after significant absences. One problem is the limited shelf life of a professional degree. For example, a physician who does not practice for ten years would have to overcome significant hurdles to get back into clinical work. On the other hand, opportunities to work in the medical sector of the economy may still be available.

However, the chance for them to return to their original occupations did not seem to matter to some of our respondents. Many of the women we interviewed said they would prefer to change professions if they returned to work in the future. Some thought of starting their own businesses. Others described transitioning to a care-giving profession. Many of the bond traders, financial managers, and attorneys we interviewed indicated that when, and if, they returned to work they had their eyes on jobs such as elementary school teacher, social worker for the elderly, or advocate for patients in hospitals.

Maintaining Status

So how can Jennifer and many other young at-home mothers manage to maintain the prestige and power that accompanied the up-scale jobs they once trained for and held? A traditional way that was more common in the past was to associate themselves with their husband's status. If she did so, Jennifer might have answered the what-do-you-do question by simply saying, "Oh, I am Paul's wife." But this kind of answer diminishes her past academic and occupational achievements. So she is more likely to mention what she used to do by saying "I am an attorney" or "I was an attorney with Brand and Cockrin but I am home with the kids for a while."

Finally, if they remain outside the workplace for long, women may choose to maintain a sense of occupational worth by serving in "quasi-professional" settings such as membership on the boards of civic associations, positions with nonprofit organizations, and aides at their children's schools.

Finally, it is difficult at this point for us to predict what these young professionals, now turned full-time mothers, will do in the future as their children grow up and they are once again free to work. The move home may only be one phase in a life of shifting pressures, opportunities, and associated identities.

Review Questions

1. What is the relationship between occupation, class, and social identity in the U.S.?

2. Shandy and Moe described Ernestine Friedl's work on the degree to which males dominate females. What is Friedl's main argument and what evidence does she use to support it?

3. At what age are women likely to move from work to home, according to Shandy and Moe?

4. What factors push women to "head home" instead of continuing to work?

5. What factors pull women to do so?

6. How do women who have left work to raise their children at home deal with the apparent loss of gender equality that comes with their domestic identity over their occupational one?

Original article from Dianna Shandy and Karine S. Moe, "Heading Home: Women, Work and Identity in America." Reprinted by permission

CHAPTER NINETEEN

Symbolizing Roles:
Behind the Veil

Elizabeth W. Fernea and Robert A. Fernea

Most societies have some things that serve as key symbols. The flag of the United States, for example, stands not only for the nation, but for a variety of important values that guide American behavior and perception. In this article, Elizabeth Fernea and Robert Fernea trace the meaning of another key symbol: the veil worn by women in the Middle East. Instead of reference to a national group, the veil codes many of the values surrounding the role of women. Often viewed by Westerners as a symbol of female restriction and inequality, for the women who wear it the veil signals honor, personal protection, the sanctity and privacy of the family, wealth and high status, and city life.

Blue jeans have come to mean America all over the world; three-piece wool suits signal businessmen; and in the 1980s pink or green hair said "punk." What do we notice, however, in societies other than our own? Ishi, the last of a "lost" tribe of North American Indians who stumbled into twentieth-century California in 1911, is reported to have said that the truly interesting objects in the white culture were pockets and matches. Rifa'ah Tahtawi, one of the first young Egyptians to be sent to Europe to study in 1826, wrote an account of French society in which he noted that Parisians used many unusual objects of dress, among them something called a belt. Women wore belts, he said, apparently to keep their bosoms erect, and to show off the slimness of their waists and the fullness of their hips. Europeans are still fascinated by the Stetson hats worn by American cowboys; an elderly Dutch woman of our acquaintance recently carried six enormous Stetsons back to the Hague as presents for the male members of her family.

Like languages (Inca, French) or food (tacos, hamburgers), clothing has special meaning for people who wear it that strangers may not understand. But some objects become charged with meaning to other cultures. The veil is one article of clothing used in Middle Eastern societies that stirs strong emotions in the West. "The feminine veil has become a symbol: that of the slavery of one portion of humanity," wrote French ethnologist Germaine Tillion in 1966. A hundred years earlier, Sir Richard Burton, British traveler, explorer, and translator of the *Arabian Nights,* recorded a different view. "Europeans inveigh against this article [the face veil] . . . for its hideousness and jealous concealment of charms made to be admired," he wrote in 1855. "It is, on the contrary, the most coquettish article of women's attire ... it conceals coarse skins, fleshy noses, wide mouths and vanishing chins, whilst it sets off to best advantage what in these lands is most lustrous and liquid—the eye. Who has not remarked this at a masquerade ball?"

In the present generation, the veil has become a focus of attention for Western writers, both popular and academic, who take a measure of Burton's irony and Tillion's anger to equate modernization of the Middle East with the discarding of the veil and to look at its return in Iran and in a number of Arab countries as a sure sign of retrogression. "Iran's 16 million women have come a long way since their floor-length cotton veil officially was abolished in 1935," an article noted in the 1970s, just before the Shah was toppled. Today [1986], with Ayatollah Khomeini in power, those 16 million Iranian women have put their veils back on again, as if to say that the long way they have come is not in the direction of the West.

The thousands of words written about the appearance and disappearance of the veil and of *purdah* (the seclusion of women) do little to help us understand the Middle East or the cultures that grew out of the same Judeo-Christian roots as our own. The veil and the all-enveloping garments that inevitably accompany it (the *milayah* in Egypt, the *abbayah* in Iraq, the *chadoor* in Iran, the *yashmak* in Turkey, the *burga'* in Afghanistan, and the *djellabah* and the *haik* in North Africa) are only the outward manifestations of cultural practices and meanings that are rooted deep in the history of Mediterranean and Southwest Asian society and are now finding expression once again. Today, with the resurgence of Islam, the veil has become a statement of difference between the Middle East and the Western world, a boundary no easier to cross now than it was during the Crusades or during the nineteenth century, when Western colonial powers ruled the area.

In English, the word *veil* has many definitions, and some of them are religious, just as in the Middle East. In addition to a face cover, the term also means "a piece of material worn over the head and shoulders, a part of a nun's head dress." The Arabic word for veiling and secluding comes from the root word *hajaba,* meaning "barrier." A *hijab* is an amulet worn to keep away the evil eye; it also means a diaphragm used to prevent conception. The gatekeeper or doorkeeper who guards the entrance to a government minister's office is a *hijab,* and in a casual conversation a person might say, "I want to be more informal with my friend so-and-so, but she always puts a *hijab* [barrier] between us."

In Islam, the Koranic verse that sanctions a barrier between men and women is called the Sura of the *hijab* (curtain): "Prophet, enjoin your wives, your daughters and the wives of true believers to draw their garments close round them. That is more proper, so that they may be recognized and not molested. Allah is forgiving and merciful." Notice, however, that veils of the first true believers did not conceal but rather announced the religious status of the women who wore them, drawing attention to the fact that they were Muslims and therefore to be treated with respect. The special Islamic dress worn by increasing numbers of modern Muslim women has much the same effect; it also says, "Treat me with respect."

Certainly some form of seclusion and of veiling was practiced before the time of Muhammad, at least among the urban elites and ruling families, but it was his followers, the first converts to Islam, who used veiling to signal religious faith. According to historic traditions, the *hijab* was established after the wives of the Prophet Muhammad were insulted by people coming to the mosque in search of the Prophet. Muhammad's wives, they said, had been mistaken for slaves. The custom of the *hijab* was thus established, and in the words of historian Nabia Abbott, "Muhammad's women found themselves, on the one hand, deprived of personal liberty, and on the other hand, raised to a position of honor and dignity." It is true, nonetheless, that the forms and uses of veiling and seclusion have varied greatly in practice over the last thousand years since the time of the Prophet, and millions of Muslim women have never been veiled at all. It is a luxury poorer families cannot afford, since any form of arduous activity, such as working in the fields, makes its use impossible. Thus it is likely that the use of the veil was envied by those who could not afford it, for it signaled a style of life that was generally admired. Burton, commenting on the Muslims portrayed in the *Arabian Nights,* says, "The women, who delight in restrictions which tend to their honour, accepted it willingly and still affect it, they do not desire a liberty or rather a license which they have learned to regard as inconsistent with their time-honored notions of feminine decorum and delicacy. They would think very meanly of a husband who permitted them to be exposed, like hetairae, to the public gaze."

The veil bears many messages about its wearers and their society, and many men and women in Middle Eastern communities today would quickly denounce nineteenth-century Orientalists like Sir Richard Burton and deny its importance. Nouha al Hejelan, wife of the Saudi Arabian ambassador to London, told Sally Quinn of *The Washington Post,* "If I wanted to take it all off [the *abbayah* and veil], I would have long ago. It wouldn't mean as much to me as it does to you." Basima Bezirgan, a contemporary Iraqi feminist, says, "Compared to the real issues that are involved between men and women in the Middle East today, the veil itself is unimportant." A Moroccan linguist, who buys her clothes in Paris, laughs when asked about the veil. "My mother wears a *djellabah* and a veil. I have never worn them. But so what? I still cannot get divorced as easily as a man, and I am still a member of my family group and responsible to them for everything I do. What is the veil? A piece of cloth." However, early Middle Eastern feminists felt differently. Huda Sharawi, an early Egyptian activist who formed the first Women's Union, removed her veil in public in 1923, a dramatic gesture to demonstrate her dislike of society's attitude toward women and her defiance of the system.

"The seclusion of women has many purposes," states Egyptian anthropologist Nadia Abu Zahra. "It expresses men's status, power, wealth, and manliness. It also helps preserve men's image of virility and masculinity, but men do not admit this; on the contrary they claim that one of the purposes of the veil is to guard women's honor." The veil and *purdah* are symbols of restriction, in men's behavior as well as women's. A respectable woman wearing conservative Islamic dress today on a public street is signaling, "Hands off! Don't touch me or you'll be sorry." Cowboy Jim Sayre of Deadwood, South Dakota, says, "If you deform a cowboy's hat, he'll likely deform you." A man who approaches a veiled woman is asking for similar trouble; not only the woman but also her family is shamed, and serious problems may result. "It is clear," says Egyptian anthropologist Ahmed Abou Zeid, "that honor and shame which are usually attributed to a certain individual or a certain kinship group have in fact a bearing on the total social structure, since most acts involving honor or shame are likely to affect the existing social equilibrium."

Veiling and seclusion almost always can be related to the maintenance of social status. The extreme example of the way the rich could use this practice was found among the wealthy sultans of pre-revolutionary Turkey. Stories of their women, kept in harems and guarded by eunuchs, formed the basis for much of the Western folklore concerning the nature of male-female relationships in Middle Eastern society. The forbidden nature of seclusion inflamed the Western imagination, but the Westerners who created erotic fantasies in films and novels would not have been able to enter the sultans' palaces any more than they could have penetrated their harems! It was eroticism plus opulence and luxury, the signs of wealth, that captured the imagination of the Westerners—and still does, as witnessed by the popularity of "Dallas" and "Dynasty."

The meaning associated with veiling or a lack of veiling changes according to locality. Most village women in the Egyptian delta have not veiled, nor have the Berber women of North Africa, but no one criticizes them for this. "In the village, no one veils, because everyone is considered a member of the same large family," explained Aisha Bint Muhammad, a working-class wife of Marrakesh. "But in the city, veiling is *sunnah*, required by our religion." Veiling has generally been found in towns and cities, among all classes, where families feel that it is necessary to distinguish themselves from strangers. Some women who must work without the veil in factories and hotels may put such garments on when they go out on holidays or even walk on the streets after work.

Veiling and *purdah* not only indicate status and wealth; they also have some religious sanction and protect women from the world outside the home, *Purdah* delineates private space and distinguishes between the public and private sectors of society, as does the traditional architecture of the area. Older Middle Eastern houses do not have picture windows facing on the street, nor do they have walks leading invitingly to front doors. Family life is hidden away from strangers; behind blank walls may lie courtyards and gardens, refuges from the heat, cold, and bustle of the outside world, the world of nonkin that is not to be trusted. Outsiders are pointedly excluded.

Even within the household, among her close relatives, a traditional Muslim woman may veil before those kinsmen whom she could legally marry. If her maternal or paternal cousins, her brothers-in-law, or her sons-in-law come to call, she covers her head, or perhaps her whole face. To do otherwise, to neglect such acts of respect and modesty, would be considered shameless.

The veil does more than protect its wearers from known and unknown intruders; it can also conceal identity. Behind the anonymity _ of the veil, women can go about a city unrecognized and uncriticized. Nadia Abu Zahra reports anecdotes of men donning women's veils in order to visit their lovers undetected; women may do the same. The veil is such an effective disguise that Nouri Al-Sa'id, the late prime minister of Iraq, attempted to escape death from revolutionary forces in 1958 by wearing the *abbayah* and veil of a woman; only his shoes gave him away. When houses of prostitution were closed in Baghdad in the early 1950s, the prostitutes donned the same clothing to cruise the streets. Flashing open their outer garments was an advertisement to potential customers.

Political dissidents in many countries have used the veil for their own ends. The women who marched, veiled, through Cairo during the Nationalist demonstrations against the British after World War 1 were counting on the strength of Western respect for the veil to protect them against British gunfire. At first they were right. Algerian women also used the protection of the veil to carry bombs through French army checkpoints during the Algerian revolution. But when the French discovered the ruse, Algerian women discarded the veil and dressed like Europeans to move about freely.

The multiple meanings and uses of *purdah* and the veil do not fully explain how such practices came to be so deeply embedded in Mediterranean society. However, their origins lie in the asymmetrical relationship between men and women and the resulting attitudes about men's and women's roles. Women, according to Fatma Mernissi, a Moroccan sociologist, are seen by men in Islamic societies as in need of protection because they are unable to control their sexuality and hence are a danger to the social order. In other words, they need to be restrained and controlled so that men do not give way to the impassioned desire they inspire, and society can thus function in an orderly way.

The notion that women present a danger to the social order is scarcely limited to Muslim society. Anthropologist Julian Pitt-Rivers has pointed out that the supervision and seclusion of women was also found in Christian Europe, even though veiling was not usually practiced there. "The idea that women not subjected to male authority are a danger is a fundamental one in the writings of the moralists from the Archpriest of Talavera to Padre Haro, and it is echoed in the modern Andalusian *pueblo*. It is bound up with the fear of ungoverned female sexuality which had been an integral element of European folklore ever since prudent Odysseus lashed himself to the mast to escape the sirens."

Pitt-Rivers is writing about northern Mediterranean communities, which, like those of the Middle Eastern societies, have been greatly concerned with family honor and shame rather than with individual guilt. The honor of the Middle Eastern extended family, its ancestors and its descendants, is the highest social value. The misdeeds of the grandparents are indeed visited on their grandchildren, but so also grandparents may be disgraced by grandchildren. Men and women always remain members of their natal families. Marriage is a legal contract, but a fragile one that is often broken; the ties between brother and sister, mother and child, father and child are lifelong and enduring. The larger natal family is the group to which the individual man or woman belongs and to which the individual owes responsibility in exchange for the social and economic security that the family group provides. It is the group that is socially honored—or dishonored—by the behavior of the individual.

Both male honor and female honor are involved in the honor of the family, but each is expressed differently. The honor of a man, *sharaf*, is a public matter, involving bravery, hospitality, and piety. It may be lost, but it may also be regained. The honor of a woman, *'ard*, is a private matter involving only one thing, her sexual chastity. Once believed to be lost, it cannot be regained. If the loss of female honor remains only privately known, a rebuke may be all that takes place. But if the loss of female honor becomes public knowledge, the other members of the family may feel bound to cleanse the family name. In extreme cases, the cleansing may require the death of the offending female member. Although such killings are now criminal offenses in the Middle East, suspended sentences are often given, and the newspapers in Cairo and Baghdad frequently carry sad stories of runaway sisters "gone bad" in the city, and the revenge taken upon them in the name of family honor by their brothers or cousins.

This emphasis on female chastity, many say, originated in the patrilineal society's concern with the paternity of the child and the inheritance that follows the male line. How could the husband know that the child in his wife's womb was his son? He could not know unless his wife was a virgin at marriage. Marriages were arranged by parents, and keeping daughters secluded from men was the best way of seeing that a girl remained a virgin until her wedding night.

Middle Eastern women also look upon seclusion as practical protection. In the Iraqi village where we lived from 1956 to 1958, one of us (Elizabeth) wore the *ahbayah* and found that it provided a great deal of protection from prying eyes, dust, heat, and flies. Parisian women visiting Istanbul in the sixteenth century were so impressed by the ability of the all-enveloping garment to keep dresses clean of mud and manure and to keep women from being attacked by importuning men that they tried to introduce it into French fashion. Many women have told us that they felt self-conscious, vulnerable, and even naked when they first walked on a public street without the veil and *abbayah*—as if they were making a display of themselves.

The veil, as it has returned in the last decade in a movement away from wearing Western dress, has been called a form of "portable seclusion," allowing women to maintain a modest appearance that indicates respectability and religious piety in the midst of modern Middle Eastern urban life. This new style of dress always includes long skirts, long sleeves, and a head covering (scarf or turban). Some outfits are belted, some are loose, and some include face veils and shapeless robes, as well as gloves so that no skin whatsoever is exposed to the public eye. However, these clothes are seldom black, like the older garments. The women wearing such clothes in Egypt may work in shops or offices or go to college; they are members of the growing middle class.

This new fashion has been described by some scholars as an attempt by men to reassert their Muslim identity and to reestablish their position as heads of families, even though both spouses often must work outside the home. According to this analysis, the presence of the veil is a sign that the males of the household are in control of their women and are more able to assume the responsibilities disturbed or usurped by foreign colonial powers, responsibilities which continue to be threatened by Western politics and materialism. Other scholars argue that it is not men who are choosing the garb today but women themselves, using modest dress as a way of communicating to the rest of the world that though they may work outside their homes, they are nonetheless pious Muslims and respectable women.

The veil is the outward sign of a complex reality. Observers are often deceived by the absence of that sign and fail to see that in Middle Eastern societies (and in many parts of Europe) where the garb no longer exists, basic attitudes are unchanged. Women who have taken off the veil continue to play the old roles within the family, and their chastity remains crucial. A woman's behavior is still the key to the honor and the reputation of her family, no matter what she wears.

In Middle Eastern societies, feminine and masculine continue to be strong poles of identification. This is in marked contrast to Western society where for more than a generation greater equality between men and women has been reflected in the blurring of distinctions between male and female clothing. Western feminists continue to state that biology is not the basis of behavior and therefore should not be the basis for understanding men's and women's roles. But almost all Middle Eastern reformers, whether upper or middle class, intellectuals or clerics, argue from the assumption of a fundamental, God-given difference, social and psychological as well as physical, between men and women. There are important disagreements among these reformers today about what should be done, however.

Those Muslim reformers still strongly influenced by Western models call for equal access to divorce, child custody, and inheritance; equal opportunities for education and employment; abolition of female circumcision and "crimes of honor"; an end to polygamy; and a law regulating the age of marriage. But of growing importance are reformers of social practice who call for a return to the example set by the Prophet Muhammad and his early followers; they wish to begin by eliminating what they feel to be the licentious practices introduced by Western influence, such as sexual laxity and the consumption of alcohol. To them, change in the laws affecting women should be in strict accord with their view of Islamic law, and women should begin by expressing their modesty and piety by wearing the new forms of veiling in public life. Seclusion may be impossible in modern urban societies, but conservative dress, the new form of veiling, is an option for women that sets the faithful Muslim apart from the corrupt world of the nonbeliever as it was believed to do in the time of the Prophet.

A female English film director, after several months in Morocco, said in an interview, "This business about the veil is nonsense. We all have our veils, between ourselves and other people. The question is what the veils are used for, and by whom." Today the use of the veil continues to trigger Western reaction, for as Islamic dress, it is not only a statement about the honor of the family or the boundary between family and stranger. Just as the changes in the nun's dress in the United States tell us something about the woman who wears it and the society of which she is a part, the various forms of veiling today communicate attitudes and beliefs about politics and religious morality as well as the roles of men and women in the Middle East.

Review Questions

1. What is the meaning to Westerners of the veil worn by Middle Eastern women? How does this view reflect Western values?

2. List the symbolic meanings of the veil to Middle Eastern women. How do these meanings relate to the Muslim concept of *purdah* and to other important Middle Eastern values?

3. There has been a resurgence of the veil in several Middle Eastern societies over the past few years. How can you explain this change?

4. Using this article as a model, analyze the meaning of some American articles of clothing. How do these relate to core values in the United States?

10

RELIGION

CHAPTER TWENTY

Religion, Magic, and World view

People seem most content when they are confident about themselves and the order of things around them. Uncertainty breeds debilitating anxiety; insecurity saps people's sense of purpose and their willingness to participate in social activity. Most of the time cultural institutions serve as a lens through which to view and interpret the world and respond realistically to its demands. But from time to time the unexpected or contradictory intervenes to shake people's assurance. A farmer may wonder about his skill when a properly planted and tended crop fails to grow. A wife may feel bewildered when the man she has treated with tenderness and justice for many years runs off with another woman. Death, natural disaster, and countless other forms of adversity strike without warning, eating away at the foundations of confidence. At these crucial points in life, many people use religion to help account for the vagaries of their experience.

Religion is the cultural knowledge of the supernatural that people use to cope with the ultimate problems of human existence.[1] In this definition, the term **supernatural** refers to a realm beyond normal experience. Belief in gods, spirits, ghosts, and magical power often defines the supernatural, but the matter is complicated by cultural variation and the lack of a clear distinction in many societies between the natural and the supernatural world. **Ultimate problems,** on the other hand, emerge from universal features of human life and include life's meaning, death, evil, and transcendent values. People everywhere wonder why they are alive, why they must die, and why evil strikes some

---

1   This definition draws on the work of Milton Yinger, *Religion, Society, and the Individual: An Introduction to the Sociology of Religion* (New York: Macmillan, 1957).

individuals and not others. In every society, people's personal desires and goals may conflict with the values of the larger group. Religion often provides a set of **transcendent values** that override differences and unify the group.

An aspect of religion that is more difficult to comprehend is its link to emotion. Ultimate problems "are more appropriately seen as deep-seated emotional needs," not as conscious, rational constructs, according to sociologist Milton Yinger.[2] Anthropologists may describe and analyze religious ritual and belief but find it harder to get at religion's deeper meanings and personal feelings.

Anthropologists have identified two kinds of supernatural power: personified and impersonal. **Personified supernatural force** resides in supernatural beings, in the deities, ghosts, ancestors, and other beings found in the divine world. For the Bhils of India, a *bhut*, or ghost, has the power to cause skin lesions and wasting diseases. *Bhagwan*, the equivalent of the Christian deity, controls the universe. Both possess and use personified supernatural force.

Impersonal supernatural force is a more difficult concept to grasp. Often called **mana**, the term used in Polynesian and Melanesian belief, it represents a kind of free-floating force lodged in many things and places. The concept is akin to the Western term *luck* and works like an electrical charge that can be introduced into things or discharged from them. Melanesians, for example, might attribute the spectacular growth of yams to some rocks lying in the fields. The rocks possess mana, which is increasing fertility. If yams fail to grow in subsequent years, they may feel that the stones have lost their power.

Supernatural force, both personified and impersonal, may be used by people in many societies. **Magic** refers to the strategies people use to control supernatural power. Magicians have clear ends in mind when they perform magic, and use a set of well-defined procedures to control and manipulate supernatural forces. For example, a Trobriand Island religious specialist will ensure a sunny day for a political event by repeating powerful sayings thought to affect the weather.

Sorcery uses magic to cause harm. For example, some Bhil *bhopas*, who regularly use magic for positive purposes, may also be hired to work revenge. They will recite powerful *mantras* (ritual sayings) over effigies to cause harm to their victims.

Witchcraft is closely related to sorcery because both use supernatural force to cause evil. But many anthropologists use the term to designate envious individuals who are born with or acquire evil

---

2   Yinger, p. 9.

power and who knowingly or unknowingly project it to hurt others. The Azande of Africa believe that most unfortunate events are due to witchcraft, and most Azande witches claim they were unaware of their power and apologize for its use.

Most religions possess ways to influence supernatural power or, if spirits are nearby, to communicate with them directly. For example, people may say **prayers** to petition supernatural beings. They may also give gifts in the form of **sacrifices** and offerings. Direct communication takes different forms. **Spirit possession** occurs when a supernatural being enters and controls the behavior of a human being. With the spirit in possession, others may talk directly with someone from the divine world. **Divination** is a second way to communicate with the supernatural. It usually requires material objects or animals to provide answers to human-directed questions. The Bhils of India, for example, predict the abundance of summer rainfall by watching where a small bird specially caught for the purpose lands when it is released. If it settles on something green, rainfall will be plentiful; if it rests on something brown, the year will be dry.

Almost all religions involve people with special knowledge who either control supernatural power outright or facilitate others in their attempt to influence it. **Shamans** are religious specialists who directly control supernatural power. They may have personal relationships with spiritual beings or know powerful secret medicines and sayings. They are usually associated with curing. **Priests** are religious specialists who mediate between people and supernatural beings. They don't control divine power; instead, they lead congregations in ceremonies and help others petition the gods.

Worldview refers to a system of concepts and often unstated assumptions about life. It usually contains a **cosmology** about the way things are and a **mythology** about how things have come to be. Worldview presents answers to the ultimate questions: life, death, evil, and conflicting values.

Finally, anthropologists also study and report on the formation of new religions, especially those that occur as a result of deprivation and stress. These **revitalization movements,** as Anthony F. C. Wallace called them in 1956, are "deliberate, organized, conscious efforts by members of a society to construct a more satisfying culture."[3] Revitalization movements are usually related to rapid change that renders a traditional

---

3   Anthony F. C. Wallace, "Revitalization Movements: Some Theoretical Considerations for Their Comparative Study," *American Anthropologist* 58, no. 2 (1956): 264-281.

way of life ineffective. For example, when one cultural group becomes dominated by another, rapid change and loss of authority may make its original meaning system seem thin, ineffective, and contradictory. The resulting state of deprivation often causes members to rebuild their culture along what they consider to be more satisfying lines.

Wallace argued that revitalization movements go through five stages:

1. *A Steady State.* This is a normal state of society in which people, through their culture, are able to manage the chronic stresses of daily life.

2. *Period of Increased Individual Stress.* Individuals in a society experience new stress caused by such events as culture contact, defeat in war, political domination, or climatic change.

3. *Period of Cultural Distortion.* Stress levels continue to rise as normal stress-reducing techniques fail to work. Social organization begins to break down, causing additional stress, and various cultural elements become distorted and disjointed.

4. *Period of Revitalization.* This period is marked by its own stages. First, a prophet or leader comes forward with a new vision of the culture that requires change. Called a *mazeway reformulation,* this vision is intended to produce a more integrated, satisfying, and adaptive culture. This is followed by the *communication* of the revitalization plan and, if it proves attractive, the plan's *organization* for wider dissemination, its *adoption* by many people, its *cultural transformation* of the society, and its *routinization* in daily life.

5. *A New Steady State.* If no additional stresses occur, the society should attain a new steady state at the end of the process.

Although not all revitalization movements are religious—the Marxist doctrine and communist revolution in Russia exemplify a political revitalization movement—most of the world's major religions probably started as revitalization movements and many smaller sects and movements fit the revitalization pattern today.

The first article, by Stanley Freed and Ruth Freed, describes how Sita, a low-caste Indian woman, is chronically possessed by the ghost of a friend who committed suicide. Stressed by the prospect of sexual relations with a new and strange husband, lack of support in her conjugal household, and the deaths of many friends and family members, ghost possession, argue the Freeds, reduces Sita's anxiety and gives her needed family support. The second article, by George Gmelch, is the latest revision of his earlier classic piece on the use of magic by American baseball players. He looks in detail at the rituals, taboos, and fetishes employed by the athletes. In the third article, Jill Dubisch illustrates the meaning and impact of ritual and pilgrimage. Using the "Run For the Wall," a motorcycle pilgrimage that involves travel from Los Angeles to the Vietnam Memorial in Washington, D.C., as an example, she shows how this difficult motorcycle ride evokes strong emotions and personal transformation among its participants. The fourth article is Horace Miner's classic article describing the body ritual of a North American group, the Nacerima. The Nacerimas concern for the health and beauty of their bodies has led them to establish an elaborate ritual system including the building of holy fonts in their houses and the presence of a variety of ritual specialists.

Key Terms

cosmology

divination

magic

mana

mythology

personified supernatural force

prayer

priest

religion

revitalization movement

sacrifice

shaman

sorcery

spirit possession

supernatural

transcendent values

ultimate problems

witchcraft

worldview

CHAPTER TWENTY ONE

Body Ritual among the Nacirema

Horace Miner

Ritual involving repeated symbolic acts can be about many things—the growth of crops, the response to death, movement from one social identity to another, community solidarity, and much more. It can also be about one's body, including how to care for it, how to make it socially acceptable, and how to make it impressive to others. This classic article written in 1958 by Horace Miner describes the extensive body ritual of a North American group, the Nacirema, whose houses contain special shrines in which body ritual takes place. From the article, it is clear that the society's elaborate variety of body rituals reveals important Nacirema cultural values.

The anthropologist has become so familiar with the diversity of ways in which different peoples behave in similar situations that he is not apt to be surprised by even the most exotic customs. In fact, if all of the logically possible combinations of behavior have not been found somewhere in the world, he is apt to suspect that they must be present in some yet undescribed tribe. This point has, in fact, been expressed with respect to clan organization by Murdock. In this light, the magical beliefs and practices of the Nacirema present such unusual aspects that it seems desirable to describe them as an example of the extremes to which human behavior can go.

Professor Linton first brought the ritual of the Nacirema to the attention of anthropologists twenty years ago, but the culture of this people is still very poorly understood. They are a North American group living in the territory between the Canadian Cree, the Yaqui and Tarahumare of Mexico, and the Carib and Arawak of the Antilles. Little is known of their origin, although tradition states that they came from the east. . . .

Nacirema culture is characterized by a highly developed market economy which has evolved in a rich natural habitat. While much of the people's time is devoted to economic pursuits, a large part of the fruits of these labors and a considerable portion of the day are spent in ritual activity. The focus of this activity is the human body, the appearance and health of which loom as a dominant concern in the ethos of the people. While such a concern is certainly not unusual, its ceremonial aspects and associated philosophy are unique.

The fundamental belief underlying the whole system appears to be that the human body is ugly and that its natural tendency is to debility and disease. Incarcerated in such a body, man's only hope is to avert these characteristics through the use of the powerful influences of ritual and ceremony. Every household has one or more shrines devoted to this purpose. The more powerful individuals in the society have several shrines in their houses and, in fact, the opulence of a house is often referred to in terms of the number of such ritual centers it possesses. Most houses are of wattle and daub construction, but the shrine rooms of the more weathly are walled with stone. Poorer families imitate the rich by applying pottery plaques to their shrine walls.

While each family has at least one such shrine, the rituals associated with it are not family ceremonies but are private and secret. The rites are normally only discussed with children, and then only during the period when they are being initiated into these mysteries. I was able, however, to establish sufficient rapport with the natives to examine these shrines and to have the rituals described to me.

The focal point of the shrine is a box or chest which is built into the wall. In this chest are kept the many charms and magical potions without which no native believes he could live. These preparations are secured from a variety of specialized practitioners. The most powerful of these are the medicine men, whose assistance must be rewarded with substantial gifts. However, the medicine men do not provide the curative potions for their clients, but decide what the ingredients should be and then write them down in an ancient and secret language. This writing is understood only by the medicine men and by the herbalists who, for another gift, provide the required charm.

The charm is not disposed of after it has served its purpose, but is placed in the charm-box of the household shrine. As these magical materials are specific for certain ills, and the real or imagined maladies of the people are many, the charm-box is usually full to overflowing. The magical packets are so numerous that people forget what their purposes were and fear to use them again. While the natives are very vague on this point, we can only assume that the idea in retaining all the old magical materials is that their presence in the charm-box, before which the body rituals are conducted, will in some way protect the worshipper.

Beneath the charm-box is a small font. Each day every member of the family, in succession, enters the shrine room, bows his head before the charm-box, mingles different sorts of holy water in the font, and proceeds with a brief rite of ablution. The holy waters are secured from the Water Temple of the community, where the priests conduct elaborate ceremonies to make the liquid ritually pure.

In the hierarchy of magical practitioners, and below the medicine men in prestige, are specialists whose designation is best translated "holy-mouth-men." The Nacirema have an almost pathological horror of and fascination with the mouth, the condition of which is believed to have a supernatural influence on all social relationships. Were it not for the rituals of the mouth, they believe that their teeth would fall out, their gums bleed, their jaws shrink, their friends desert them, and their lovers reject them. They also believe that a strong relationship exists between oral and moral characteristics. For example, there is a ritual ablution of the mouth for children which is supposed to improve their moral fiber.

The daily body ritual performed by everyone includes a mouth-rite. Despite the fact that these people are so punctilious about care of the mouth, this rite involves a practice which strikes the uninitiated stranger as revolting. It was reported to me that the ritual consists of inserting a small bundle of hog hairs into the mouth, along with certain magical powders, and then moving the bundle in a highly formalized series of gestures.

In addition to the private mouth-rite, the people seek out a holy-mouth-man once or twice a year. These practitioners have an impressive set of paraphernalia, consisting of a variety of augers, awls, probes, and prods. The use of these objects in the exorcism of the evils of the mouth involves almost unbelievable ritual torture of the client. The holy-mouth-man opens the client's mouth and, using the above mentioned tools, enlarges any holes which decay may have created in the teeth. Magical materials are put into these holes. If there are no naturally occurring holes in the teeth, large sections of one or more teeth are gouged out so that the supernatural substance can be applied. In the client's view, the purpose of these ministrations is to arrest decay and to draw friends. The extremely sacred and traditional character of the rite is evident in the fact that the natives return to the holy-mouth-men year after year, despite the fact that their teeth continue to decay.

It is to be hoped that, when a thorough study of the Nacirema is made, there will be careful inquiry into the personality structure of these people. One has but to watch the gleam in the eye of a holy-mouth-man, as he jabs an awl into an exposed nerve, to suspect that a certain amount of sadism is involved. If this can be established, a very interesting pattern emerges, for most of the population shows definite masochistic tendencies. It was to these that Professor Linton referred in discussing a distinctive part of the daily body ritual which is performed only by men. This part of the rite involves scraping and lacerating the surface of the face with a sharp instrument. Special women's rites are performed only four times during each lunar month, but what they lack in frequency is made up in barbarity. As part of this ceremony, women bake their heads in small ovens for about an hour. The theoretically interesting point is that what seems to be a preponderantly masochistic people have developed sadistic specialists.

The medicine men have an imposing temple, or *latipso*, in every community of any size. The more elaborate ceremonies required to treat very sick patients can only be performed at this temple. These ceremonies involve not only the thaumaturge but a permanent group of vestal maidens who move sedately about the temple chambers in distinctive costume and headdress.

The *latipso* ceremonies are so harsh that it is phenomenal that a fair proportion of the really sick natives who enter the temple ever recover. Small children whose indoctrination is still incomplete have been known to resist attempts to take them to the temple because "that is where you go to die." Despite this fact, sick adults are not only willing but eager to undergo the protracted ritual purification, if they can afford to do so. No matter how ill the supplicant or how grave the emergency, the guardians of many temples will not admit a client if he cannot give a rich gift to the custodian. Even after one has gained admission and survived the ceremonies, the guardians will not permit the neophyte to leave until he makes still another gift.

The supplicant entering the temple is first stripped of all his or her clothes. In everyday life the Nacirema avoids exposure of his body and its natural functions. Bathing and excretory acts are performed only in the secrecy of the household shrine, where they are ritualized as part of the body-rites. Psychological shock results from the fact that body secrecy is suddenly lost upon entry into the *latipso*. A man, whose own wife has never seen him in an excretory act, suddenly finds himself naked and assisted by a vestal maiden while he performs his natural functions into a sacred vessel. This sort of ceremonial treatment is necessitated by the fact that the excreta are used by a diviner to ascertain the course and nature of the client's sickness. Female clients, on the other hand, find their naked bodies are subjected to the scrutiny, manipulation and prodding of the medicine men.

Few supplicants in the temple are well enough to do anything but lie on their hard beds. The daily ceremonies, like the rites of the holy-mouth-men, involve discomfort and torture. With ritual precision, the vestals awaken their miserable charges each dawn and roll them about on their beds of pain while performing ablutions, in the formal movements of which the maidens are highly trained. At other times they insert magic wands in the supplicant's mouth or force him to eat substances which are supposed to be healing. From time to time the medicine men come to their clients and jab magically treated needles into their flesh. The fact that these temple ceremonies may not cure, and may even kill the neophyte, in no way decreases the people's faith in the medicine men.

There remains one other kind of practitioner, known as a "listener." This witchdoctor has the power to exorcise the devils that lodge in the heads of people who have been bewitched. The Nacirema believe that parents bewitch their own children. Mothers are particularly suspected of putting a curse on children while teaching them the secret body rituals. The counter-magic of the witchdoctor is unusual in its lack of ritual. The patient simply tells the "listener" all his troubles and fears, beginning with the earliest difficulties he can remember. The memory displayed by the Nacirema in these exorcism sessions is truly remarkable. It is not uncommon for the patient to bemoan the rejection he felt upon being weaned as a babe, and a few individuals even see their troubles going back to the traumatic effects of their own birth.

In conclusion, mention must be made of certain practices which have their base in native esthetics but which depend upon the pervasive aversion to the natural body and its functions. There are ritual fasts to make fat people thin and ceremonial feasts to make thin people fat. Still other rites are used to make women's breasts larger if they are small, and smaller if they are large. General dissatisfaction with breast shape is symbolized in the fact that the ideal form is virtually outside the range of human variation. A few women afflicted with almost inhuman hyper-mammary development are so idolized that they make a handsome living by simply going from village to village and permitting the natives to stare at them for a fee.

Reference has already been made to the fact that excretory functions are ritualized, routinized, and relegated to secrecy. Natural reproductive functions are similarly distorted. Intercourse is taboo as a topic and scheduled as an act. Efforts are made to avoid pregnancy by the use of magical materials or by limiting intercourse to certain phases of the moon. Conception is actually very infrequent. When pregnant, women dress so as to hide their condition. Parturition takes place in secret, without friends or relatives to assist, and the majority of women do not nurse their infants.

Our review of the ritual life of the Nacirema has certainly shown them to be a magic-ridden people. It is hard to understand how they have managed to exist so long under the burdens which they have imposed upon themselves. But even such exotic customs as these take on real meaning when they are viewed with the insight provided by Malinowski when he wrote:

"Looking from far and above, from our high places of safety in the developed civilization, it is easy to see all the crudity and irrelevance of magic. But without its power and guidance early man could not have mastered his practical difficulties as he has done, nor could man have advanced to the higher stages of civilization."

Review Questions

1.   Where are the Nacirema located?

2.   Describe the main body rituals that occur in Nacireman household shrines.

3.   What kinds of ritual specialists does Miner describe for the Nacirema in this article? What do they function to do for people?

4.   What is the *latipso,* and for what is it used?

5.   What do you think the psychological functions of Nacireman body ritual are, and how do these fit with Malinowski's theory about the functions of religion and magic described in the earlier article on baseball magic?

11

COLONIALISM AND THE MODERN WORLD SYSTEM

CHAPTER TWENTY TWO

Globalization

Several times a week, a small island freighter leaves Granada's Saint George's harbor loaded with fuel drums, crates of processed food, boxes containing manufactured goods, and an occasional motor scooter or car. When its hold is filled, 60 or 70 passengers, many of them women, troop across the gang plank and settle down among the freight or take a seat in a small cabin set aside for them on the upper aft deck. They are bound for their small island home, Carriacou, located about 35 miles by sea to the north. Most are returning from overseas work in New York, Britain, or mainland Europe, where they worked for a few years as maids and cleaners or at other service jobs. Carrying gifts of CD players, clothing, shoes, and other items manufactured outside their island, they will be greeted warmly by their relatives, whom they have alerted by phone or e-mail about the time of their arrival. Most returnees have already wired home money they saved from their off-island work and are beginning to think about using it to build a house or buy items that will make their lives easier and more secure.

    The people returning to Carriacou illustrate a major trend that is sweeping the world: globalization. **Globalization** consists of powerful forces that reshape local conditions on an ever-intensifying scale.[1] Although places such as Carriacou may seem peripheral to globalization, the impact of international money, tourists, transportation, goods, and the movement of the island's peoples to other parts of the world have all affected the way people live there. And their experience is repeated in many other parts of the world.

    Globalization may occur on several levels. In the most general and formal sense, we can talk about it as a world system. The **world system** is often defined in market terms and links nations and people together economically. More accurately, it is **transnational;** it consists of companies and patterns of exchange that transcend national borders and may evade control by individual governments. An international company may have a headquarters located in Bermuda; manufacturing facilities in Atlanta, Mexico, and Shanghai; customer service representatives in Mumbai; and investors from thirty or forty different countries. Japanese cars and motorcycles sold in the United States reflect the transnational world system. So do the tuna caught by American trawlers in the Atlantic and shipped overnight to Japan to make sushi.

The world system affects local conditions by providing goods, stimulating production, and introducing ideas. As a result, local people can easily find themselves both motivated by and at the mercy of world markets. For example, the government of India, through its state and district development offices, encouraged tribals living in Southern Rajasthan to dedicate some of their cropland to sericulture (silk worm production). Local farmers borrowed money to build "cocoon houses," and to underwrite the cost of fertilizing mulberry bushes for the silk worms to eat. The World Bank advanced money for a small cocoon processing factory. The program was a success—farmers doubled their money each year; women earned wages in the processing plant—until, that is, the Chinese government arbitrarily lowered the price of the silk its farmers produced by half. Unable to compete, the Indian program failed, disrupting the lives of people who embraced it. Stories like this should not come as a surprise to American workers who have lost jobs to "outsourcing," and to factory workers in other countries who are now employed to take their place.

The international movement of people also illustrates globalization. **Refugees,** people who immigrate to other parts of the world because it is too dangerous for them to stay in their homeland, have moved to many countries. **Guest workers** (people granted permission to work in a country other than their own) are found in many parts of the world. Legal immigrants (and illegal immigrants) diversify populations in many nations. The result is that some societies are becoming **multicultural;** people with different cultural backgrounds live side by side. Just as companies can be transnational, so can immigrants, workers, and refugees. People who originate from the same cultural areas often communicate with one another, calling or e-mailing home, wiring money to each other, and forming a visiting network. Tourism is the world's largest industry and regularly brings people with different backgrounds into contact.

Finally, globalization is marked by cultural diffusion. **Cultural diffusion,** or cultural borrowing, represents the movement of cultural ideas and artifacts from one society to another. Coca Cola has diffused from the United States to many parts of the world; sushi has diffused from Japan to the United States and Europe. So have musical styles, forms of dress, words, and a variety of other cultural items.

In almost every case, societies that borrow aspects of another group's culture adapt them to their own ways of life. Borrowed items usually undergo **cultural hybridization;** they are a mixture of the borrowed and the local. A hamburger in China will probably not taste exactly like one cooked on the backyard grill of an American family. Curry in the United States tastes different from the "real thing" prepared in India. (Note that as the local size of immigrant populations rise, more genuine, meaning closer to its ethnic origins, food becomes available to the original residents as well.)

The articles in Part Nine illustrate several of these points. The first, by Dianna Shandy, is an updated version of an article included in the previous edition. It describes the ordeal faced by Nuer refugees as they attempt to gain admittance and establish a life in the United States. Fleeing the civil war that has wracked their home in southern Sudan, Nuer refugees must develop the skill and determination to pass through a series of bureaucratic hurdles to reach and adjust to life in the United States. Personal initiative, education, using U.S. Non governmental organizations (NGOs), and the sharing of information about what works are keys to their success. The second article, by Sharon Bohn Gmelch, stresses the importance of tourism as a global phenomenon. It is the world's largest business and is not only economically important but also a major agent of culture change. In the third article, Ian Condry describes a form of pop culture, hip-hop, that has spread from the United States to Japan. Reviewing more general globalization theory, he shows how hip-hop has been hybridized in the Japanese context and how anthropologists, with their emphasis on Local settings, can show what globalization means to people as they conduct their daily lives.

Key Terms

cultural diffusion	multicultural
cultural hybridization	refugees
globalization	transnational
guest workers	world system

CHAPTER TWENTY THREE

Cocaine and the Economic Deterioration of Bolivia

Jack Weatherford

The demands of the world market have eroded local subsistence economies for centuries. Lands once farmed by individual families to meet their own needs now grow sugarcane, cotton, grain, or vegetables for market. Deprived of their access to land, householders must work as day laborers or migrate to cities to find jobs. Villages are denuded of the men, who have gone elsewhere for work, leaving women to farm and manage the family. The rhythm and structure of daily village life are altered dramatically. In this article, Jack Weatherford describes the impact of a new world market for cocaine on the structure and lives of rural Bolivians. Fed by an insatiable demand in Europe and the United States, the Bolivian cocaine trade has drawn males from the countryside, disrupted communications, destroyed families, unbalanced the local diet, and upset traditional social organization.

"They say you Americans can do anything. So, why can't you make your own cocaine and let our children come home from the coca plantations in the Cha-pare?" The Indian woman asked the question with confused resignation. In the silence that followed, I could hear only the rats scurrying around in the thatched roof. We continued shelling corn in the dark. The large house around us had once been home to an extended clan but was now nearly empty.

There was no answer to give her. Yet it was becoming increasingly obvious that the traditional Andean system of production and distribution built over thousands of years was now crumbling. Accompanying the destruction of the economic system was a marked distortion of the social and cultural patterns of the Quechua Indians. Since early in Inca history, the village of Pocona where I was working had been a trading village connecting the highlands, which produced potatoes, with the lowlands, which produced coca, a mildly narcotic plant used by the Incas. Over the past decade, however, new market demands from Europe and the United States have warped this system. Now the commodity is cocaine rather than the coca leaves, and the trade route bypasses the village of Pocona.

Bolivian subsistence patterns range from hunting and gathering in the jungle to intensive farming in the highlands, and since Inca times many parts of the country have depended heavily on mining. In the 1980s all of these patterns have been disrupted by the Western fad for one particular drug. Adoption of cocaine as the "drug of choice" by the urban elite of Europe and America has opened up new jungle lands and brought new Indian groups into Western economic systems. At the same time, the cocaine trade has cut off many communities such as Pocona from their traditional role in the national economy. Denied participation in the legal economy, they have been driven back into a world of barter and renewed isolation.

The vagaries of Western consumerism produce extensive and profound effects on Third World countries. It makes little difference whether the demand is for legitimate products such as coffee, tungsten, rubber, and furs marketed through legal corporations, or for illegal commodities such as opium, marijuana, cocaine, and heroin handled through criminal corporations. The same economic principles that govern the open, legal market also govern the clandestine, illegal markets, and the effects of both are frequently brutal.

Before coming to this Bolivian village, I assumed that if Americans and Europeans wanted to waste their money on cocaine, it was probably good that some of the poor countries such as Bolivia profit from it. In Cochabamba, the city in the heart of the cocaine-producing area, I had seen the benefits of this trade among the *narco chic* who lived in a new suburb of houses styled to look like Swiss chalets, Spanish haciendas, and English country homes. All these homes were surrounded by large wrought-iron fences, walls with broken glass set in the tops, and with large dogs that barked loudly and frequently. Such homes cost up to a hundred thousand dollars, an astronomical sum for Bolivia. I had also seen the narco elite of Cochabamba wearing gold chains and the latest

Miami fashions and driving Nissans, Audis, Ford Broncos, an occasional BMW, or even a Mercedes through the muddy streets of the city. Some of their children attended the expensive English-speaking school; much of Cochabamba's meager nightlife catered to the elite. But as affluent as they may be in Bolivia, this elite would probably not earn as much as working-class families in such cities as Detroit, Frankfurt, or Tokyo.

Traveling outside of Cochabamba for six hours on the back of a truck, fording the same river three times, and following a rugged path for the last twenty-five kilometers, I reached Pocona and saw a different face of the cocaine trade. Located in a valley a mile and a half above sea level, Pocona is much too high to grow the coca bush. Coca grows best below six thousand feet, in the lush area called the Chapare where the eastern Andes meet the western edge of the Amazon basin and rain forest.

Like the woman with whom I was shelling corn, most of the people of Pocona are older, and community life is dominated by women together with their children who are still too young to leave. This particular woman had already lost both of her sons to the Chapare. She did not know it at the time, but within a few months, she was to lose her husband to the same work as well. With so few men, the women are left alone to plant, work, and harvest the fields of potatoes, corn, and fava beans, but with most of the work force missing, the productivity of Pocona has declined substantially.

In what was once a moderately fertile valley, hunger is now a part of life. The daily diet consists almost exclusively of bread, potato soup, boiled potatoes, corn, and tea. The majority of their daily calories comes from the potatoes and from the sugar that they put in their tea. They have virtually no meat or dairy products and very few fresh vegetables. These products are now sent to the Chapare to feed the workers in the coca fields, and the people of Pocona cannot compete against them. The crops that the people of Pocona produce are now difficult to sell because truck drivers find it much more profitable to take goods in and out of the Chapare rather than face the long and unprofitable trip to reach such remote villages as Pocona.

Despite all the hardships caused by so many people being away from the village, one might assume that more cash should be flowing into Pocona from the Chapare, where young men easily earn three dollars a day—three times the average daily wage of porters or laborers in Cochabamba. But this assumption was contradicted by the evidence of Pocona. As one widowed Indian mother of four explained, the first time her sixteen-year-old son came home, he brought bags of food, presents, and money for her and the younger children. She was very glad that he was working in the Chapare. On the second visit home he brought only a plastic bag of white powder for himself, and instead of bringing food, he took away as much as he could carry on the two-day trip back into the Chapare.

The third time, he told his mother that he could not find enough work in the Chapare. As a way to earn more money he made his mother bake as much bread as she could, and he took Mariana, his ten-year-old sister, with him to sell the bread to the workers in the Chapare. According to the mother, he beat the little girl and abused her repeatedly. Moreover, the money she made disappeared. On one of Mariana's trips home to get more bread, the mother had no more wheat or corn flour to supply her son. So, she sent Mariana away to Cochabamba to work as a maid. The enraged son found where Mariana was working and went to the home to demand that she be returned to him. When the family refused, he tried but failed to have her wages paid to him rather than to his mother. Mariana was separated from her family and community, but at least she was not going to be one more of the prostitutes in the Chapare, and for her mother that was more important.

The standard of living in Pocona was never very high, but with the advent of the cocaine boom in Bolivia, the standard has declined. Ten years ago, Pocona's gasoline-powered generator furnished the homes with a few hours of electric light each night. The electricity also allowed a few families to purchase radios, and occasionally someone brought in a movie projector to show a film in a large adobe building on the main square. For the past two years, the people of Pocona have not been able to buy gasoline for their generator. This has left the village not only without electricity but without entertainment and radio or film contact with the outside world. A few boys have bought portable radios with their earnings from the Chapare, but their families were unable to replace the batteries. Nights in Pocona are now both dark and silent.

In recent years the national economy of Bolivia has been virtually destroyed, and peasants in communities such as Pocona are reverting to barter as the only means of exchange. The value of the peso may rise or fall by as much as 30 percent in a day; the peasants cannot take a chance on trading their crops for money that may be worth nothing in a week. Cocaine alone has not been responsible for the destruction of the Bolivian economy, but it has been a major contributor. It is not mere coincidence that the world's largest producer of coca is also the country with the world's worst inflation.

During part of 1986, inflation in Bolivia varied at a rate between 2,000 and 13,000 percent, if calculated on a yearly basis. Prices in the cities changed by the hour, and on some days the dollar would rise at the rate of more than 1 percent per hour. A piece of bread cost 150,000 pesos, and an American dollar bought between two and three million pesos on the black market. Large items such as airplane tickets were calculated in the billions of pesos, and on one occasion I helped a man carry a large box of money to pay for such a ticket. It took two professional counters half an hour to count the bills. Workers were paid in stacks of bills that were often half a meter high. Because Bolivia is too undeveloped to print its money, the importation of its own bills printed in West Germany and Brazil was one of the leading imports in the mid-1980s.

Ironically, by no longer being able to participate fully in the money economy, the villagers of Pocona who have chewed coca leaves for centuries now find it difficult to afford the leaves. The narcotics industry pays such a high price that the people of Pocona can afford only the rejected trash from the cocaine industry. Whether chewed or made into a tea, the coca produces a mild lift somewhat like a cup of coffee but without the jagged comedown that follows a coffee high. Coca also reduces hunger, thirst, headaches, stomach pains, and the type of altitude sickness known as *sorroche*.

Were this all, coca use might be viewed as merely a bad habit somewhat like drinking coffee, smoking cigarettes, or overindulging in chocolates, but unlike these practices coca actually has a number of marked health benefits. The coca leaf is very high in calcium. In a population with widespread lactose intolerance and in a country without a national system of milk distribution, this calcium source is very important. The calcium also severely reduces cavities in a population with virtually no dental services outside the city. Coca also contains large amounts of vitamins A, C, and D, which are often lacking in the starchy diets of the mountain peasants.

Without coca, and with an excess of corn that they cannot get to market, the people of Pocona now make more *chicha,* a form of home-fermented corn beer that tastes somewhat like the silage that American dairymen feed their cows. It is ironic that as an affluent generation of Americans are decreasing their consumption of alcohol in favor of drugs such as cocaine, the people of Pocona are drinking more alcohol to replace their traditional coca. *Chicha,* like most beers, is more nutritious than other kinds of distilled spirits but lacks the health benefits of the coca leaves. It also produces intoxication, something that no amount of coca leaves can do. Coca chewing is such a slow process and produces such a mild effect that a user would have to chew a bushel of leaves to equal the impact of one mixed drink or one snort of cocaine.

In many ways, the problems and complaints of Pocona echo those of any Third World country with a cash crop, particularly those caught in the boom-and-bust cycle characteristic of capitalist systems. Whether it is the sisal boom of the Yucatan, the banana boom of Central America, the rubber boom of Brazil, or the cocaine boom in Bolivia, the same pattern develops. Rural villages are depleted of their work forces. Family and traditional cultural patterns disintegrate. And the people are no longer able to afford certain local products that suddenly become valued in the West. This is what happened to Pocona.

Frequently, the part of a country that produces the boom crop benefits greatly, while other areas suffer greatly. If this were true in Bolivia, benefits accruing in the coca-producing area of the Chapare would outweigh the adjustment problems of such villages as Pocona. As it turns out, however, the Chapare has been even more adversely affected.

Most of the young men who go to the Chapare do not actually work in the coca fields. The coca bush originated in this area and does not require extensive care. One hectare can easily produce eight hundred kilograms of coca leaves in a year, but not much labor is needed to pick them. After harvesting, the leaves are dried in the sun for three to four days. Most of these tasks can easily be done by the farmer and his family. Wherever one goes in the Chapare one sees coca leaves spread out on large drying cloths. Old people or young children walk up and down these cloths, turning the drying leaves with their whisk brooms.

The need for labor, especially the labor of strong young men, conies in the first stage of cocaine production, in the reduction of large piles of leaves into a small quantity of *pasta*, or coca paste from which the active ingredient, cocaine, can then be refined. Three hundred to five hundred kilograms of leaves must be used to make one kilogram of pure cocaine. The leaves are made into *pasta* by soaking them in vats of kerosene and by applying salt, acetone, and sulfuric acid. To make the chemical reaction occur, someone must trample on the leaves for several days—a process very much like tromping on grapes to make wine, only longer. Because the corrosive mixture dissolves shoes or boots, the young men walk barefooted. These men are called *pisacocas* and usually work in the cool of the night, pounding the green slime with their feet. Each night the chemicals eat away more skin and very quickly open ulcers erupt. Some young men in the Chapare now have feet that are so diseased that they are incapable of standing, much less walking. So, instead, they use their hands to mix *the pasta,* but their hands are eaten away even faster than their feet. Thousands and possibly tens of thousands of young Bolivian men now look like lepers with permanently disfigured hands and feet. It is unlikely that any could return to Pocona and make a decent farmer.

Because this work is painful, the *pisacocas* smoke addictive cigarettes coated *with pasta*. This alleviates their pain and allows them to continue walking the coca throughout the night. The *pasta* is contaminated with chemical residues, and smoking it warps their minds as quickly as the acids eat their hands and feet. Like Mariana's brother, the users become irrational, easily angered, and frequently violent.

Once the boys are no longer able to mix coca because of their mental or their physical condition, they usually become unemployed. If their wounds heal, they may be able to work as loaders or haulers, carrying the cocaine or transporting the controlled chemicals used to process it. By and large, however, women and very small children, called *hormigas* (ants), are better at this work. Some of the young men then return home to their villages; others wander to Cochabamba, where they might live on the streets or try to earn money buying and selling dollars on the black market.

The cocaine manufacturers not only supply their workers with food and drugs, they keep them sexually supplied with young girls who serve as prostitutes as well. Bolivian health officials estimate that nearly half of the people living in the Chapare today have venereal disease. As the boys and girls working there return to their villages, they take these diseases with them. Increasing numbers of children born to infected mothers now have bodies covered in syphilitic sores. In 1985, a worse disease hit with the first case of AIDS. Soon after the victim died, a second victim was diagnosed.

In an effort to control its own drug problem, the United States is putting pressure on Bolivia to eradicate coca production in the Andean countries. The army invaded the Chapare during January of 1986, but after nearly three weeks of being surrounded by the workers in the narcotics industry and cut off from their supply bases, the army surrendered. In a nation the size of Texas and California combined, but with a population approximately the size of the city of Chicago, it is difficult for the government to control its own territory. Neither the Incas nor the Spanish conquistadores were ever able to conquer and administer the jungles of Bolivia, where there are still nomadic bands of Indians who have retreated deep into the jungle to escape Western encroachment. The army of the poorest government in South America is no better able to control this country than its predecessors. The government runs the cities, but the countryside and the jungles operate under their own laws.

One of the most significant effects of the coca trade and of the campaigns to eradicate it has come on the most remote Indians of the jungle area. As the campaign against drugs has pushed production into more inaccessible places and as the world demand has promoted greater cultivation of coca, the coca growers are moving into previously unexplored areas. A coca plantation has been opened along the Chimore river less than an hour's walk from one of the few surviving bands of Yuqui Indians. The Yuquis, famous for their eight-foot-long bows and their six-foot arrows, are now hovering on the brink of extinction. In the past year, the three bands of a few hundred Yuquis have lost eleven members in skirmishes with outsiders. In turn, they killed several outsiders this year and even shot the missionary who is their main champion against outside invaders.

According to the reports of missionaries, other Indian bands have been enlisted as workers in cocaine production and trafficking, making virtual slaves out of them. A Bolivian medical doctor explained to me that the Indians are fed the cocaine in their food as a way of keeping them working and preventing their escape. Through cocaine, the drug traffickers may be able to conquer and control these last remnants of the great Indian nations of the Americas. If so, they will accomplish what many have failed to do in the five-hundred-year campaign of Europeans to conquer the free Indians.

The fate of the Indians driven out of their homelands is shown in the case of Juan, a thirteen-year-old Indian boy from the Chimore river where the Yuquis live. I found him one night in a soup kitchen for street children operated in the corner of a potato warehouse by the Maryknoll priests. Juan wore a bright orange undershirt that proclaimed in bold letters Fairfax District Public Schools. I sat with him at the table coated in potato dust while he ate his soup with his fellow street children, some of whom were as young as four years old. He told me what he could remember of his life on the Chimore; he did not know to which tribe he was born or what language he had spoken with his mother. It was difficult for Juan to talk about his Indian past in a country where it is a grave insult to be called an Indian. Rather than talk about the Chimore or the Chapare, he wanted to ask me questions because I was the first American he had ever met. Was I stronger than everyone else, because he had heard that Americans were the strongest people in the world? Did we really have wolves and bears in North America, and was I afraid of them? Had I been to the Chapare? Did I use cocaine?

In between his questions, I found out that Juan had come to Cochabamba several years ago with his mother. The two had fled the Chapare, but he did not know why. Once in the city they lived on the streets for a few years until his mother died, and he had been living alone ever since. He had become a polilla (moth), as they call such street boys. To earn money he washed cars and sold cigarettes laced with pasta. When he tired of talking about himself and asking about the animals of North America, he and his two friends made plans to go out to one of the nearby *pasta* villages the next day.

Both the Chapare (which supplied the land for growing coca) and highland villages such as Pocona (which supplied the labor) were suffering from the cocaine boom. Where, then, is the profit? The only other sites in Bolivia are the newly developed manufacturing towns where cocaine is refined. Whereas in the past most of this refining took place in Colombia, both the manufacturers and the traffickers find it easier and cheaper to have the work done in Bolivia, closer to the source of coca leaves and closer to much cheaper sources of labor. The strength of the Colombian government and its closeness to the United States also make the drug trafficking more difficult there than in Bolivia, with its weak, unstable government in La Paz.

Toco is one of the villages that has turned into a processing point for cocaine. Located at about the same altitude as Pocona but only a half-day by truck from the Chapare, Toco cannot grow coca, but the village is close enough to the source to become a major producer of the *pasta*. Traffickers bring in the large shipments of coca leaves and work them in backyard "kitchens." Not only does Toco still have its young men at home and still have food and electricity, but it has work for a few hundred young men from other villages.

Unlike Pocona, for which there are only a few trucks each week, trucks flow in and out of Toco every day. Emblazoned with names such as Rambo, El Padrino (The Godfather), and Charles Bronson rather than the traditional truck names of San José, Virgen de Copacabana, or Flor de Urkupina, these are the newest and finest trucks found in Bolivia. Going in with a Bolivian physician and another anthropologist from the United States, I easily got a ride, along with a dozen Indians, on a truck which was hauling old car batteries splattered with what appeared to be vomit.

A few kilometers outside of Toco we were stopped by a large crowd of Indian peasants. Several dozen women sat around on the ground and in the road spinning yarn and knitting. Most of the women had babies tied to their shoulders in the brightly colored *awayu* cloth, which the women use to carry everything from potatoes to lambs. Men stood around with farm tools, which they now used to block the roads. The men brandished their machetes and rakes at us, accusing us all of being smugglers and *pisacocas*. Like the Indians on the truck with us, the three of us stood silent and expressionless in the melee.

The hostile peasants were staging an ad hoc strike against the coca trade. They had just had their own fields of potatoes washed away in a flash flood. Now without food and without money to replant, they were demanding that someone help them or they would disrupt all traffic to and from Toco. Shouting at us, several of them climbed on board the truck. Moving among the nervous passengers, they checked for a shipment of coca leaves, kerosene, acid, or anything else that might be a part of the coca trade. Having found nothing, they reluctantly let us pass with stern warnings not to return with cocaine or *pasta*. A few weeks after our encounter with the strikers, their strike ended and most of the men went off to look for work in the Chapare and in Toco; without a crop, the cocaine traffic was their only hope of food for the year.

On our arrival in Toco we found out that the batteries loaded with us in the back of the truck had been hollowed out and filled with acid to be used in making *pasta*. *Chicha* vomit had been smeared around to discourage anyone from checking them. After removal of the acid, the same batteries were then filled with plastic bags of cocaine to be smuggled out of Toco and into the town of Cliza and on to Cochabamba and the outside world.

Toco is an expanding village with new cement-block buildings going up on the edge of town and a variety of large plumbing pipes, tanks, and drains being installed. It also has a large number of motorcycles and cars. By Bolivian standards it is a rich village, but it is still poorer than the average village in Mexico or Brazil. Soon after our arrival in Toco, we were followed by a handful of men wanting to sell us *pasta*, and within a few minutes the few had grown to nearly fifty young men anxious to assist us. Most of them were on foot, but some of them circled us in motorcycles, and many of them were armed with guns and machetes. They became suspicious and then openly hostile when we convinced them that we did not want to buy *pasta*. To escape them we took refuge in the home of an Indian family and waited for the mob to disperse.

When we tried to leave the village a few hours later, we were trapped by a truckload of young men who did not release us until they had checked with everyone we had met with in the village. They wondered why we were there if not to buy *pasta*. We were rescued by the doctor who accompanied us; she happened to be the niece of a popular Quechua writer. Evoking the memory of her uncle who had done so much for the Quechua people, she convinced the villagers of Toco that we were Bolivian doctors who worked with her in Cochabamba, and that we were not foreigners coming to buy *pasta* or to spy on them. An old veteran who claimed that he had served in the Chaco War with her uncle vouched for us, but in return for having saved us he then wanted us to buy *pasta* from him.

The wealth generated by the coca trade from Bolivia is easy to see. It is in the European cars cruising the streets of Cochabamba and Santa Cruz, and in the nice houses in the suburbs. It is in the motorcycles and jeeps in Toco, Cliza, and Trinidad. The poverty is difficult to see because it is in the remote villages like Pocona, among the impoverished miners in the village of Porco, and intertwined in the lives of peasants throughout the highland districts of Potosí and Oruro. But it is in communities such as Pocona that 70 percent of the population of Bolivia lives. For every modern home built with cocaine money in Cochabamba, a tin mine lies abandoned in Potosi that lost many of its miners when the world price for tin fell and they had to go to the Chapare for food. For every new car in Santa Cruz or every new motorcycle in Toco, a whole village is going hungry in the mountains.

The money for coca does not go to the Bolivians. It goes to the criminal organizations that smuggle the drugs out of the country and into the United States and Europe. A gram of pure cocaine on the streets of Cochabamba costs five dollars; the same gram on the streets of New York, Paris, or Berlin costs over a hundred dollars. The price increase occurs outside Bolivia.

The financial differential is evident in the case of the American housewife and mother sentenced to the Cochabamba prison after being caught with six and a half kilograms of cocaine at the airport. Like all the other women in the prison, she now earns money washing laundry by hand at a cold-water tap in the middle of the prison yard. She receives the equivalent of twenty cents for each pair of pants she washes, dries, and irons. In Bolivian prisons, the prisoner has to furnish his or her own food, clothes, medical attention, and even furniture.

She was paid five thousand dollars to smuggle the cocaine out of Bolivia to the Caribbean. Presumably someone else was then to be paid even more to smuggle it into the United States or Europe. The money that the American housewife received to smuggle the cocaine out of the country would pay the salary of eighty *pisacocas* for a month. It would also pay the monthly wages of two hundred fifty Bolivian schoolteachers, who earn the equivalent of twenty U.S. dollars per month in pay. Even though her price seemed high by Bolivian standards, it is a small part of the final money generated by the drugs. When cut and sold on the streets of the United States, her shipment of cocaine would probably bring in five to seven million dollars. Of that amount, however, only about five hundred dollars goes to the Bolivian farmer.

The peasant in the Chapare growing the coca earns three times as much for a field of coca as he would for a field of papayas. But he is only the first in a long line of people and transactions that brings the final product of cocaine to the streets of the West. At the end of the line, cocaine sells for four to five times its weight in gold.

The United States government made all aid programs and loans to Bolivia dependent on the country's efforts to destroy coca. This produces programs in which Bolivian troops go into the most accessible areas and uproot a few fields of aging or diseased coca plants. Visiting drug-enforcement agents from the United States together with American congressmen applaud, make their reports on the escalating war against drugs, and then retire to a city hotel where they drink hot cups of coca tea and cocktails.

These programs hurt primarily the poor farmer who tries to make a slightly better living by growing coca rather than papayas. The raids on the fields and cocaine factories usually lead to the imprisonment of ulcerated *pisococas* and women and children *hormigas* from villages throughout Bolivia. Local authorities present the burned fields and full prisons to Washington visitors as proof that the Bolivian government has taken a hard stance against drug trafficking.

International crime figures with bank accounts in New York and Zurich get the money. Bolivia ends up with hunger in its villages, young men with their hands and feet permanently maimed, higher rates of venereal disease, chronic food shortages, less kerosene, higher school dropout rates, increased drug addiction, and a worthless peso.

Review Questions

1. List and describe the major effects of the cocaine trade on rural Bolivian life.

2. Why have the production of coca and the manufacture of cocaine created a health hazard in Bolivia?

3. Why has the cocaine trade benefited the Bolivian economy so little?

4. How has the cocaine trade disrupted village social organization in Bolivia?

This article was published in *Conformity & Conflict* Copyright ©1986 by Jack Weatherford. Reprinted by permission.

CHAPTER TWENTY FOUR

Malawi Versus the World Bank

Sonia Patten

Market economics rules in most industrialized countries, especially since the decline of communism. In market systems, goods are produced for sale, prices affect demand and vice-versa, and demand drives production. Underlying the system is the profit motive to get the greatest gain for the least cost. The market not only applies to manufacturing and providing services in industrialized societies but also governs agriculture although most governments interfere with it to some extent in that economic sphere. It is no wonder that most economists from industrialized nations believe that the free market system is the key to development in nonindustrialized societies, and this has led institutions such as the World Bank and the International Monetary Fund (IMF) to drop social and agricultural support programs in favor of market-based development as a requirement of receiving loans.

There is a problem, however, at least initially, with the market-based approach to development especially as it applies to agriculture. In many nonindustrialized societies, a majority of the people farm small plots of land in order to feed their families and meet social obligations to kin and neighbors. When floods, draught, exhausted soils, and other factors reduce yields and people face starvation, only government aid, not market-based programs, can help them. That is the point Sonia Patten makes in this article as she discusses conditions in the small south African country of Malawi. She notes that international lending agencies required the Malawian government to cease underwriting the cost of fertilizer in favor of a market-based system. As a result, the exhausted land produced less maize and people began to starve. Eventually, the government

of Malawi overruled their international lenders and reinstituted
a program to provide fertilizer to farm families. The result was
a grain surplus, the end of famine, and improved health for the
nation's citizens.

This article is about the impact a group of economic organizations called the "Washington Consensus" has on rural families living in the small southern African nation of Malawi. The "Washington Consensus," which is located in Washington, D.C., as the name implies, and its associated economists and policymakers created a situation in Malawi that forced rural farmers there to trade a day's labor for a days food, dismantle their homes to sell timbers and roofing for cash so they could purchase food, beg for food, or go hungry. One can challenge statements about the causal relationships between macro-level and micro-level socioeconomic decisions and events, but in this instance the connections seem clear. A review of "Washington Consensus" policy and the information provided by women in ten rural Malawi households over a period of eighteen months helps us understand just how individuals and families struggle to survive when macro-level economic policies have an adverse impact on them.

The "Washington Consensus" refers to a set of economic prescriptions derived from policies of the International Monetary Fund (IMF) and the World Bank (both headquartered in Washington, D.C.) and endorsed by the U.S. Treasury Department. The goal for these policies and prescriptions is to bring about basic economic reform in poor nations, rapidly moving their economies in the direction of capitalism and incorporation into the global marketplace. When a government applies for a loan from these international lending agencies, it must agree to abide by a structural adjustment program (SAP) based on these economic policies and prescriptions. Thus, the conditions for securing a loan include the following: (1) cuts in spending for health, education, and all forms of social welfare; (2) privatization of all state-owned enterprises; (3) opening the economy to foreign competition and direct foreign investment; (4) allowing the market to determine interest rates; (5) managing currency exchange rates to keep them stable. Additionally, governments are to broaden the tax base in order to collect more revenue, deregulate labor markets, and stop using public monies to subsidize commodities, thus increasing the cost to consumers. It is this last point, the withdrawal of subsidies, that I will focus on. The commodity in question is commercial fertilizer, an absolutely essential agricultural input for even the smallest subsistence farmer.

Malawi is one of the poorest nations in the world. It has a population of about thirteen million people, 95 percent engaged in rain-fed agriculture, mostly on smallholdings of about one to four acres. It takes about two-thirds of an acre per person to have a reasonable chance of producing sufficient food to meet subsistence needs for a family. The nation has more or less reached the limit of its possible area of cultivation, and is suffering from the problems that accompany deforestation as people have cut trees to clear land for firewood for cooking and brick-making. There is no longer a fallow period for cropland—farmers plant all of their land every year.

The staple crop is white maize (corn); it is consumed at every meal. Over 90 percent of cultivable land in Malawi is planted to maize. It is hard on the soil, rapidly leaching it of nutrients, especially nitrogen. Presently, if commercial fertilizer high in nitrogen is not applied during the growing season, the amount of maize harvested is greatly diminished. Households are unable to meet their subsistence needs and have no surplus to put on the market. The "season of hunger," that period of time between family consumption of the last store of maize from the previous harvest (any time between early September and late December) and the beginning of the next harvest (in late March or April) grows longer, and families have to find a way to cope.

Fertilizer subsidies have a long history in Malawi. They began in 1952 while the country was still a British colony. The objectives of the subsidy were to ensure distribution of a vital agricultural input at a low cost to even the most geographically remote smallholder farmer, thus increasing output of maize, the priority crop, and to maintain soil fertility. The subsidies continued after independence and into the 1970s. In 1981 the country experienced a balance of payments problem and turned to the World Bank and IMF for assistance in the form of loans. Thus, Malawi has been indebted to and under the influence of these international lending agencies longer than any other African nation, and the involvement continues up to the present. As early as 1984, the World Bank and IMF began attributing problems in the economy to government subsidy policies, particularly with regard to commercial fertilizer. By 1985 the government began progressive reduction of the fertilizer subsidy. By the 1990s, there was complete deregulation and liberalization of the fertilizer and seed markets in Malawi, under the tutelage of the international lending institutions. The process was finalized in 1994/95 with complete removal of all types of subsidies and price controls on all agricultural inputs and products. At the same time there was 40 percent depreciation in the value of the currency and inflation soared from 20 percent to 53 percent.

This was an absolute crisis for small farmers. Harvests fell and malnutrition rose. By the month of June, most rural families were reduced to eating two meals a day. Over a third of rural families were running out of stored maize by September and 80 percent by September. More than 25 percent of under-five children were underweight and more than half were stunted by long-term malnutrition. The country was struggling with the heavy burden of HIV/AIDS, and life expectancy had fallen to 37 years. World Bank economists had begun to get a sense that all was not well, all was not going according to plan, and perhaps a social safety net was needed to "catch" those who were most vulnerable. A number of fertilizer programs were begun to try and meet the needs of smallholders and allow them to have a greater likelihood of producing sufficient food to feed their families.

Government programs like the Starter Pak Initiative and Targeted Input Programme were created to distribute free or subsidized fertilizer. The results were mixed at best.

Big farmers were not eligible for these programs, which relied on the distribution of vouchers to smallholders through village headmen. A voucher could then be exchanged for a 50 kg bag of fertilizer free or at a subsidized price, depending on the program. But headmen sometimes sold the vouchers rather than distribute them. And big farmers would have vendors with coupons buy bags of fertilizer at the subsidized price, then pay the vendors a fee for this service, and re-sell the bags for a handsome profit. The supply of subsidized fertilizer was quickly depleted, long before most small farmers had secured any. Another social safety net program put rural men and women to work building roads, and at the end of several days of work, they were paid with a 50 kg bag of fertilizer. It took so much work to earn a bag that many people refused to participate, saying it seemed like a kind of slavery.

How did individual households cope with these dire circumstances? This is what I learned from ten women in one village where few families could afford a sufficient amount of fertilizer. Some of the families were able to secure one bag, allowing them one application on their maize crop; it takes three applications during a growing season for optimal results. Most of the families used no fertilizer at all. In 2005, all but one family consumed all of their stored food by September, and some as early as August. Normally August is the time of year when weddings take place, when ancestors are honored. These events require contributions of food from each household, but in 2005 the village headman decreed that no household should make these contributions because everyone was suffering from insufficient food.

The first strategy that families turned to in the hunger crisis was to skip meals. When there is sufficient food, people eat *nsima* (maize porridge) three times a day—breakfast, lunch and supper. When there is a food shortage, breakfast is no longer prepared. As the situation continued to deteriorate, women began to mix maize flour, the regular ingredient for *nsima,* with maize bran, which is usually used for animal feed. The next step was to use cassava rather than maize for the noon meal. Cassava is nutrient poor, and most people in the Central Region don't like it. By this time men and women were actively seeking work that they could exchange for food—a day's work in a rich farmer's fields in exchange for enough maize flour to prepare a meal. If such work could not be found, people began to sell off their assets in order to buy maize, which was in short supply and thus very expensive. They sold animals, bricks, sheets of corrugated metal roofing, timbers that had supported their houses—whatever they had that could be sold for money or exchanged for maize. The absolute last resort was to sell land or exchange land for maize. And I was told that some older women who had no family in the vicinity were so desperately hungry that they went door to door begging for something to eat.

It is during this season of hunger that the land must be prepared and the next crop planted and cultivated. When hunger is great, maize will be harvested and cooked while it is still green and other foodstuffs like pumpkins will be cooked when they are small. People can't wait for them to mature—they might starve in the interim.

So how it is that World Bank and IMF economists would mandate a policy that causes so much human suffering? The current president of Malawi, Bingu wa Mutharika, must have asked the same question. He is an economist trained at a prominent U.S. university, and is well aware that Western nations heavily subsidize their farmers. After the disastrous 2005 harvest that required emergency food aid for five million Malawians, he reinstated and deepened fertilizer subsidies over the protests of the U.S. The result? The 2007 maize harvest was so big that Malawi is exporting hundreds of thousands of tons to neighboring countries. The national granaries are full. Acute hunger in children has fallen so sharply that the UN-donated powdered milk stockpiled for treating hungry children has been sent on to other African nations still in need. In sum, it appears that the policies generated by the Washington Consensus may need to be reconfigured when it comes to public investment in African agriculture, especially agriculture practiced by subsistence farmers who are unable to produce enough grain for sale to pay for the fertilizer that will ensure a surplus.

Review Questions

1. What is the "Washington Consensus"?

2. What are the five points of the Washington Consensus' Structural Adjustment Program (SAP)? What is the economic theory behind them?

3. What is the history of farm support in Malawi and how did taking loans from the World Bank and IMF change that history?

4. Why is chemical fertilizer so important to farming in Malawi?

5. When it followed SAP guidelines, the government of Malawi ceased to provide fertilizer for its farmers. How did that impact the country's people and agricultural output?

6. What happened when the government of Malawi recently again began to provide fertilizer for its farmers? What does that say about World Bank and IMF policy?

12
POSTCOLONIALISM

CHAPTER TWENTY FIVE

The Kindness of Strangers: The U.S. and Iraq

Robin Fox

We typically view the era of Western colonialism and more recently some aspects of U.S. foreign policy as systems of exploitation. Colonials, we claim, were there to extract raw materials and tap cheap labor; today the U.S. also wants raw materials, especially oil, as it enters the affairs of other countries. Although there is ample evidence to support this view, we should recognize another motive for Western intervention in other countries: the gift of civilization and for Americans, our view of freedom and democracy. In this selection, Robin Fox stresses this last point. He notes that like Protestant missionaries, we believe that the "love of freedom" and "democracy" are part of human nature. All we need to do is give it to people, and they will naturally see the light. When people don't accept the gift, we treat them as if we are stern parents "helping" them to do what is best for them. Our invasion of Iraq was certainly about oil, but it was just as much about bringing democracy to the "Iraqi people." But Iraq was cobbled together after World War 1 by the British, and its people direct their loyalty not to the state but to family, clan, tribe, and sect. Rather than a part of human nature, democracy, Fox concludes, defies human nature and takes work to create and maintain.

Since Laocoön's warning to his fellow Trojans went so tragically unheeded, the course of history has been strewn with the corpses of ungrateful nations which, despite the misery that stemmed from their inability to govern their own affairs, bitterly resented and actively resisted the firm and forceful help of others. The strangers gift of peace, order, and prosperity is less welcome to us than the death, chaos, and poverty that are our own doing. For in the end they are our own, and that is what matters to us. Like truculent adolescents, we do not want to be told how to do things or have them done for us; we want to make our own, even fatal, mistakes. We will take what we can use from what is offered, but we want, at last, to do it ourselves: to manage our own lives, however badly. The main thing about the stranger, after all, is that he is strange. He is not like us; he will never understand us. Our greatest fear, perhaps because the possibility is often so seductive, is that we will become like him and lose our selves. The stranger's gift never comes without strings, and we do not want to be tied.

We of the post-Enlightenment Anglophone West are among the most earnest of the givers. We are not, like our medieval Catholic ancestors, really proponents of the Crusade and the holy war against the heathen. We are at heart Protestant missionaries. We want to bring the good news and the benefits of civilization to the benighted of the earth. And if they don't want it, then like Protestant parents, and entirely for their own good of course, we must sternly make them accept it. Certainly, we hoped to make profits and attain political power in the process, but these were small prices the benighted had to pay for the incomparable gifts we had to offer. Critics of colonialism miss the point if all they see is the profits and the power. Our civilizing mission was, and still is, as dear to us as the jihad is to Muslims. Even when it is not Protestantism per se that we are offering, it is the children of the Protestant Ethic that we know as democracy, liberty, equality, and the free market. Our learned men tell us we are the foreordained bearers of a truth so fundamental that with its triumph history will come to an end, there being nothing left for mankind to achieve. If this is so, how can the benighted so stubbornly, and even violently, refuse our gift of a free leg up onto the stage of world history?

There is no question that we went into Iraq to defend our oil interests: that, at least, was the rational part. But the holy warriors of the White House saw a far greater opportunity. They could plant the banner of liberal democracy in the heartland of Arab totalitarianism, and thus change the world for the better. To do this was to collaborate with the inevitable progress of mankind—a sure winner of a policy. We would simply give the inevitable progress a friendly shove in the right direction. The "Iraqi People" (much invoked) would greet us as liberators and gratefully accept our gift of free elections. How could they possibly prefer the savagery of Saddam and the hegemony of the brutes of Baath? Once rid of these monsters, the "Iraqi People"—like people everywhere, as "lovers of freedom"— would set up a representative democracy modeled on our own. Ballot boxes and purple finger paint would be provided, political parties would be free to form, the press would be unrestricted. This model democracy would stand as a rebuke and an example to the monstrous regimes in the Middle East, which would gradually succumb to the same happy fate. What is more, it would be an Arab democracy, thus saving the Arabs from the embarrassment of Israel being the only democratic state in the region. Since democracies are inherently peaceful, the more of them in the region the better, and the better for our "national security." And above all, as the guarantors of this liberal democratic paradise, we would have a continuing benign influence in the area, which would, incidentally, protect our oil interests.

For the missionaries this was a chance too good to be missed. Saddams regime was ripe for the plucking. There was no way its army could stand up to the superior Western forces, and once the army was disbanded, the criminals tried, and "de-Baathification" completed, the grateful freed "People of Iraq" would take it from there. They would need help and firm guidance from the missionaries, of course. They would make mistakes, and there would be all the baggage of dictatorship to unpack. But it had been done in Japan and Germany with startling success (both totally misleading examples, as it happens), why not in Iraq? To suggest otherwise, said George W. Bush, was to suggest that the "Iraqi People" were inherently incapable of "freedom and democracy." That was to be condescending and colonialist. Everyone everywhere wanted these benefits, and only wicked regimes prevented them from realizing these universal human goals, toward which, we must not forget, mankind was inevitably evolving anyway.

I am not caricaturing this position. Those who would see the ideology as a cynical cover for the arms industry, Halliburton, and Big Oil are missing what is truly at issue here, and what is much more frightening. The colonial powers always look out for their economic and strategic interests; it would be foolish of them not to. But they have also always believed the "civilizing mission" to be just as important. This was justified partly by religion—bringing Christianity to the heathen—but was also seen as an end in itself: the production of an industrial, peaceful, democratic (sometimes socialist) world.

As societies evolved from military to industrial institutions, so would peace and democracy spread around the globe. Free-trade advocates repeat it today: the more we are dependent on each other through trade, the less likely will we be to fight each other. Trade requires the rule of law, the rule of law promotes democracy, and democracies don't fight each other—we know the logic. This is the fundamental belief of the missionaries. We have a precious gift that we can give the nations of the world, and whether they want it or not, we are going to give it to them. If they think they don't want it, then they must be re-educated, with force if necessary, to realize that they do. History is going to end in universal liberal democracy, so they might as well learn to co-operate with the inevitable.

The problem for liberal and radical critics of Bushism in the West is that they really believe this too. It is no longer fashionable to think that some form of communism or socialism will be the inevitable end product, but some kind of democratic open society is seen as the only alternative for the decolonized peoples of the world. It is hard to find any fervent postcolonialist who will agree that, having thrown off the imperial yoke, the ex-colonial peoples should be free to choose dictatorship, theocracy, tribalism, nepotism, clitoridectomy, or the rule of warlords. Respect for "indigenous cultures" goes only so far. The left-liberals assume as fervently as the Bushites that people everywhere aspire to a state of liberal democratic polity where human rights and the rights of women will be assured and tolerance and religious freedom will be institutionalized. It is to their constant embarrassment that this does not happen, and fifty years later the excuse that the failure lies in the pernicious aftereffects of colonialism is wearing thin; they do not really believe it themselves. (They have substituted neocolonialism, neoliberalism, globalization, transnational corporations.) But the alternative is hard to bear for the progressive mentality that assumes we can indeed write our own script and exclude all those factors of "human nature" that seem so stubbornly to resist our enlightened blandishments.

Against this naive optimism of the missionaries of whatever stripe, we can set an opposing view that is historical and what we might call naturalistic. It sees that the institutions we so prize are not the *product of a* freedom-loving human nature but the result of many centuries of effort to *overcome* human nature. However desirable they may be, they are not natural to us. We maintain them with constant vigilance and the support of hard-won economic, political, legal, and social structures. These have taken literally thousands of years to put in place. In England universal suffrage had to wait until 1928, when women under thirty were finally included. In the United States it was only after the Voting Rights Act of 1965 that we can be said to have achieved true democracy. Far from being a fact of human nature, the voluntary ceding of power after elections, the basic feature of liberal democracy, actually flies in the face of nature. It is self-evidently absurd. Our political opponents are always disreputable and their accession to power will be the ruin of the country. Listen to the rhetoric of campaigns: allowing the opponents to take over amounts to almost criminal malfeasance. Yet that is what we do after a mere counting of heads—cede control to the villains and incompetents.

The cynic will say that we allow this to happen only because we know there is no real difference between political parties in these systems, and so we join in a conspiracy of the willing to take our turns. Even so, this willingness that we take for granted is an amazing, unusual, and fragile thing. Our Western democracies still struggle with nepotism and corruption whose energetic persistence should tell us something. How could we believe then that we could walk into a country like Iraq and do in a few months, or even a few years, or even several decades, what millennia had failed to evolve spontaneously? Because the "Iraqi People," like everyone else, "loved freedom"?

For a start, there are no "Iraqi People." The phrase is pure rhetoric. Iraq as a "nation" (like the "nation" of Kuwait) was devised by the compasses and protractors of Gertrude Bell when the British and French divided up the Middle East after World War 1. We know well enough the ethnic-religious division into Kurd, Sunni, and Shiite. But what is not understood is that Iraq, like the other countries of the region, still stands at a level of social evolution where the family, clan, tribe, and sect command major allegiance, and the idea of the individual autonomous voter, necessary and commonplace in our own systems, is totally foreign, and would not make sense to the "average Ahmed."

I received a call in 2003 from a *New York Times* reporter, John Tierney, who was baffled by what he discovered in his Baghdad hotel. Each week there was a lavish wedding in the dining room and ball-room. It looked very Western until he discovered that the bride and groom were inevitably cousins, and, more than that, they were most often paternal parallel first cousins, as the jargon has it; they were the children of two brothers, and if they were not that close, then the bride was usually from the same paternal clan as the groom. Occasionally, a woman from the mother's paternal clan was married, as in the case of Saddam Hussein. When questioned about this, the young people told the reporter, "Of course we marry a cousin. What would you have us do, marry a stranger? We cannot trust strangers." Such a system of close-cousin marriage, the commonest form of preferred marriage in Arab society, literally keeps the marriage in the family. These groups are inward-looking and suspicious of strangers. It is the "Mafia solution" to life: never go against the family. Trust is only possible, ultimately, between close relatives, and preferably those of the paternal clan. The idea of voluntarily doing anything for strangers has to be worked at. It is another of those things we in Western democracies do every day without thought. It is "human nature" for us. We give large sums of our money to complete strangers to distribute to other strangers for purposes often unknown to us. This is taxation. It is everywhere hated, but absolutely necessary to run a complex society. We trust strangers to do things absolutely essential to our lives and welfare. We take it for granted they will do them: they are doing their jobs. But this is as foreign to much of the world as our odd acceptance of the relinquishment of power. And to that same world it borders on the immoral as well as the insane. In those places where the state cannot be trusted with the welfare of individuals, they turn to the older and wiser certainty of kinship.

When there was no electricity in Baghdad, the reason was that as soon as copper cable was laid, the Iraqis came out in the night and stole it. Copper brought a good price. When the troops expostulated with those caught and tried to make them see that their theft was against the "Iraqi People," the indignant thieves demanded to know who these "Iraqi People" were who stood between them and the feeding of their starving families. They were responsible not for some mythical Iraqi People but for their kin: their cousins who were their spouses. The few ambulances in Baghdad cannot function properly to get the injured from bombings to the hospitals. The armed clansmen of the injured commandeer the ambulances and turn out the unrelated wounded. Firefights often break out between armed groups competing for the ambulances. Remember the graphic scene in *Lawrence of Arabia* when the tribal chief Auda, played by Anthony Quinn, is told he should join in the attack on the Turks in Aqaba for the sake of "the Arabs." "What tribe is that?" he asks. He recites the tribes he knows, but demands to know what tribe is "the Arabs" that he should sacrifice for them. "The English" he understands as a tribe he can ally with against his enemies, including the Turks if it suits him. Thus some of the sheikhs in Anbar ally with the Americans against Al Qaeda and its allies if it suits them. But their and Auda's sole concern is with their tribal advantage. This was Auda's highest moral imperative. And Auda loved freedom above all other things.

If this tribal "mentality" is closer to the default system of human nature than is our cherished individualistic democracy, then we ignore its appeal at our peril. The marriage of close cousins may appear to us backward, unhygienic, or immoral, but it is the pattern that has dominated the world until fairly recently. If we could get into God's memory, we would find that the majority of marriages throughout history have been with close cousins. In the West we had to move from tribalism, through empire, feudalism, mercantile capitalism, and the Industrial Revolution to reach our present state of fragile democracy (shrugging off communism and fascism along the way). We were helped in the shedding of dominant kinship groups by the relative individualism of the Angles and Saxons with their emphasis on the independent nuclear family, and then by Christian monogamy and the banning of cousin marriages by the Church. And we had to do it by our own efforts, to pull ourselves up by the social bootstraps, to make it stick. We have seen in Germany, in Italy, and in Spain how fragile this really is. Russia never did make it. France is always problematic. Latin America and the Balkans continue to be a mess. But in making this move we had to change the entire communalistic, ritualistic, kinship-dominated society that is natural to us. We had to transform "nepotism" and "corruption" from tribal virtues into criminal offenses, and we have to keep at it all the time. I live in New Jersey and I stare into the pit.

The future is hypothetical. The old formula "no bourgeoisie, no democracy" still holds. What independent professional class there was in Iraq, with its need for the rule of law to guarantee contracts, was destroyed by Saddam. It is something we cannot re-create with any amount of aid or surges, nor can we force it upon the "Iraqi People." The price of failure, says Bush, is too high. But failure was written all over this enterprise from the start. The goals set, beyond the toppling of Saddam, were impossible, and the real mystery is why our leaders ever thought they could be achieved. The administration may, by increased force and bribery (the "Iraqi People" understand both very well), patch up some kind of "order" for a while. But it cannot create the whole civil infrastructure and the sea change of values that underpin a functioning liberal democracy. To do that you have to turn tribesmen into citizens.

These White House children of the Protestant Ethic should understand how hard won is the open society we live in, how much it is the work of centuries of struggle and suffering, how fragile it is, and how we *had to do it for ourselves*. Our fundamentalist Islamic opponents have on their side the atavistic attractions of the closed society, and we should take them at least as seriously as they take us. Before we try to make them over in our image, we should remember how unnervingly recent was our own makeover, and act with becoming humility and caution. A helping hand here and there may not be amiss, but we should never be surprised at the rejection of the stranger's gift.

Review Questions

1. According to Fox, how do people usually act when strangers try to give them things?

2. What mission has characterized Western colonial intervention in other peoples countries?

3. Americans believe that people everywhere long for something. What is it, and how does this belief relate to our actions toward Iraq?

4. Why is the phrase "Iraqi people" wrong, according to Fox?

5. Where do most people in Iraq place their loyalty, and how does this affect how they see the U.S. presence in their country?

6. Why is it important to know who Iraqis marry, and what does this tell us about political structures in Iraq?

7. How has democracy emerged in the world, and what does that say about human nature and prospects for U.S. success in Iraq?

13

GLOBAL CHALLENGES AND ANTHROPOLOGY

CHAPTER TWENTY SIX

Cross-Cultural Law: The Case of the Gypsy Offender

Anne Sutherland

Every society recognizes a list of legal statutes, which anthropologists call substantive law, that define right from wrong. In the United States, for example, it is against the law for an individual to marry more than one person at a time. But what is proper in one country may be a crime in another. Unlike the United States, for example, in Iran it is legal for a person to be married simultaneously to more than one person. So what happens when members of one society live within and under the legal jurisdiction of another? This is the question explored by Anne Sutherland in this article on the legal plight of a young Gypsy man who is arrested for using the Social Security number of a relative on a car loan application. Despite the claim that using different identities of family members is a common Gypsy practice designed to hide their identities, and that he had no intention to defraud anyone by doing so, the young man receives a six-month jail term.

It is often the case that a law made for one set of purposes has another, unintended impact on a particular group. A recent law making the use of a false social security number a federal felony is intended to help prosecution of major drug crime syndicates, but it has a special impact on Gypsies in the United States. Gypsies, traditionally a nomadic people, frequently borrow each others' "American" names and social security numbers, viewing them as a kind of corporate property of their kin group or *vitsa*. They also often lack birth certificates and must obtain midwife or baptismal certificates to use for identification purposes when they try to obtain credit, enter school, or apply for welfare.

In this article, I shall examine the case of a nineteen-year-old Gypsy man who was convicted under the new social security law and served six months in jail. Arguments for the defense in the case followed three lines of reasoning: 1) that this law unfairly singled out Gypsies for punishment; 2) that there was no intent to commit a crime; and 3) that in using the social security numbers of relatives, Gypsies were following a time-honored tradition to remain anonymous and separate from non-Gypsy society.

Facts of the Case

In the fall of 1991 in St. Paul, Minnesota, a nineteen-year-old Gypsy man was convicted of the crime of using his five-year-old nephew's social security number to obtain credit to purchase a car. When the purchase was questioned by the car dealership, he returned the car and was arrested on a felony charge of using a false social security number. After he was arrested, police searched the apartment where he was staying. They found lists of names, addresses and social security numbers, leading them to suspect an organized crime ring.

In *The United States of America v. S.N.,*[1] it was "alleged that the defendant, S.N., while in the process of obtaining a new Ford Mustang from a car dealership, used a social security number that was not his own with intent to deceive." Under the statute 42 U.S.C. 408 (g)(2), a person who, with intent to deceive, falsely represents his or her number to obtain something of value or for any other purpose, is a felon.

In Mr. S.N.'s case there is no specific allegation that he intended to deprive another person permanently of property because the focus of the charging statute is false representation of numbers. The underlying purpose which motivates a person to falsely represent his or her number may be an essentially innocent purpose, but the statute, at least as it has been interpreted, does not appear to impose a burden of proof as to wrongful purpose.

The statute punishes the means (false number) which a person may employ to achieve any number of ends and it punishes those means

---

1   *United States* v. *Sonny Nicholas,* U.S. District Court, State of Minnesota, CR 4-91-137 (1991). Quotes from Philip Leavenworth, memorandum in support of a motion to declare 42 U.S.C.408(g)(2) unconstitutional.

as a felony. The lawyer for the defense argued that the statute's failure to address the nature of the purpose to which false credentials are used is a serious flaw in the law and may punish those who would use the number for petty misconduct as felons. He also argued that there is a potential for discriminatory impact on Gypsies who use false credentials to conceal themselves from mainstream society. A Gypsy household may obtain a telephone by providing a false social security number and even if they pay the telephone bill without fail for years, they are felons under this law. S.N. not only made the payments for his car, but he returned it when the number was questioned. He is still a felon under this law.

The defense lawyer argued that the law is objectionable for two reasons. First, the law's disproportionate impact on the Gypsies is objectionable under the equal protection guaranteed in the Fifth Amendment of the U.S. Constitution. He argued that the law denies Gypsies equal protection of the law by irrationally and disproportionately punishing at the felony level certain traditional Gypsy actions which cause no positive injury to anyone. As evidence he used material from my book, *Gypsies: The Hidden Americans*, for testimony that Gypsies routinely use false social security numbers to acquire credit but do pay their bills and are available for repossession in case of default of payment. They get phone service, buy houses and cars and other household items on credit and have a record of payment that is probably better than the general population *(United States v. S.N., 1991)*. They do this primarily to remain unknown by mainstream society rather than to cause loss or injury to any person.

Second, as the defense lawyer pointed out, there is a Supreme Court decision that requires the government to prove felonious intent when it seeks to punish a person for wrongful acquisition of another's property. S.N. maintained that he used a false social security number because of a Gypsy tradition to remain anonymous and because his own number had been used by other Gypsies. The government argued that there was a "ring" of Gypsies in the area where S.N. was living. At S.N.'s residence a number of false credentials and social security numbers were found which had been used to obtain cars illegally. Some of these cars are still missing. In other words, there was evidence that false identity had been used recently in the area to steal. In this case, however, S.N. had not stolen anything and was not being accused of stealing, but only of using a false social security number.

Because of the evidence of a ring of car thieves in the area, the prosecution hoped to use the threat of prosecution against S.N., the only Gypsy they had been able to arrest, to plea bargain for information regarding the other people involved in the alleged ring. These other people had disappeared immediately as soon as S.N. was arrested.

One of the problems in the case was that both the prosecution and even the defense had difficulty obtaining complete and accurate information on S.N. For example, they had difficulty determining his "real" name, a moot point for the Gypsies since they have a practice of using many "American" names although they only have one "Gypsy" name *(nav romano)*. The Gypsy name of *o Spiro le Stevanosko* (or Spiro the son of Stevan) uses the noun declension characteristic of the Sanskrit-rooted Rom language and is not immediately translatable into English since it does not employ a surname. Spiro's identity can be pinned down by finding out what *vitsa* (a cognatic descent group) he belongs to so that he will not be confused with any other Spiro le Stevanoskos. The Spiro of our example is a *Kashtare* which is part of a larger "nation" of Gypsies or *natsia* called *Kalderasha* (coppersmith). For his "American" names he may take any of a number used by his relatives such as Spiro Costello, John Costello, John Marks, John Miller, Spiro John or Spiro Miller. His nickname is Rattlesnake Pete.

The Anthropologist as Cultural Broker

S.N.'s defense attorney contacted me after finding that he was less confused about S.N. after reading my book about Gypsies. He sought my help in determining whether S.N. was a Gypsy, what his name was, and any other cultural information (such as the use of social security numbers by Gypsies) that would help him with his case.

Consequently, one cold autumn day I drove to the federal holding prison, one and a half hours from the city, and met S.N. He was a thin young man, perpetually fearful of pollution from contact with non-Gypsies and suffering from the effects of several months of what for him was solitary confinement since he had not seen any of his people since being incarcerated. The telephone was his only link with people to whom he could relate, people from his own culture who spoke his language. His main contact was with a non-Gypsy woman who lived with one of his relatives. She was his link with the world he had known and the only "American" household he had been in before prison. Since my primary task was to determine if he was a Gypsy, first I talked to him about his relatives in Los Angeles and his *vitsa* (Yowane) and tried to establish what section of the *vitsa* I personally knew. This exchange of information about *vitsa* and Gypsies of mutual acquaintance is a normal one between Gypsies. The purpose was to establish a link between us.

Then I asked him about why he was in Minnesota. He talked about a seasonal expedition he and his brothers and cousins make to Minnesota to buy and sell cars and fix fenders before winter sets in. He claimed not to know where his brothers and cousins had gone or how he got into his present predicament.

For S.N., the most immediately effective action I could take was to see that he got the food he needed to stay "clean" in jail. When I met him he had lost fifteen pounds and was suffering demonstrable distress and nervousness. He was upset at being cut off from his culture and people for the first time in his life. In addition, he was distressed at being incarcerated and fearful for his safety. More importantly, he was worried he would become defiled or *marime*. A major concern of his was that if he ate food prepared by non-Gypsies who did not follow rules of cleanliness considered essential in the Gypsy culture, he would become *marime,* a condition of ritual impurity that would result in his being shunned by his relatives and other Gypsies. To protect himself, he avoided eating prison food in the hopes that when he was released from prison he would be able to return to his family without a period of physical exile, also called *marime* (or "rejected" as the Gypsies translate it into English). I arranged for his lawyer to provide him with money to buy food from the concession because it is packaged and untouched by non-Gypsies and therefore considered clean by Gypsy standards. He bought milk in cartons, candy bars and soft drinks and other packaged foods that, though they may lack in nutrition, at least were not defiling and kept him from starvation.

A further complicating factor for S.N. was that he spoke English as a second language. He had only a rudimentary ability to read, thus straining his grasp of his defense. And his only contact with relatives was by telephone since neither he nor they could write with any ease. Even though his limited English made it difficult for him to follow his own trial, the court did not provide a translator.

The Trial

The trial was held in Federal Court and centered around the constitutionality of a law that unfairly targets a particular ethnic group and the question of intent to commit a crime. My testimony was intended to establish that Gypsies may use false identification for a number of cultural reasons which may have no connection to any intent to commit a crime. For a traditionally nomadic group with pariah status in the wider society and a pattern of secretiveness and autonomy, concealing identity is a long-established pattern.

This pattern is widespread in all Gypsy groups in Eastern Europe, Western Europe, Russia, Latin America and the United States. It is a mechanism they have developed over centuries to protect themselves from a wider society that has persecuted them or driven them away. The recent case of the German government paying large sums to Romania to take back Gypsy refugees is only the latest in a historically established tradition of discrimination against Gypsies. The persecution of Gypsies in the Holocaust, in medieval Europe and in the early part of the 20th century in the United States has been well documented. Current events in Eastern Europe have shown a resurgence of extreme prejudice against Gypsies. Interviews in recent *New York Times* articles have pointed to a hatred of Gypsies so deep that there is talk of extermination.[2] Because of the history of violence against them, Gypsies have developed elaborate mechanisms of secrecy and have hidden their identity in order to survive. It will not be easy to get them to change this pattern that has stood them in good stead for so many centuries.

The purpose of my testimony was to establish that S.N. *was* a Gypsy and that Gypsies often use false identification without intent to defraud. They do so because as members of a *vitsa*, or cognatic descent group, identification is corporate in nature. Members of the group have corporate access to property owned by other members of the group. That property includes forms of identification.

An additional problem in the S.N. case was the question of identification from photographs. Here we encountered the age-old problem that members of one culture and race have trouble identifying individuals from another culture and race. In simple terms, to many non-Gypsies, all Gypsies look alike. Part of the case involved clearing up erroneous identification of S.N. in photos provided by the prosecution.

I was also asked to testify on my own personal experience with discrimination against Gypsies by the Minneapolis Police Department. One instance of discrimination I related to the court occurred during a talk I gave to some twenty police officers to help them understand Gypsy culture. When I had spoken about the strong sense of family and community among the Gypsies and how much they value their children, a police officer suggested that since the main problem law enforcement officers have is how to detain the Gypsies long enough to prosecute them, removing Gypsy children from their homes on any pretext would be an effective way to keep the parents in town.

Prejudice against Gypsies often goes unrecognized even by culturally and racially sensitive people. The assistant district attorney prosecuting S.N. offered me an article that he used to understand the Gypsies, entitled "Gypsies, the People and their Criminal Propensity"[3]

---

2   See *New York Times*, November 17 and 28, 1993, for recent accounts of extreme
     prejudice against Gypsies.
3   Terry Getsay, *Kansas State FOP Journal*, Parts I, II, and III (1982): 18-30.

which quotes extensively from my work, including the fact that Gypsies have several names and that the same or similar non-Gypsy names are used over and over. The article concentrates on "criminal" behavior and never mentions the possibility that there are Gypsies who may not engage in criminal activities. In one section, quotations from my book on the ways Gypsies deal with the welfare bureaucracy were placed under the title, "Welfare Fraud," although by far most of the practices I described were legal. These concluding words in Part II are representative of the tone of the article:

> Officers should not be misled into thinking these people are not organized. They are indeed organized and operate under established rules of behavior, including those that govern marriage, living quarters, child rearing, the division of money and participation in criminal acts.

The implication of such statements is inflammatory. Gypsies have a culture, history, language and social structure, but that fact is distorted to imply that their social organization is partly for the purpose of facilitating criminal behavior. Their culture is viewed as a criminal culture. Gypsies have been fighting this view for hundreds of years. It is the view that they still combat in their relations with law enforcement and the criminal justice system. It is the view that was promoted by the prosecution in this case.

In spite of the best efforts of S.N.'s attorney and my testimony that use of a false social security number did not necessarily indicate intent to commit a crime, he was convicted of illegally using a social security number and served about six months in jail.

Conclusions: Anthropology and Cultural Differences in the Courtroom

Anthropologists are often called in as expert witnesses in cases involving cultural difference. Most Native American legal cases, such as the *Mashpee* case reported by James Clifford,[4] center around Indian status, treaties and land rights. In St. Paul, a number of Hmong legal cases highlighted the conflict between traditional marriage (specifically, the age at which children may marry) and the legal status of minors in American law. With the Gypsies, there is yet another set of cultural issues in their contact with American law.

---

4   "Identity in Mashpee," in *The Predicament of Culture* (Cambridge: Harvard University Press, 1988), pp. 277-346.

First is the question of the cultural conflict between a historically nomadic group and the state bureaucracy of settled people. Identification— a serious legal issue in a bureaucratic society composed of people with fixed abodes and a written language—has virtually no meaning for the nomadic Gypsies who consider descent and extended family ties the defining factor for identification.

Second is the conflict between Gypsy religious rules regarding ritual pollution and prison regulations. The Gypsies avoid situations, such as a job or jail, that require them to be in prolonged contact with non-Gypsies. Jail presents special problems because the Gypsies can become *marime*, that is, defiled by unclean food and living conditions. The psychological trauma that results from isolation from their community is compounded if they then emerge from jail and have to undergo a further isolation from relatives because of becoming *marime* in jail.

Finally, this case illustrates a cultural clash between the Rom Gypsy value on corporate kinship and the American value on individual rights. The rights and status of an individual Rom Gypsy is directly linked to his or her membership in the *vitsa*. Furthermore, the status of all members of the *vitsa* is affected by the behavior of each individual *vitsa* member. Since they are so intricately linked, reciprocity between *vitsi* members is expected. Members of a *vitsa* and family share economic resources, stay in each other's homes, help each other in work and preparation of rituals, loan each other cars, information, identification, and money. They also share the shame of immoral or incorrect behavior by one member and the stigma *(marime)* attached to going to jail. For the Gypsies, the American ideal of each individual having only one name, one social security number, or a reputation based entirely on their own behavior is contrary to their experience and culture.

The analysis of an event such as a trial, especially an event that brings to the fore cultural difference, can be instructive for both cultures. In this article I have tried to present fundamental differences in the practices of American culture and U.S. law and the practices of Roma law and Gypsy culture. Understanding difference does not necessarily resolve conflict, but it can lead to a more humanitarian application of the law to different cultures. The United States, a country based on immigration and diversity, is in no position to ignore the cultural foundations of different ethnic groups, nor are different cultures in the United States exempt from a law because it is contrary to custom. However, the more aware the legal system is of cultural histories and custom, the greater its capacity for justice.

S.N. chose to pursue his case through the U.S. legal system. He made this choice partly because of the influence and advice of a brother who was married to an American lawyer. The rest of his family strongly opposed this decision, preferring to do it the way they always have, by fleeing or lying to avoid contact with the legal system. While he was in jail, the Gypsies in his community held a *Kris* (formal meeting) to explain his decision to work through the American courts rather than the traditional Gypsy way and to raise money for his defense. The outcome of that trial was that on his release S.N., as well as his brother and brother's wife, who was his lawyer, were "rejected" *(marime)* and totally ostracized by his family. At the same time, the conditions of his probation stipulated that S.N. could not associate with his family, and he was released early into the custody of his brother and his brother's wife. Ironically, in the end, both U.S. and Roma law were in agreement on the consequences of his "crime" but for opposite reasons. The American legal system viewed S.N.'s family as "criminal associates"; his family, on the other hand, viewed S.N. and his brother as *marime* for rejecting Gypsy culture. Nevertheless, the strength of Gypsy culture has always been its ability to keep its closely knit ties, and today S.N. and his brother are back in the bosom of the family.

As the world changes into the next millennium, more people than ever before in human history are on the move as migrants, immigrants, guest workers, refugees and even as tourists. At this time in history, many people are living in places that do not share their cultural and legal traditions. Studies of society and legal systems must search for ways to deal with this cultural encounter. Gypsies have probably the longest recorded history of continuous movement and adaptation to other societies and cultures. Their treatment is a barometer of justice and civilization.

Review Questions

1. What aspect of the "crime" committed by a young Gypsy man is due to cross-cullural difference, according to Sutherland?

2. How did the police interpret the lists of social security numbers and other evidence found in the young man's apartment? How did their interpretation of this evidence differ from the Gypsy's?

3. How does this case illustrate the role cultural anthropologists can play in everyday American life?

4. Can you think of other cases where immigrants or culturally different people run afoul of American substantive law?

Original article from Anne Sutherland, "Cross-Cultural Law: The Case of the Gypsy Offender." Copyright ©2010 by Anne Sutherland. Reprinted by permission

CHAPTER TWENTY SEVEN

Medical Anthropology: Improving Nutrition in Malawi

Sonia Patten

Applied anthropologists work in many settings. They may conduct government program evaluations, work on forest conservation projects, market or advertise products, staff rural development programs, establish foreign offices for nongovernmental organizations or corporations, or advise hospital staff, among other things. In this article, Sonia Patten describes her role as an applied medical anthropologist on a project aimed at the improvement of infant and child nutrition in the African nation of Malawi. As a medical anthropologist, her job was to collect cultural baseline data that would help to shape the program and make it appropriate to village conditions in Malawi.

Malawi—Welcome to the Warm Heart of Africa. This is the sign that greets travelers when they arrive in this southeastern African republic. The warm, open response to visitors that I have enjoyed each time I have traveled to Malawi contrasts starkly to the poverty that plagues its citizens.

Malawi is a small landlocked nation in southeast Africa that lies south of Tanzania, east of Zambia, and west of Mozambique. The country is long and thin with its axis running north and south along the Great African Rift Valley. Part of the valley holds Lake Malawi, the third largest lake in Africa, which accounts for more than 20 percent of the country's total area of 119,100 square kilometers. Malawi is one of the ten poorest countries in the world. Its economy is based predominately on agriculture, which accounts for half the gross domestic product and virtually all the exports. Cotton, tobacco, and sugar are most likely to be sold to other countries. However, despite exports, food security for both households and the nation is a chronic problem, with annual "hungry seasons" a fact of life and the specter of famine never far from people's minds. Maize, or white corn, is the staple food for the nation, and it is rare when the nation's rain-fed agriculture produces enough of it to adequately feed the population. The Malawi government faces the enormous challenges of strengthening the economy, improving educational and health facilities, and dealing with the serious environmental issues of deforestation and erosion. The country depends heavily on the International Monetary Fund, World Bank, and bilateral and multilateral donor assistance. It was a small project funded by the U.S. Agency for International Development (USAID) that brought me as a medical anthropologist to Malawi several times during the 1990s.

Medical anthropology is difficult to define because it covers such a wide scope of research and practical programming. In the broadest sense, it can be defined as the study of human health in a variety of cultural and environmental contexts. Over the past three decades, medical anthropology has become a distinct and important area within anthropology. Presently it has three major areas of emphasis. One is the study of cultural differences in health beliefs and systems of healing such as alternative therapies, shamanism, and folk concepts of disease. A second consists of biomedical studies of human adaptations to disease, including nutrition, genetics, and demography. The third is applied medical anthropology, which focuses on the application of anthropology to health-related problems and possible solutions.

Medical anthropologists often carry out research as members of interdisciplinary teams, where their main contribution is to discover a people's cultural conceptions of health, illness, and the more general cultural context within which ideas about health are situated. It was as an applied medical anthropologist that I came to be a member of such an interdisciplinary team that would work in Malawi.

In the early 1990s, I was on the faculty at one of three universities that had joined together to apply for a USAID grant under a program called University Development Linkages Program (UDLP). Two of the universities were American and one was the agricultural college that forms part of the University of Malawi system. A major goal of the UDLP was to strengthen developing nation colleges and universities by giving them access to U.S. faculties and other American university resources.

The program also sought to increase the involvement of U.S. faculty members with faculty in developing nations so that students at U.S. institutions would benefit from an internationalizing of the curriculum.

In this case, scientists from participating universities were asked to devise and implement a project that would benefit all collaborating institutions of higher education. Many teams of UDLP scientists that applied for grants designed projects intended to strengthen curricula at developing nation institutions. Our team, however, opted to design and implement a project addressing a major problem, child undernourishment in Malawi. We recognized that three out of five children in the country were undernourished. Worse, the mortality rate for children under five was 24 percent or nearly one in four. The problem was caused by the fact that children received insufficient protein and calories, which left them vulnerable to a host of infectious diseases, potential mental impairment, serious deficiency diseases such as kwashiorkor and marasmus, and premature death. This is the story of the people from two central Malawi villages and three universities as we worked to craft a program to reduce child undernourishment and increase child survival on a sustainable basis.

Faculty members who were participating in this effort represented a number of disciplines: anthropology, human nutrition, cooperative extension, animal science, veterinary medicine, and crop science. Several of the participating faculty members from Malawi had grown up in small villages, still had extended family in those villages, and were familiar with economic and cultural factors contributing to child undernourishment there. From them and from field research we learned that mothers breastfeed their babies for two to three years, which assured that the children received sufficient protein and calories during these early years. However, that changed when the children were fully weaned. The indigenous weaning food is a gruel of water and maize flour, and babies receive small amounts of it beginning at about four months of age. When mothers wean their toddlers, it is this gruel that the children eat day after day. It is a nutritionally inadequate weaning food and children soon begin to show its effects—swollen bellies, stunted growth, and increased susceptibility to malaria, measles, and other infectious diseases. The weaning food is made from the same crop, maize, that constitutes the staple food for adults, a boiled maize flour dish called *nsima*. The problem of a nutritionally inadequate weaning food is not unique to Malawi—it plagues many developing nations. In these countries there is often a high-carbohydrate food such as corn or rice that makes up as much as 90 percent of children's daily intake. If people survive into adulthood, their bodies have made an adaptation to this low-protein diet. But young children do not thrive.

As our project searched for ideas about how to create a plan for addressing child nutrition, we decided to focus on a simple approach that would use indigenous resources and be manageable at the local level. This was the introduction of a protein and calorie-rich additive, goat milk, to the local weaning food. Although goats are plentiful in Malawi villages, they are meat goats, not dairy goats. They are like walking bank accounts, to be sold when a family needs money to pay school fees for the children, healthcare, and rites of passage such as weddings and funerals. It would be a bold step to secure approval from male village political leaders and elders for the introduction of milk-producing goats to provide milk for young children. Dairy goats would be put directly into the hands of women, not men. Would it work? Would women be willing to learn new animal management and food handling techniques? Would they have time to carry out the additional labor that would be required? Would the goat milk be given to the children who needed it? Would husbands or brothers take the valuable animals away from the women? Would the goats and the children flourish? As time went on, we learned the answers to all these questions and more. And the village women contributed very valuable insights and suggestions that made the project a model that has been adopted elsewhere in Malawi.

The Program

Our work began with a series of planning meetings. Our goal was to create a program that would enable women to raise and keep dairy goats on a sustainable and manageable basis, and use the milk that was produced to supplement their children's diets and increase food security for their families. The plan we generated would have three parts: (1) generation of a database on the milk production and biological characteristics of goats; (2) development and implementation of demonstrations and outreach programs for distributing milk goats to rural women and teaching them how to care for the animals; and (3) formation and implementation of outreach programs for rural women so they could learn how to safely handle goat milk and use it as a regular part of the diet, especially for their children who were under five years of age. At our planning meetings we had to figure out what we were actually going to do, and in what sequence.

The animal scientists on the team knew that milk goats introduced into local villages would have to be hardy or they would die. They wanted to try out some breeding experiments using local goats and imported breeds of dairy goats to see just what kind of a crossbred doe would result in the best combination of high milk production and ability to adapt to life in the village. So they worked out a breeding scheme using local Malawi goats and imported Saanen dairy goats from South Africa, Damascus goats from Cyprus, and Anglo-Nubian goats from the U.S. The breeding experiments were carried out at the farm that the Malawi members of our team used for teaching and research.

This kind of research can't be done in a hurry. Arranging for the importation of animals is a complex process because one has to find a supplier, arrange for payment, arrange for shipment (very few airlines are willing to transport large animals internationally), work out how to feed and water the animals while they are in transit, secure permits from the Malawi Ministry of Agriculture, and quarantine the animals for a period of weeks when they arrive in country. Only then can the breeding research begin.

To our dismay, none of the imported Anglo-Nubian goats survived for very long in Malawi. And several of the Damascus goats also died. The Saanens, however, proved to be the hardier—not surprising, since they originated from relatively close by South Africa where environmental conditions were similar to those in Malawi. And when bred with local Malawi goats, the resulting crossbreeds turned out to provide substantial weekly milk yields that would be enough for the goats' kids as well as for the young children of rural families. So the team decided to import more Saanens and continue the crossbreeding program. Crossbred does would be distributed to village women and most of the crossbred bucks would be sold to support the project. As the program developed, team members discovered that some local does produced relatively high average milk yields; this finding became important as the project unfolded.

My work as the team anthropologist involved the human side of the project. With the help of team nutritionists and the extension expert, I designed a survey to collect baseline cultural information in the villages where the milk goats would be distributed. It was important to document such things as women's daily activities, the meaning and use of goats, relationships between men and women, and ways children were fed in the target villages before the milk goats were introduced. Later we would look for changes we hoped would occur after the new goats arrived and for unexpected problems.

To proceed with the social research, we selected three villages, all relatively close to the college campus in a rural setting about 25 km from the capital city of Lilongwe. To proceed, however, it was necessary to obtain permission from the people in each community. To do so we held meetings with the village headmen, men and women elders, mothers of young children who would be affected by our project, and anyone else from the village who was interested in learning about the program.

In the Central Region of Malawi where we were working, most people belong to the Chewa ethnic group. The Chewa have a matrilineal descent system and practice matrilocal residence. Thus, Chewa men and women inherit clan and lineage membership from their mothers. It is this membership that gives people the right to farm plots of land surrounding their villages. When women marry, most continue to live in the village of their birth with a group of related females—mother, maternal grandmother, mother's sisters and their children, sisters and their children, and eventually, adult daughters and their young children. When young men marry, most move to the villages of their brides. The village political leader is usually, but not always, a man. He cannot be the son of the prior headman because a son is not part of his father's matriline. Instead, he is likely to be the son of the prior headman's sister—a maternal nephew. This system creates a situation where almost all of the women and the powerful men in a village are maternal kin to one another.

To introduce the project, we had to recognize the matrilineal nature of village social organization and the need for people's approval. We met with groups of interested women and men and the headmen in two villages. We explained what we were proposing to do. We said we wanted to find out how the young children in the village were doing in terms of growth and health. Then we intended to make milk goats available to women who had children under five years old because we felt the children would benefit from goat milk in their diet. We noted that it would not cost the women any money. (Most rural women lack the means to purchase even local goats, because they cost from $30 to $50. Dairy goats would be much more expensive.) We said that women who received milk goats would be asked to return the first healthy kid, whether male or female, to the college farm and that this would constitute payment for the animal. We told them that women who took the goats would be asked to attend demonstrations to help them learn how to care for the animals, handle the milk, and feed the milk to their children. We also said that someone from the project would come to the village each week to weigh and measure the participants' children to see if goat milk in their diet was having an effect on weight and height of their youngsters.

Village women were uniformly positive about the project—they wanted to participate. But men, including the headmen, were more skeptical. They worried about the impact on social relations of such valuable animals going to women—it didn't seem appropriate— couldn't the goats be given to the men of the village? The goats were not to be sold or slaughtered, we said. They would be there for the benefit of the children, and their care would involve extra work for the women. Everyone knew that children were suffering because of mal-nourishment—sometimes a child would become so seriously malnourished that relatives had to take it to the district hospital for nutritional rehabilitation. This meant a three-week hospital stay with a family member right there to feed and care for the child. The cost to the family was considerable. And the death of a child was a great sorrow. So eventually the men agreed that the project should go forward. The headmen agreed that the goats should belong to the women and said they would resolve any disputes over ownership in favor of the women.

When we were ready to talk with people in a third village about the project, we learned something that quickly dissuaded us from continuing there. It seemed that there was animal theft going on in the area, and the prime suspects were a family living in the third village! Until the local system of justice had solved these crimes and dealt with the perpetrators, we could not take the risk of working in that village. Animal theft became a problem in the other two villages as well. The rural economy in Malawi has weakened in recent years because of droughts, floods, soil depletion, deforestation, erosion, low prices for commodities, and high rates of inflation. The annual hungry season, the period of time between when people consume the last of the food they have stored to the time when the next crops are harvested, used to begin in December and end in March. Now the hungry season often begins in September. People must reduce the amount of food they eat at a time when they have to carry out the heaviest agricultural labor, preparing fields and planting them when the annual rains begin. Both men and women do this work and nearly all agricultural labor is done by hand. In the depth of the hungry season, people may turn to eating maize bran, the portion of the maize kernel that they normally feed to their animals, in order to have something in their bellies to assuage the hunger pangs. Under conditions such as these, it is no surprise that theft of animals is on the rise in the countryside.

Women in the two villages who received milk goats responded vigorously to the threat of theft once a few animals had been stolen. They began to take their milk goats with them as they went to work in the fields, tethering them nearby rather than letting them range free. They built pens against the sides of their mud or brick houses, to provide shade and security. At night they brought the animals into their houses so the whole family could guard them.

Our research team hired two young women who were both native speakers of the local language, Chichewa, and who had grown up in villages. We asked them to administer the baseline survey in the two villages and to continue working on the project. They would help to distribute animals to village women and later pay weekly visits to the recipients to weigh and measure their young children. One of these young women remained with the project throughout, and is dedicated to working with the villagers. She has been a key to the success of our work.

The baseline survey of households with children under five years of age revealed some interesting and useful information. Women headed 30 percent of the households; there was no adult male regularly living with them. Almost 75 percent of the women were nonliterate. A total of 35.4 percent of the children were underweight for their age and 57.7 percent were stunted (short for age). These figures are close to the national averages for a preharvest season, (i.e., the hungry season). A surprising finding was that children in female-headed households were less likely to be undernourished or stunted. We can only speculate about why this was the case. Perhaps it has to do with groups of related women sharing resources in the interest of their children's well being.

We gave women who participated in the baseline survey the opportunity to volunteer to receive a milk goat, with the understanding that they would attend demonstrations that taught ways to manage the animals and keep them healthy, how to milk goats, how to keep the milk from spoiling, and how to add it to their children's food. We also pointed out that they would have to return first-born kids to project personnel so the does could eventually be distributed to other women, but that all kids born after that would be theirs to keep. The female goats would increase their flock of milk-producers, and the males could be sold to give the women much-needed cash. All women who received milk goats would also be provided with a bucket for milking, a pan for cooking, and a measuring cup to help them track milk production.

The program proved popular. Very quickly the project had more participants than it could accommodate, and we had to create a waiting list. We gave priority to those women who had children under five that were most seriously undernourished. Other women on the waiting list agreed to this. We also provided animals to some grandmothers who were raising young grandchildren orphaned when their parents died of AIDS. Care for AIDS orphans has become a major problem in Malawi, and is reflected at the village level. It is common to see women, already struggling to care for immediate family members, stressed to the maximum as they undertake to feed and house children left behind by relatives who have succumbed to the disease.

Team members designed and began to present demonstrations for village women on goat management, goat health, milking, safe milk handling, and incorporation of milk in their children's food. Recipes using local ingredients and goat milk were developed and tested in the home economics kitchens at the college, and taste-tested by the women participants and their children at the village-based demonstrations. The recipes that passed the taste test were routinely used by the women; those that didn't were rejected.

When the women received their animals, all of the does were either pregnant or already had young kids. This is when project field assistants began their weekly visits to the villages. During each visit, the participating women gathered in a central area of the village with their children. Each woman would have her child or children weighed in a sling scale that was suspended from a tree branch. Once a month, team members measured the upper arm circumference and height of the children. The fact of high child mortality was brought home to me in a very graphic way during this process when some women initially objected to having their children's height measured because they thought it was too much like measuring the children for coffins. A few women persisted in their objection. In these cases, our field assistants could only estimate observable changes in height. The field assistants also asked women about the general health of their children during the previous week, the milk production of their goats, and the health of their goats. If a goat was ill, the field assistant arranged for a veterinary assistant or the team member who was a veterinarian to travel to the village and examine the animal. If there was a significant health problem with a child, the field assistant notified faculty team members who would then take the information to the nearest clinic where they could arrange transport of the woman and child to a hospital if that was called for. Almost all the women who received animals were committed to caring for them and using the milk for their children. Ninety-eight percent of the recipients returned the first kid to the project. This is an astonishingly high rate of return and it implies that rural women would be very good risks for other kinds of so-called "payback schemes" that make local efforts to improve economic security sustainable.

We were gratified to see that those children who began to receive even small amounts of goat milk as an ingredient in their daily diets showed steady weight and height gains even when they were sick. In time, however, we began to see children hit growth plateaus or even lose ground temporarily. We learned from village women themselves why this was happening. Women who made up village committees approached the project team with a proposal for a solution. They told us that their milk goats had to have at least two kids before they could get a second high-yield doe, and this meant that there were periods of time when no milk was available for their children. The women asked if we could teach them how to grow soybeans. They were all familiar with soybean flour as a food for undernourished children because this is what they received when they took their malnourished children to maternal and child health clinics for treatment. Their plan was to grow soybeans and grind them into flour to feed their children when no goat milk was available.

Our project team went back to the drawing board and figured out how to incorporate this new effort. The team purchased soybean seed and distributed 5 kg of it to each woman in the two villages. The village headmen approved of this effort and in some instances designated land for use by those women who needed it. Malawi team members developed and presented demonstrations on how to grow and process soybeans. The women agreed to pay back the 5 kg of seed after their first harvest, again a way to perpetuate the program over time and make it sustainable, and all did so. Women have now completed three or four successful growing seasons with soybeans, and many are growing and storing enough beans to see them through the periods of time when their does produce no milk. They also save enough seed for the next planting season.

It also became clear after a short period of time that we would have to change the goat crossbreeding program. The college farm could not breed enough hardy milk goats to keep up with the demand. The animal scientists on our team looked for local Malawi goats that were the highest milk producers and these, when pregnant or with a kid, were distributed to women on the waiting list. Simultaneously, plans were made to build buck stations in each of the villages and to provide each station with a Saanen or crossbred buck to breed with local goats. Village headmen oversaw the building efforts and other men and women helped to feed and water the buck. When a doe comes into heat, the owner can bring it to the station to be inseminated. In this way the Saanen genes for high milk production spread more rapidly into the village flocks. The villagers know that their bucks must be exchanged for others about every three years in order to avoid inbreeding.

I returned to Malawi for a short visit in the summer of 2004 and found that many positive features of the project were still in place. In discussions with groups of women who had received dairy goats, I learned that two-thirds of them still had their original project animals. The remaining third had lost their original animals to disease or injury, but not before the goats had delivered offspring that survived. Only one woman had sold her animal before it had given her viable kids; this is tantamount to a farmer selling or eating her seed! But the woman's situation was quite difficult. Her husband was seriously ill and could not assist with farm work, and as a consequence she had been unable to raise sufficient maize to provide for household subsistence. She was desperate for cash in order to purchase food, and it was out of this desperation that she sold her milk goat.

Several women had a sufficient number of animals that they were able to meet the nutritional needs of their young children and sell surplus goats, keep her animals was in the fortunate position of having a husband who was employed, albeit at a relatively low wage, at a government facility. His small but steady income protected the family from having to sell assets such as animals in order to afford staple food. The women who had sold their milk goats were hopeful that, in a year of good harvest, they would be able to purchase a milk doe.

When I expressed my concern and disappointment about these developments to a Malawian who was a key member of the project team, he suggested that I should think about this in another way—if women had not had these valuable animals to sell for a good price in order to see their families through this difficult time, they might have been forced to resort to such dire acts as dismantling their houses to sell the timbers and sheets of metal roofing. This is one of the last resorts of rural dwellers when faced with chronic hunger and the need for cash to purchase food. So the women were buffered from such a drastic move. And they were convinced of the value of milk goats for the physical health of their young children and their own economic well being. They are resilient and resourceful women, and they viewed the setback as only temporary.

Review Questions

1. What are the social and environmental conditions that lead to child malnutrition in Malawi, according to Patten?

2. What programs did the project team come up with to improve child nutrition in Malawi, and what steps did they take to implement it?

3. How is anthropology useful for programs such as the one described by Patten in this article?

4. In what ways did team members involve local people in the design and implementation of the program?